Lizzie Pye

EDWARD BLISHEN

Lizzie Pye

HAMISH HAMILTON
LONDON

First published in Great Britain 1982
by Hamish Hamilton Ltd
Garden House 57–59 Long Acre London WC2E 9JZ

Copyright © 1982 by Edward Blishen

ISBN 0–241–10781 4

Phototypeset by Tradespools Ltd, Frome, Somerset
Printed in Great Britain by The Pitman Press
Bath

Blishen, Edward
    Lizzie Pye.
    1. Blishen, Edward   2. Authors, English—
    20th century—Biography
    I. Title
    828'.91409   RP6052.L57Z/

    ISBN 0-241-10781-4

To Nance; Joy & Ken; Jon & Carol; Nick & Sam; Christine &
Peter; & Kathryn,

all of whom she loved—though, of course, she sometimes got
them muddled up

PART ONE

I

'Now I can be untidy,' said my mother, clapping her hands. 'I don't have to worry about fingermarks. He used to drive me mad ... Fingermarks on the kitchen cupboard. Fingermarks on the gas stove. He'd come in from the garden and go round and look for fingermarks.' She clapped her hands again. 'I can be as grubby as I like.' She astonished me by looking upwards and making with one finger a little triumphant gesture at the ceiling. It was in that general direction that she supposed my father now existed: or was ... undergoing his ordeal of non-existence.

Her eyes filled at once with tears. 'My dear husband,' she said.

It was two days after his death. She'd loved him amazingly, and found him amazingly abominable: and being with her during those two days had been like being present at the fall of an unpopular government. Part of my mother was out on the streets, shouting raucously and waving revolutionary flags. Part was grieved beyond words. She was toppling statues and releasing political prisoners, and had never known such hopefulness and such agony.

Well, she had herself been his prisoner for fifty-four years: that had been the term of their marriage. They'd met thirteen years before that. My handsome, dark-natured father had had her tormented and steadfast love for the best part of three quarters of a century. And now, at last, she'd been rescued. She wished it had been some other hero than Death who had set her free; but she couldn't help being grateful, and kept finding images for the effect of it. Weeping night after night at the thought of the defeat of her cruel and charming jailer, she would tell me each day, in some different way, how it felt to be

3

at liberty. 'It's as if there'd been a great piece of concrete on my head and now it's gone.' 'It was tension all day long—*all day long*—and now I'm beginning to feel relaxed.' And then ... some attempt to explain to me, but mostly to herself, why she had clung to him all those years. 'What can you do? If you love a man, and he's going to murder you, you still stick there to be murdered.' Her characteristic vehemence. I treasured it as a child, my small mother suddenly making a rampart of her chin and beginning to fire from behind it.

Yet there was another way of looking at her refusal ever to break with him. She'd often spoken of the advice she'd been given before her marriage, in 1919, by relatives certain she was to be unhappy. Whatever occurred, she was not to walk out. Walk out, and she would never get back again! *Stay where you were*, for that was the only way a woman could make herself secure against—oh, whatever terrible things happened to someone who'd abandoned her home. No matter what just cause for anger you had, never let him drive you away!

Suddenly she asked my sister how he would be in his coffin. He'd be wearing some sort of gown, said Betty, horrified by the question and her own vagueness. My mother chewed her lip, and was all tears again. Nothing, I think, had hurt her more than having to surrender him to the undertaker. It was unnatural that anyone else should determine how he looked, on the most casual occasion ... let alone this one, so cruelly important.

Then she said: 'As long as he's comfortable.'

And I thought it the most astonishing thing she'd said yet. So grotesque ... what comfort could a corpse have? ... and yet so soberly true to her feeling. While there was a trace of him anywhere, whatever form it took, she was concerned with its well-being.

And my dead father was, in any case, still a property to be directed, sent on journeys, housed. The undertaker had told me how he would be transferred from the hospital to the undertaker's own chapel. 'We'll bring him in,' he said. 'He's still at Southampton but ... we'll bring him in.' He made it sound a strenuous feat that we could rely on him to perform fearlessly. I saw my father as ... perhaps a yacht whose crew had been drowned. They'd send out tugs and the empty thing

4

would be brought to harbour. 'We've brought him in,' the undertaker assured me, ringing later to fix some detail.

I thought of my mother in an oddly similar way—that is, in sea terms. Being with her was like watching over some terrifyingly frail craft that was tossing in incredible storms: of grief, relief and terror.

She was resolved to reverse the whole tendency of things that he'd established. After his retirement from the Civil Service he had shut them into a bungalow on the south coast, and kept the rest of the world at a prickly distance. My sister and I had not always found it easy to effect an entry. The policeman's language did not seem unfitting. With most of their neighbours he'd limited his contact to brief salutes that always had some edge of sarcasm. Well, as a small boy walking him home from his evening bus I'd thought it must be the proper way to say 'Good evening'—sardonically.

Now it was going to be different. She was full of plans. She would invite this neighbour and that in to tea: and would accept invitations from them, as he'd always said she shouldn't. She was taking quiet stock of her little kingdom: dreaming of being free of it, staying up late, watching television as and when she wished: being a notable hostess. Once again she would make those little cakes brimming over at the edges that were a marvel of my boyhood: and people would talk about them. Or, as mother saw it, they would rush into the street proclaiming their excellence. 'She said she could hardly wait to get home and tell them about my cakes.' I heard her saying it, throughout the 1920s and 1930s. Now she said, again clapping her hands: 'I'm going to do all the things my dear husband didn't want me to do. Am I wicked?'

And I felt wretched, faced with that quivering excitement. It had surely come too late: this opportunity of realising her dream. She was so tremulously confident and hopeful, all knuckles, making determined fists of her small hands; and during these astonishing days she had spawned scheme after scheme. But she was, for goodness' sake, the frailest eighty-three, a persistent little bag of bones: and nearly blind.

Typically she'd said nothing to my father about her growing blindness: she'd always shielded him from what was worrying. But he had slowly guessed it. She'd bring letters to him, newly delivered, with a nonchalant pretence of not having bothered to see who they were from. That might work for a while; but my father knew that the last woman he was married to was one given to breezy incuriosity. And she'd given up her habit of reading a letter as if it were *War and Peace*, making an intense serial study of it spread over days. My mother could always have passed rigorous examinations on the contents of letters. On top of all that, she'd stopped reading newspapers—at the end, I guess, stopped pretending to read them. And that made it impossible for him to continue his own pretence that all was well with her.

I'd been turning over old photos, and had noticed that in nearly every one in which she'd figured through the years—on beaches, on the lawn at our old home at Barton-on-the-Hill, anywhere—my mother had her nose in a newspaper. The photos didn't show what I easily imagined: her mouth moving as she transferred the print to her mind. Her imperfect education meant she often got things wrong: she could think she was reading about China when she was reading about Chile. Usually she wasn't concerned with either of those countries, however, but with murders, disgraces, little—at best, local—horrors. She was feeding her sadness about people. She loved them, on the whole, but would never cease to grieve over their tendency to provide the material for lamentable stories. I see my mother in her middle years, when my father had made her a character in a lamentable story of their own—if he was at meetings of office committees to a late hour three times a week, what were these cinema tickets carelessly left in a pocket of his jacket? ... I see her consoling herself with a general view of the world in which it was common for men to take girls from the office to the pictures. Of course, to get into the newspapers it had to end in disgrace, scandal, perhaps murder: and I guess my mother saw these as threats to be kept at bay with her larger housewifery, as with her smaller skills she drove back the dust, all manner of untidiness ... *fingermarks*!

It struck me now that it was odd for her to have left fingermarks round the place for my father to complain about. That too must have been an effect of her blindness: and his

6

persecution of her by discovery and denunciation of the marks would have been a cruel, frightened part of his attempt not to know what was happening.

Well, she was determined to go on living here, alone: looking after the bungalow, the garden, as if it were a substitute for looking after him. And I guess that's how she thought of it: but it was also, of course, her liberated kingdom. And she was ready with answers to every objection. Yes, the telephone would become enormously important: what she'd do was to get us to write out the vital numbers in huge figures and pin them all over the place. She made it sound an irresistible project. You'd have to be the most charmless spoilsport to throw doubt on it.

She was talking to me about this as she stood at the stove, preparing a meal: and didn't see that the cloth she was holding was trailing down into a flame. It became a little torch, and with a cry quickly smothered she crushed it out against the side of the sink. She talked then with such desperate gaiety that I couldn't bring myself to remark on what had happened.

It was impossible that she should live alone: it was impossible that she shouldn't.

2

So many languages she spoke in.

'You know,' she said, 'always, when he zipped up my dress, he used to kiss my neck.' And I could see him doing this—with that cocky charm of his, that he'd shared with his five brothers. It was something they'd learned as boys in the slums of West London ... A brisk, half-mocking flirtatiousness, always ready. I'd been aware of that, too, as a child: how, when they were gathered, they would pay their attentions to each other's wives, so that my uncles and aunts seemed always to generate an atmosphere inexplicably thrilling. Part of the warmth I felt in them, when they were at their best, had its roots in a tendency to encircle waists, stroke arms and blow kisses, and at certain moments to burst into a particular kind of thrustful laughter. Looking back, I see how erotic it all was: and indeed there were always more names involved in their current histories (as discussed with a guardedness that I thought of as an interesting secondary language, perfectly easy to follow) than was justified by the simple marital facts. There was on the edge of it all an excitement of Ednas, Hildas, Dorises . . .

In this discharge of a lifetime, my mother's brimming soliloquy during those days after his death, it was remembered gallantries that inspired one of the languages in which she spoke: that of barely clouded adoration. She recalled him as she'd first known him—beautiful, she said, in gaiters and a jacket with shining buttons. A van boy at Selfridge's. Cheeky grin. And they were so right for his legs—gaiters. If she'd had her way, he would never have worn anything else to the very end. He would even have gone to work as a civil servant in highly polished leather, setting off the cocky glamour of his legs. But he'd worn, too, at that remote date—1906, my goodness, though dates were meaningless—an immense overcoat, swamping him: it had been given to him, and his mother had no skill in abbreviating overcoats. He was very proud of it, and she quickly learned not to laugh. She'd gone home with him for the first time, and my grandmother had said, in the opening aside of a relationship full of them: 'Do you know how old he is? He's thirteen—that's all.'

My mother made no comment on this memory—but I saw at once that my grandmother must have disliked her on sight, for her plain simplicity and good nature. A goose! And when she set out to startle that sixteen-year-old innocent with the truth about my father's age (he'd have claimed to be seventeen, of course), it was, I'd bet, with malice. The little goose had wandered into quite the wrong kind of farmyard! Here all the animals were sexual predators, given to strutting about on their jauntily turned legs from the earliest age! Off you go, goose!

8

But this was an obstinate goose, and she was determined to pass into the possession of her unsuitable lover ...

'They said I was a poor morsel,' said my mother, getting it wrong as she always did: and referring to the attitude of her mother and her aunts and uncles on her mother's side. It was they, a mass of remembered kindness, but not her father or her sisters, who thought her a poor mortal, doomed to damage if she went round with that lecherous van boy. 'They said he was a rotter! They said they were all rotters! I don't know if they knew things I didn't.' My mother, whose uncertainty on this point must have been cleared up long since, looked back, I guess, to a time when she would not hear anything bad said about him—or them. She'd have shut her ears, and made a stubborn deafness of herself whenever these kindly people offered their warnings.

Her father was a builder's labourer, Irish she said, illiterate: given to fits of generosity and sweetness, but to far more common fits of black anger. He was often drunk. He'd married my other gentle grandmother when she was pregnant, victim of the son of the house where she'd been a maid: and *her* son, the illegitimate one, my mother now told me, had not as a boy been allowed in the house. He had to sleep in the streets and doorways. He'd made his own angry life, somehow: I remembered him, rarely met, as a man of great soreness, with a habit of scorn towards his own relations balanced by an exaggerated respect for his wife's. A milk roundsman. As a child I treasured the thought of him, on the one hand—not everyone had a milk roundsman in the family—and shrank from him on the other: having a child's awareness of that explosive bitterness in him. ...

My mother was exactly like *her* mother, good-natured, straight: and clearly my grandfather detested them both. Now she told me how, in one of their wretched lodgings, he'd insisted that the lino be taken up and washed not only on top but underneath, and the floorboards washed too—'until you could have eaten off them.' Her flashy sisters, all unsuitably named after flowers, shameless Daisy and incontinent Violet, had refused to do it, and he'd accepted their refusal, making my mother do it instead, in a coarse apron. She spoke of the apron, seventy years later, with an undiminished angry

9

emphasis—all her life having loved the dainty and despised the coarse. 'I don't know why he didn't like me.'

I thought two things as she poured this out: how right that friend of mine was who held that folk tales and fairy tales were still the truest of realistic narratives: and that one of the most stunning things about human life was the length of it and the brevity of it. Well, here was my mother, in 1973, still caught up in unfinished situations, open-ended scenes dating from about 1899. Life, my God, was a three-volume novel written hastily on the back of a postcard.

And of course there was that other language she spoke in: running with no hint of irony or hypocrisy alongside the first: the language of her long disappointment in him.

Well, half a century of disappointment *was* a lot of disappointment. . . .

Somewhere about this point in her outpouring she reached a moment when even a newly-freed prisoner, determined to be dramatically indifferent to the old prison timetable, had to go to bed. She didn't like bedtime, for it was now totally in the hands of grief and shock. But off she went: and kissing me goodnight, with the lingering soft kisses that must have been a vital ingredient in the unlikely spell she'd cast over the strutting van boy, she said: 'Thank you for a very nice day.'

Well, *that* was the most extraordinary thing she'd said! My father had been dead two days, and his death had been to her like nothing so much as a dagger plunged in her heart: and she'd been full of the twisted story of the past, the agonised story of the present, the tremblingly hopeful story of the future. And her comment on all this, to her shrugging, sighing, smiling listener, was to thank him for . . . oh, what were the conventional words? . . . making such an enjoyable day possible.

What she'd enjoyed was the almost unbearable liberty of being herself.

3

'He didn't like you, you know,' she said.

My mother's characteristic bluntness—based on her typical refusal of pretence. Eight years later, when she was on her deathbed, I was to lean over her—she'd recognised no one for days—and reflect that here was a tender-hearted woman who was never sentimental: and at that moment, aware of some anxious shadow a few inches from her failing eyes—engaged in her last furious struggle to prove that anxiety was out of place—she muttered: '*Go away!*' I think Kate, my wife, who was with me, was concerned that I might have been hurt by my mother's dying brusqueness. But I laughed with helpless pleasure. She could not more exactly have illustrated my point: that the last gift she had was tact. Or, as she always insisted on calling it: *tack* ...

Now, using her second language, she was talking about my father's view of me. He'd expressed it of late, it seemed, largely in terms of many variations in his will.

It had been, for her, one of the torments of those last years. He'd gone to his solicitor again and again with some new idea for reducing, or delaying, my inheritance, and increasing, or hastening, my sister's.

'Wait till I get you home!' he'd cry on Sunday evening walks, when I'd trodden on his gleaming shoecaps or thrown too many thistle-heads at my sister—who, having enjoyed *that* game, then enjoyed the other of getting me into trouble by bursting into deliberate tears. His last will and testament had clearly seemed to him an ultimate way of dealing with me when he had himself, so very finally, reached home. He'd tan my arse, as he would have put it, with fiercer and fiercer codicils. The last, said my mother—at her own urging more generous than its predecessor—left two thirds to my sister, a third to me. He'd gone again after that to the solicitor, with some scheme for postponing my sour windfall until I was seventy. The solicitor had said, really this was far enough. It would be impossible to defend such a will. He must refuse to draft it. 'He came home with his tail between his legs,' said my mother. But it was not a tail given to being in that position. In no time at all it was on its way aloft again. 'I think,' he told her, in that order of reasonable voice that warned those who knew him that he was about to be spectacularly unreasonable, 'that after Christmas I'll go into Bournemouth and find a new solicitor. I'd like to make a new will.' That had been a week before his death.

'He knew it tormented me,' she said. 'He knew it made me cry.'

Apart from wishing to punish me for being his hopelessly uncongenial son, he thought of himself, I guess, as keeping as much of his money, for as long as possible, out of Kate's eager hands.

There was never a hope that Kate would seem to him anything but a monster. It was a definition of a monster: someone who married one of his children. Over the years, manufacturing his own evidence, he'd built up a picture of Kate as a termagant; a snob; a negligent mother; a person incapable of feeding her family to accepted average standards; and as someone who spent much of her time longing for the deaths of her in-laws and planning the disposal of the money that would then fall into her lap.

On every point it was a view of Kate that missed the reality by millions of miles. And sometimes, furious though its falsity made me, I'd reflect that it was not a view of Kate, anyway. He had no independent views of anyone. His ideas about wives were based firmly on family situations as he had perceived them as a child and young man. A wife, being a woman, was untrustworthy: was a ready bearer of malice: having secured her cocky man, was engaged in subduing his cockiness. There was no one who didn't think incessantly about what might be wrung from others, but women thought of such things harder than men. It was all part of a terrible view of marriage and the family as essentially predatory arrangements and organisations.

When I married Kate Brown, I'd married a positive impurity. Certainly this was so eugenically. If one of our sons threw a tantrum, when small, my father would make an announcement. 'We say he gets that from the Browns. Kathleen's father especially.' Then, since he couldn't claim actually to have seen Mr Brown hurl himself screeching to the ground and kick his heels: 'Bad temper. Comes out in all sorts of ways.' Tom or Dan at this point having begun to claw the ground, my father might add: 'Touch of Kathleen's mother, too.' I found this particularly odd. If Mrs Brown had a weakness, it was a grave incapacity to behave badly. Her displeasure was of the smouldering kind: she might have glowered at the ground, but would never have clawed it.

Much of the time this sort of thing was said, mercifully, out of Kate's hearing: when it wasn't, she was inclined to provide what my father saw as evidence in support of his theory. 'That's what I mean. People take things personally. I'm only making a remark.' Curious phrases of my father's, both. Reply to some blistering attack on your appearance, character or outlook, and you were taking things personally. And he had always defended his right to make the most slanderous statement on the grounds that it was merely a remark.

When Tom's or Dan's behaviour began again to have elements of virtue in it, my father would say: 'That's better! You've got your good side, haven't you, Daniel'—or 'Thomas'. A proposition to which, to be fair to them, our sons never assented. But it was clear that whichever was at the moment involved was now exhibiting characteristics deriving from my half of the mixture that Kate and I had thoughtlessly created.

My father's view of the disastrous effects of polluting our blood with that of the Browns was at times so melodramatic that you'd have thought Kate and I had assembled our sons amid flashes of lightning at midnight in some private laboratory in Transylvania. ...

My mother said: 'For the first time I'm looking forward without tension to Kate's coming.'

4

Kate arrived next day, bringing one of my mother's best friends—our Jack Russell, Sally. She was a stern little dog, who'd have startled no one had she worn pince-nez. Arrived anywhere, she made a quick, inimical tour of the place: and then leapt up on what was most comfortably to be leapt on, making herself defensively compact there and yawning with rapid nervousness. Her yawns were enormous, and like everything else she did had a condemnatory quality about them. But touch her, however slightly, and at once she'd be on her back, offering herself to caresses. And if they were given, she'd allow the tip of her tongue to appear—except that it wasn't allowed, it fell helplessly out of her mouth, ran helplessly round her lips. I never grew accustomed to the speed with which this puritan became this wanton. In general, she reminded me of the teacher of whose severe love I'd felt confident when I was eight or nine: Miss Baker, prevented by her official position and some pointless fuss about age from declaring her passion, but hinting at it with unprecedented grants of ten out of ten for my compositions. When Sally lay there to be adored, belly up, it was as if Miss Baker *had* declared herself—had flung herself to the floor and rolled over in the classroom of my memory: and I could imagine no sexual fantasy more shocking.

Sally lay now upside down on a couch beside my mother: two small creatures both with double worlds inside them. Her eyes were distant, as though she were abstractedly appraising the bliss of being stroked. My mother wept, but not unhappily. 'He did love you, you know! He'd let you do anything!' And it was true. Every now and then a creature was able to claim exemption from my father's distaste for living things.

But Sally was certainly the only one he'd ever complacently watched pissing on a lawn of his. She'd leave a brown patch, but he smiled wryly ... I'd think at times that it was the unlikelihood of her ever making a claim to status that earned her his amazing approval. It wasn't possible that she'd suddenly allege she'd been a principal in the Civil Service, had grown prize roses, or was related to some person whose name was frequently in the newspapers. ...

Mother's hand were running now over the stretch of her belly, following the feathery pattern of her bright white hair. I felt what she felt—the small givings and girdings of Sally's flesh. My mother's hands were life, and Sally was life under those hands: and the dog's body and my mother's hands ran together, in a patterned stir of life. And I suddenly saw my father lying in—how ridiculous to think so, but it was how I thought of it—*astounded* stiffness in that absurd undertaker's absurd chapel; and that made me think strangely of this fluttering of flesh and nerve that was life, and the rhythm of my mother's hands, and the answering rhythms of the dog's small body.... And I felt how intensely, at this grieving moment, my mother was alive.

We *couldn't* tell her that her dream was an impossible dream, and that she must become a dependant in someone else's impatient house.

To fade, perhaps, into being like Kate's grandmother, who had died at the age of 101 soon after we'd gone to live at Barley Wood. For some time before her death, she'd been quite blind. 'It's all black and silent,' she said. 'A black gulf. ...' And our little son Dan, alas, was afraid of her groping attempts to embrace him. He found himself in those trembling blind arms and couldn't bear either the blindness or the frantic longings that caused her to tremble. 'Granny wants so much love,' she declared, when she had him at last: and he wept bitterly and struggled to escape. I'd sit with him on my knee, and a hand in the old woman's hand, trying to comfort them both together, and give her a sense of being close to her great-grandson: but it was kissing and hugging that she wanted. She wanted someone with her in the blackness, and she wanted warmth: and these needs made her as passionate as a young girl.

People wished to be good to her, but it was often too much. She always needed to know what was happening, and it was an occupation in itself to make the attempt to penetrate her deafness. Kate's parents, Jim and Dorothy, were often curt: there was nothing else they could be, if they were to get on with their own lives. They'd had the old woman with them for almost as long as Kate could remember: and there was a time when they'd had Jim's mother, too, deeply distressed by widowhood. She, Jim's mother, had gone away once, and lived for a while with a sister of Jim's: but then one day she was back. And Kate, about fourteen at the time, remembered shouting at her—telling her to go away again, to leave them alone. It was a troublesome memory for Kate—shouting like that at an old, lonely woman. But she knew, she said, what it meant to her mother, the strain, and never being able to go out freely. She was shouting at her distracted grandmother on behalf of her distracted mother.

And it seemed to me there was so much easy nonsense talked about old age. They said what a splendid woman little granny was! It must be marvellous to have a mother who'd lived to be a hundred! Wonderful memories, of course! And the reality was so different—irritabilities and sadnesses on both sides, the worse for being unacknowledged; and worse than that, for being, in the deepest sense, unintended. It was not what anyone had ever meant to happen.

And then she became a gaunt old lady who simply couldn't die. For month after month she couldn't die. She could not any longer bear her false teeth: speech became difficult. She lay in bed and longed to go, and couldn't understand what cruelty kept her here. 'Always thirsty and always tired,' she told me. 'I only want to go to sleep and not wake up.' And suddenly she prayed aloud for death—an intense, quivering petition. I didn't know what to say ... went on holding her thin dry hand.

It was more than six weeks before her prayer was answered. And when she was buried, in a hillside cemetery that looked down on fields where I'd played as a child, I had a feeling I'd never have expected. There were Jim and Dorothy, arm-in-arm, behind the coffin, and then Kate and I, arm-in-arm, behind them, on this fresh, blowy August morning: and I felt a

16

deep pleasure in having, and conformably taking, my place in the ritual. It was quietly stirring, being accepted in this other family. I suspected my pleasure of being, at least partly, histrionic. The slow tread ... the way the morning dashed aside the clouds on its breezy face, and they returned, and again were scattered ... and the long view of the valley of my childhood ... 'Who'd recognise the rebellious, awkward young man of half a dozen years ago in this solid mourner ...?' And so, disgracefully, on.

And in that over-polished coffin, little granny being lowered—wearing the nightdress and white stockings she'd had ready, in a box under the bed, for so many patient—and then, at the end, so many impatient—years. ...

And all that time she'd been an intrusive footnote in other people's lives. Which was precisely what my mother did not wish to be. Patient longer even than Kate's grandmother, she'd waited for the moment when, her beloved torturer gone, she could resume her life as it had been more than fifty years earlier. Well, so often during this week she'd sounded like a girl, a young woman. Dammit, who could bring himself to hold this eager youngster back on the grounds that she was eighty-three, was kept going by digitalis, and was virtually blind?

Her doctor could do so, as Kate and I discovered when we went to see him. A kindly, intelligent man, resigned to the problems that arose when most of your patients were over sixty, he turned out not to have understood the relationship between my parents. He thought my father so powerful that my mother must have been powerless beyond belief. She must have been his merest appendage. The only future for her, clearly, as a dependant. We must use guile to accustom her to the idea of living with one of us—Betty or me. 'An honourable but difficult fate for you,' he said, smiling sternly.

'But I do think you've misunderstood my mother,' I said. 'She has guts, you know ...' I was half-minded to tell him what sort of guts: about her running away from home, at thirteen, because her father was making his incestuous way through his daughters, and my mother had said to herself (as she'd reported lately to me): 'Lizzie, you can do better than this.' Lizzie Pye—known during the brief disrupted period of her schooldays as 'Piecrust.' A genius in the manufacture of crusts of any kind, she'd never thought of this nickname as anything but an accolade. It was part of her eager faint memories of schooling. Learning was another challenge she'd gladly have accepted, if life hadn't constantly been snatching such things out of her grasp. She'd wanted very badly, she'd told me the day before, to learn to play the piano. 'Especially the twiddly bits.' Music as one long monstrous twiddle had been a lure, and a joke, to her when I was an adolescent, musically infatuated. She'd make wild gestures with her hands to represent the activity of a conductor, a man who presided over the production of the amazing spaghetti of music.

My mother always had a wistful sense that she'd been excluded from the best of human activities, all marked by their being extravagant tangles . . . All advanced activity was a matter of being twiddly.

'You've missed,' I wanted to say to that excellent doctor, 'not only my mother's courage, but her very considerable sense of humour.'

He'd write to her, he said, and point out how much better it would be if she crept under my wing, or Betty's. . . .

5

And coming away from his surgery, I remembered the not entirely cowardly response she'd made to my father's fairly impossible behaviour when, late in the war, he'd been returned to London from a posting in Nottingham.

He'd been gone for two years, and in my mother's view it was a cunningly contrived absence during which he'd certainly not have permitted the national emergency to prevent him from taking large numbers of girls from the office to large numbers of cinemas. I think she saw him making up for the restrictions imposed on him by life in London, so close to home, by engaging in multiple adulteries—infidelity on an unprecedented scale. How could the Midlands resist those cocky legs? The news of his return had her ... well, if it *had* been cricket; which, as he played it, it certainly was not ... standing on the boundary, hands gratefully cupped to catch this culpable sitter. She girded herself for the agony of his presence, and glowed with the justice—and, of course, the delight—of it.

For me, living at home, the news was monstrous. 'This means,' squalled my diary, 'the violation of a thousand small freedoms. It means continuous Forces Programme. Our mild little anarchy is coming to an end: a most uncomfortable wilfulness is returning.' I set out to console the household with an imitation of the front page of a newspaper. OLD MAN RETURNING, screamed the headlines. RE-ESTABLISH-MENT OF TYRANNY AT 10 MANOR ROAD. POPU-LACE PREPARES FOR ATROCITIES. In an interview I was quoted as saying ('handsome 23-year-old President of the Republic'): 'I shall fight on for the liberation of this dining room.' (It was the room in which we everlastingly sat. The sitting room was the room in which we never sat, except at Christmas and when uncomfortable guests were expected.) 'A vigorous attack will be maintained against the Forces Pro-gramme. Gardening will be crushed wherever it appears.' My father was being sent to the headquarters of the London Fire Service on the Embankment. REACTION AT LAMBETH, said further headlines. CIVIL SERVANTS FLEE.

On his last visit he'd been full of war news: the details of some canteen intrigue in the office. He was chairman of the canteen committee: a body, it seemed, as furiously divided as any in other wartime centres of power. Only on the train journey home had the malevolent strategy of his opponents become clear to him. Or rather, it had become clearly obscure: as he told us of it, the obscurity was more evident than the clarity. He'd write, he said, to his superior, revealing (it was his word) the plot. That evening, he held forth in a speech closely modelled on addresses to the nation widely familiar at the time: and I dared not move, for at each fidget my mother would look at me with the sort of sympathy that seems to print the word on the air in capital letters: and then, with a total absence of *tack*, at the clock.

And then he was wholly back. He still found it difficult to speak to us in the usual small domestic manner. He addressed us hugely. In coming home, he said, he'd merely anticipated the end of the war by nine months. It seemed he'd come home simply to do that. 'If only people realised ...' he kept saying. In Nottingham he'd been at the very navel of things. Back here on the ... knee, or mere ankle, he spoke to the rustics with an oddly drawling amusement. They need not think in Lambeth that he was going to be bound by conventional office hours! As for his successor in Nottingham: '*He* need not think he's going to put on my mantle!'

Poor man! London almost at once poured huge numbers of buckets of cold water over him. From his first day there he came home disconcerted. The change of office, he said, was like moving from a country club to a prison. He brought with him a file, ostensibly to show me the sort of work he had to do. I read this through—a question of paying a quarterly charge on a connection between two water mains. My father's chief, a much younger man, had written a very clear minute: and directed my father to draft a letter modelled on it. 'You can write it,' he said to me. And I suddenly saw that he was frightened of producing a weak letter as his first performance. I was frightened myself, then, and produced a few lame, inept words: and with sinking heart saw him make a note of them. His prose style was cumbrous: mine, when it was a matter of connections between water mains, and not weather, or landscape, or people, or women's breasts, which at that time entered largely into my writing (or minutely, because in the manner of the day those splendid objects—of which my experience was wholly literary—could be enormously heavy or as inconsiderable as apples) ... my official prose was as bad as his. I tried for his sake to urge myself to greater effort, but uselessly. I could feel he wasn't sure, was still nervous: and I was miserable because I couldn't do better for him. Then he said: 'This is how young Tewkesbury and I used to work in Nottingham—we'd talk matters out, and then I'd throw it to

20

him and say, "Write something on those lines." ' Tewkesbury was a youngster with literary leanings who reviewed books for one of the Nottingham newspapers: and suddenly I saw that for two years in the Midlands he'd been my father's ghost-writer, his prose style itself: the amiable source of much of his swagger.

Nottingham had made my poor father incapable of London! It had even made a lieutenant of him in the Home Guard. Back in Barton-on-the-Hill he was told there was no room for another officer. He'd have to revert to being a private. 'I'm afraid,' he informed the dining room at 10 Manor Road, 'that I shan't go down there very often and shall turn up in civvies, whether they like it or not.' Later he proposed to leave his gaiters (the war had re-equipped him with those) white like an officer's: he'd not black them like a private's. 'Let them find out for themselves!'

And the collapse of my father's brief holiday from marriage and every kind of official realism brought out, in the end, the worst in him: and compelled my mother to display the guts that, thirty years later, her doctor did not believe her to possess.

It was his ear that he always, as it were, fell back on at times like this when his morale was under attack. He had a genuinely ruined ear: shellfire in the First World War had shattered the drum. But over the years it had turned from a straightforward source of discomfort to a reason why, at chosen moments, all criticism of his character and conduct should be absolutely withdrawn and replaced with over-whelming sympathy. If possible, the sympathy should be servile and cloying.

He didn't this time call immediately upon the services of his ear. Instead, he tried the effect of teaching the London Fire Service a lesson by being abominable to the other occupants of the dining room at 10 Manor Road: my mother, my sister and myself, lunatically intimate in this tiny space. After two years, it seemed suddenly, again, quite insane—all of us in that little room. In the evening, my father eating; the wireless on: Betty and I reading; my mother being shocked by the newspaper, exactly as if it had been the first she'd ever read. If what was on the wireless was something I'd chosen, he'd cry at intervals, truculently: '*Nonsense!*' Once, it was one of Beethoven's piano concertos. Absurd to try to listen to music in these circumstances, but there were times when I could not bear not to. 'What's that supposed to be!' cried my father, in tones suggestive of a withering inability even to ascribe it to some such broad category as: Music. He spoke very loudly about the course of the war, giving his definitive account of the reputations of British and German generals: urging armies in various directions; full, still, of the sense of intoxicated importance he'd acquired in Nottingham. Mother said he'd produced half a dozen boxes of silver cutlery, as if from a waistcoat pocket. The origin of this expensive metal was not explained. 'Who's going to clean the things?' she cried. It seemed that the chairmen of wartime canteen committees did not find it impossible, morally or practically, to use their positions to raid the nation's stock of silverware.

I remember thinking how awful to contemplate was the repetitive banality of life for the women penned in such houses. I wandered disconsolately one day, soon after my father's return, into my sister's room, where she was lying with a heavy cold, and looked out of the window and commented for her on the world outside. It was near evening on a November day eighteen months from the end of the most hideous war in human history. The sky was an attractive wintry blue: and as I watched, a few mauve clouds were rubbed out by the spreading of blue dusk. Men and women went past, leading dogs. Now and then—and it seemed a great incident—a window banged. Small children, lost in their own fierce world, in which the road was a battlefield, ran up and down, hot-eyed. And I wondered what the future held for them—specifically, for the little girls among them. The daily trudge to and from the dustbin?

Inside the huge, melodramatic general fate, all those tiny individual destinies. Like my mother's. She was not then by any means entirely my friend. Or rather, she was my most precarious ally. Deeply, we were on the same side. We were together against my father's pomposity and the pure boredom that resulted when he spoke—as, nowadays, he mostly spoke—at length. There was always, between my mother and myself, the ... reverse, I suppose, of a gentlemen's agreement.

22

It was an agreement of riff-raff. All my life I'd enjoyed her coarse little whispers, directed against my father's absurdities. I was, and would remain, a kind of welcome drain down which she could pour the overflow of satire he inspired in her. But at the same time, she was distinctly against me. I was, dammit, a major reason for his dissatisfaction with things. If, just here and there, I would conform to his notion of what a son should be—in the surely not difficult matter of a bowler hat, a tendency to read much less and to be far more light-hearted in my taste for music, less morbid, more merry, spaghetti!—if I'd adjust myself in such matters, then life in the war-swept dining room would be very much easier. Dear Mother!—torn between the rebel who was glad there was another dissident at hand, and the woman who was inevitably under my father's influence, saw things at times in his way: because he *was* her original ally, and it was still so much a matter of those feelings she'd had about the overcoat that swamped him when he was thirteen. She wanted to laugh, but an inclination just as strong was to make him feel absolutely at home in his intolerable solemnity—the swamping overcoat of his character. 'As long as he's comfortable.'

But an indignant Fire Chief wrote to the head of my father's division to say he'd received a letter, over 'an unintelligible signature', that was 'not worth the paper it was written on.' My father was so shocked that he didn't keep this to himself. We were as appalled as he was; but didn't make a sufficient demonstration of our understanding that it was a bad moment for a civil servant tumbling from the empyrean of Nottingham down, down to the stunningly hard earth of Lambeth. An aeroplane, friendly or not, passed over as he was telling of it: and my mother chose that moment to express inattentively an exasperation she'd felt for four years. 'Oh, go home!' she cried. '*We know you can drive it!*' My sister and I laughed—with real delight. My mother's naïve sarcasm summed up an aspect of the fury we'd all felt during those murderous years: that in some ways we were suffering from a great outbreak of exhibitionism, especially in the case of young men given an apocalyptic opportunity to show off with elaborate machines. When Betty and I laughed, alas, my mother had one of those giddy fits in which she took herself to be a major source of amusement. 'You needn't think we're quoting in our shoes!' she cried (getting it all wrong) after the disappearing defender—or would-be assassin, as the case might have been.

My father was furious at being upstaged by an aeroplane, and had ear trouble more or less from that moment.

It was not a battle, this one between us and him, for which medals were given out. But the Battle of My Father's Ear looms large in my own personal history book. He was no commonplace hypochondriac. Once he'd established the fact of his malaise, he was ready to discuss nothing else. He wanted us all to join in a free-ranging canvass of the physiological possibilities. Since when he did A, B happened, was it fair to deduce that C was the cause: or was he failing to take into account D, E and F? Of course, the problem might be something none of us had thought of: say, G, H or I. Someone at work had even thrown out J as a possibility. 'You see,' he told my exhausted mother. 'That bubble has moved ... If I hold my head like this, *the bubble moves!*' My mother, who'd confided to me her view of the bubble ('blasted'), began nervously to grin. 'I know you regard it as funny,' he said, hideously tragic. 'But I can only say I'm glad you've never had anything like it. No one in this house has had anything like it. If you were suffering like me, we'd have to have a woman in to do the housework.' He glared at my mother and snatched at a newspaper, hiding behind it with an explosive volley of pages straightened and furiously re-arranged. 'Why the hell don't people put newspapers in order when they've done with them! Some people don't even know that ... page five comes after page four, not page eight!' My mother, famous muddler of newspapers, was uncertain whether to glare back, or giggle. ...

Great happenings in the world were upstaged for weeks by great happenings in my father's ear.

There was, as I remember, one light moment. It was when my old school-friend Ben came on a visit. He was himself a civil servant—temporarily diverted to unadministrative duties of a dangerous character, largely in the Atlantic. My father forgot his agony for a moment, greeting Ben with what I'd come to recognise as his hearty laughter for serving lads. Ben—with his severe brow, ill-described as a 'lad'—cheered him enormously with a disrespectful reference to the London Fire Service. My father then spoke with positive levity of his problem of hearing. 'I'm wondering,' he said, 'what they do with deaf civil servants.' 'You should get a job in the Foreign Office,' said Ben. 'That's what R. A. Butler did ... He sat on the front bench and pretended not to hear questions about non-intervention in Spain.' My father can have had no sympathy whatever with this remark, but was ready to forgive Ben anything for his libellous view of Lambeth.

But when Ben left, my father's grin went with him. 'I don't know whether to leave the cottonwool out of my ear or not ...' he said. My mother said, with exhausted indifference: 'I'm not able to tell you.'

The climax came the next evening, his first words on entering the house being, 'My ear got all stuck up again today.' My mother laughed hysterically. 'I didn't expect sympathy,' he said. She presented him with his dinner. 'I may not,' he said, 'need all this. I feel rather sick. I'm always sick.' 'Oh,' said my mother. 'Then don't eat it.'

And I thought what an amazing feat this was of my father's—to kill the sympathy in a woman so recklessly inclined to be sympathetic. But now she was enraged. She had had hours of his ear—entire and bitter evenings of his ear— total weekends of his ear. 'I must think,' she snapped, 'of some name of something *I*'ve got!'

'Be thankful, my dear,' intoned my father, 'that you keep—'

'Well,' she cried. 'You were going to say?'

'—that you can keep going,' he said, suddenly at the bottom of the stairs down which they were duelling, his rapier most uncertainly held. She was pressing furiously after him.

'I could easily go to bed!' she cried.

'And so could I,' was his feeble parry. Then he leapt desperately on to a balustrade; clutched at a ledge; appeared above her. He seemed completely to have recovered.

'If it wasn't for the fear of being left alone,' he flashed.

It seemed my mother was beaten by a most outrageous stroke. Was he suggesting that this woman who'd given her life to looking after him ... wouldn't look after him?

But she caught at an overhanging branch—swung herself upwards—and was high above him. 'You'll find it's no good,' she cried, 'putting lovely flowers on the grave and big words on the stone!' And with a general gleam of steel, left the room.

6

And the grave was his, and she sat waiting for his funeral as she'd waited for any other momentous event: the beginning of a holiday, a state visit to in-laws of doubtful friendliness. She had dressed hours too soon, and was opening and shutting the handbag in her lap. And I thought how often I'd seen her do that—without, till this moment, being precisely aware of the habit. Click—open: click—shut. Sitting in cafés; in dentists' waiting rooms; or waiting for my father to join the train when we were off to the seaside. He'd always remained on the platform till the very last second. I'd often wondered if he knew it made her nervous, and had done it from cruelty: or if it had been quite thoughtless. Such an old question, asked about so many of my father's acts.

Asked most severely now: for I'd inquired, the day before, where the photographs were of herself when young, her uncles and aunts and cousins, those snaps of her mother taken when she was attending some convalescent home in St Leonard's before the First World War. And now that I remembered— the photographs of Aunt Polly, whom I'd known only in her last bedridden years: and Uncle Bill, with young and *straight* legs: and Auntie Flo, in that photograph in which her hair hung in a silky blonde bang over one eye—I'd fingered that often as a boy, strangely excited by that vanished eye, the visible one seeming to be set in a vampish wink, and a silky dress flowing ...

And my mother told me that before he left Barton-on-the-Hill, he tore them all up. One afternoon, clearing things out before their departure, he'd gone through the album and torn up everything of hers. He'd kept the photographs of his own youth, his own family, but everything of hers had gone. And I couldn't bear the thought of it—of the loss of those few reminders of her past, and of his action. That last I knew at once I'd never be able to bear. Or rather, I'd always find unendurable the impossibility of knowing why he did it. Could there be an explanation rooted in mere clumsy thoughtlessness? Must the explanation not be some terrible, cruel one?

'Why didn't you stop him, dear?' I made myself ask. And *she* made herself answer: 'I was too frightened. ...'

She'd given her instructions for today, for our behaviour at the funeral: 'Now, no emotion! Please! No emotion!' Astonishing woman!—I'd never have guessed she'd say that! And then I saw how consistent it was with so much in her that was the stuff of the grim tactician. It was necessary to keep at bay the threat that her feelings would burst all bounds. So we would behave as if we had no feelings ... She sat, with her handbag in her lap. Click—open: click—shut. ...

The question of her future had become astonishingly unresolved. Last night a sensible man, her next-door neighbour, had said: 'I must point out that in no circumstances will the doctor agree to her living alone. She has a heart condition. And a neighbour, even living next door, can be a long way away.' This kindly man had been one of my father's monsters: he'd ensured that by having once been the manager of something or other. 'Manager my arse! Couldn't manage a wheel-barrow!'

But Betty and I were unconvinced. We'd even stared hard at each other and confessed that we'd rather she died of burning than that her valiant spirit should be broken. In duelling terms, she was now on an empty stage, all her opponents conquered. Could we step in and declare her victory a defeat?

Well, after the funeral she'd come to London with my sister: it was almost Christmas: she'd stay, rest, re-examine things: and then—then—*then* we'd decide.

And of course—it seemed strange every time we stepped outside the circle of our private story—this was the end of

27

1973. My father had died when everything seemed to be dying.

The local council had decreed that no electric light should be used: and when Kate and I called on the registrar, on our way back to London from the funeral, we found him sitting with his candle, cross with councils; and he was very slow and sour about registering my father's death.

How odd, I thought, for my father to have gone at a moment when he could have added his voice, more jubilantly morose than at any similar occasion in the past, to those abusing the miners! To my father, these men who put their lives at risk to provide him with coal, in all its uses, were a great stage army of malcontents and traitors.

But the night before he himself was burned, I'd left Kate and Betty with my mother and gone walking: ending in one of the local pubs. And that was full of men and women whom, oddly, I couldn't bear to think of my father being allied with. At that moment, I tried to separate him from them. I tried not to hear his voice when their voices declared:

'Bring Enoch in! He'll sort the boys from the men!'

Or:

'I'd take the bloody lot and drop them in Northern Ireland!'

My father, minor official and perfectionist in the matter of documents (my childhood had been all paperclips, and at times I'd thought he could hardly address me on any subject without untying a file), had his final documentation conducted by a minor official of reluctant bent, who appeared to regard my story—that my father was dead and had a few hours earlier been cremated—with only the most cautious credulity. He was barely to be convinced as to the name I offered, the address; my father's having left a widow. He turned the death certificate over and over in the light of the candle—which seemed much of his mind about these matters, inclined to gutter with doubt, and die.

I think, alas, my father and he might have got on sourly well.

7

A schoolfriend met in quite another pub told me that my old English master, Williams, had died.

So strange!—within a few days of each other, my father, who'd hated the idea of my going to university: and Williams, who'd done his absent-minded best to get me there.

The absurd speed with which things happened!—though, again, if you looked at life from a slightly different angle, how sluggish it was! This galloping tortoise—or creeping hare—of a life! When I first knew Williams he was a young teacher aged twenty-four, fresh from Oxford with novels, great poems, a famous critical work or two all impending in his neat head. Seeing I was lonely and longing to write, he'd invited me to send him letters ... to Swansea, when he was home there during the holidays. And I'd done it, and he'd instantly and gravely and marvellously answered. I had his letters still—but didn't need them: knew every word by heart. 'You mentioned your ambition to become a writer, and you have recognised the difficulties involved in such a choice. When a young man asks me whether he should take up writing for a career, in nine cases out of ten I say—No! In your case I say—Yes, because I think that you will be willing to suffer the endless disappointments which are the lot of the artist. ... Few men earn as much as J. B. Priestley, but you may get there. The great thing is not to be attracted too much by the modes of the moment. ...'

Oh, I didn't care if I failed to earn as much as J. B. Priestley! I didn't care if I failed to earn anything! The very word 'artist' thrilled me through and through. Look here, Dad: Mr Williams accepts that I'm an artist! But I must beware ... tiptoe past my father, if possible! For Williams had

29

quoted Marvell:

> The grave's a fine and private place,
> But none, I think, do there embrace.

'You and I can embrace everything,' he had written, intoxicatingly, 'provided that we are careful not to knock against the dead bodies. The corpses are so numerous, that you have to be cunning to get through the crowd. As long as your heart is in the right place, you'll manage. But don't shout at the dead men—they can't hear. Don't grasp their hands—the skin is shrivelled and their bones alone make a noise. They walk, but, my, how they rattle! And one of the best ways in which to get through a crowd is to look like the rest for a time: when you are through and breathing the pure air, you will be glad of this advice. Do you realise that I am nearly out myself? And, believe me, I am young to get through. Some men never succeed because they will argue with the corpses; others show they are alive, and the dead bodies just sway heavily against them, until the living man is suffocated, dies without protest, and is made a Mason, or a Town Councillor.'

Every word still remembered, still exciting—and here was Williams dead, aged sixty-seven, and he'd *never* got through! Nothing had come of it—not a novel, not a poem—one small critical work, made much of, sadly much of by Williams himself for forty years after it was written. One way of looking at it was to say he'd talked his life away. That Welsh flow that had been so marvellous in the classroom, filling it with words, had become a substitute for . . . whatever was more substantial than talk. He became someone much given to dreaming not only a life for himself but lives for others. For years I'd not been able to meet him without being taken through some scheme that would lead me to a doctorate, the headmastership of some astounding school ('I think it's not beyond your grasp, Edward'), the authorship of a fair sort of novel. (I'd noticed sadly that Williams didn't after all want me to get very far as a literary man. When I began to be published, he'd take me to task about misprints. 'You may think I'm being a pedant, Edward, but there's no writer worth his salt who hasn't watched over his proofs like a hawk!') And over the years I'd realised that the man who was all the fireworks I ever knew at school had become a burnt-out stick. The generous liberator had remained in the trap.

But sadder than that!—he'd once told me a story that made me realise he was never, in any true fashion, a firework of any kind. It was the story of his night out with Dylan Thomas. Well, that first letter he'd ever written me, from Swansea in 1935, had referred to a young friend of his who'd just gone up to London to pursue his literary career. Williams had reviewed this young man's first book of poems—and he enclosed the review. It ended (with words that again I don't have to check): 'Now Dylan has left us and gone up to London; and we know he will do well there. For Dylan is no playboy of the West End whirl.'

It was—dramatic irony and all—one of the first two acclamatory reviews that Dylan Thomas received: and it was here that Williams's story began. The poet had invited the two reviewers to dinner, in London—at the Dorchester! And so Williams, very happy, had gone to the hotel one evening after school: and had found the other critic there; and they'd waited for Dylan. They'd waited long after the hour fixed. Then Dylan came—but not, Williams thought, in the dress of a man who truly intended to dine, and to dine others, at the Dorchester. And indeed, leaning a little, Dylan suggested they go out first for a beer or two: but he meant a beer or three or four ... or eight or nine. ... Many beers, in many pubs. My dear teacher, always cautious about drink, sipped at half a pint here and half a pint there, and grew hungrier and hungrier, and more and more conscious of being nothing much but a tiring fixed smile on the edge of conversational rallies of which Dylan was the centre. More and more Williams was on the edge, more and more he was famished, more and more he was deeply disappointed. Very late indeed they arrived at a top-floor flat in Soho: and here, in his schoolmaster's sober dress, Williams lost touch altogether with his host, and crept away in time, but only just in time, to catch the last train back to Barton.

And with hunger, and disappointment, and the effect of a long day's teaching, he fell asleep—deeply: being shaken awake by a railway guard. It was morning; the train was in a siding; Williams was just able to reach school for assembly. He was—in his storytelling he made a great point of this—in yesterday's shirt, and unshaven.

Hearing of Williams's death, at this moment, I had no wish to make morals out of it. I'd last seen him in hospital after a stroke, when he'd told me about his friendship with the physiotherapist. Well, you see, she was Czech, and was startled and pleased when Williams, amateur violinist, talked about Smetana and Janáček. 'She plays the cello,' said Williams, out of the monstrously lolling corner of his stricken mouth. 'We'll make a trio, with a friend of mine. You and Kate will be very welcome to come and listen to us.' His habit of futures, I noticed, was—thank God—indomitable. And then he said: 'You know—there's an old man down there, at the end of the ward ... left school at thirteen, full of *strange* knowledge. Oh, it's not bad here, Edward. But I would like to get home again.'

And his habit, I thought, of being stirred by promise—even if (and I'd seen the poor old man at the end of the ward) it was dying eighty-year-old promise—was still alive, too.

I'd thought as a boy that Williams and my father were at opposite ends of the earth, but now I thought, with infinite sadness, that they'd been united in unfulfilment.

8

In a sense, it was the best Christmas she'd ever had. She sat among us on Boxing Day, when we all gathered at my sister's, like a little, enchanted, heart-broken girl. If only once he'd accepted the invitations we'd sent him to share Christmas with us! She'd proposed it again this fatal year, but he'd said she could never risk the journey. He would not endanger her like that—not at this season! And she sat there, glowing and blooming with the strange health of her grief—and with that natural health he'd never trusted in her, which said 'Pish!' to heart conditions—and lamented that he wasn't with us. And I knew that if he *had* been, his merriment might almost have exceeded hers. He'd certainly have been astounded by the perfectly obvious success of such an occasion.

And—as she was—he'd have been charmed by our son Tom, in some cast-off waistcoat and a straw hat I'd brought back once from Kenya: being enchantingly silly, exactly as when he was a little boy. *Then* he and my mother had had a secret comic relationship much like the one I'd shared with her for so many years. 'You little worm,' she once called him, and he'd retorted by calling her, 'You big worm.' To each other they were still 'Worm'. I thought how unlikely it was that, looking forward from the vantage-point of a thirty-year-old—say, from our Barley Wood days—yesterday, a quarter of a century ago—I'd have guessed that I'd come to have a mother in her mid-eighties, and a son in his mid-twenties, who addressed each other, with great complaisance on both sides, as 'Worm'.

She had a slogan that she carefully pronounced in the hearing of each person present—and any stray visitor who appeared. 'I love my home!' A few years later the techniques of persuasion might have seen her in a T-shirt (which she'd have delighted in wearing) that made this declaration: I LOVE MY HOME. 'When Brian is ready, I am ready,' she said, more mysteriously in the case of the stray visitor; who might not at once have realised that she meant that, when my brother-in-law had a moment to spare, he could drive her straight back to the bungalow, without any fear that he was rushing her. She was totally prepared. The idea of doing anything else was totally absent.

My sister said she was determinedly unobtrusive. She clearly loved being there, but didn't want anyone to conclude that that was where she, in any even faintly permanent sense, wished to be. She had cultivated a touchingly temporary look. As for her heart—'Well,' she said, 'I know it goes too fast sometimes. I'll just have to see it goes slower.'

She was, justly, doubtful of my competence in the matter of handling my father's estate, and the other chores of bereavement. In fact, I was leaning heavily on the good sense of my brother-in-law, who had a positive liking for such matters, and wouldn't have minded being called upon regularly to manage a bereavement or two in terms of documents. 'Remember,' said my mother, holding my hand, 'that you're next of *king*.' Being next of king—she gave my hand little slaps—I must pull myself together and try to resemble my father just a little in his careful attention to laws and rulings. She was very fond of Brian, but had incorrigibly the view my father had of persons incorporated into the family by the insecure link of marriage—they might well be plotting to grab everything and run for it. I won a little of her uncertain admiration by asking her to provide signatures for various documents. After assembling these—writing was a monumental activity for her, and required the tongue to hold the lips apart, for fear of what the teeth might do—she *patted* my hand: repeating, 'Remember—you're *next of king!*'

And a few days later she was full of pride because they'd gone out the previous evening and hadn't come home till midnight. She couldn't imagine what my father would have thought of that—he who'd had her in cotton wool by eight or nine o'clock every evening for years: by protecting her, I'd often thought, protecting himself. She'd stepped out into the midnight air, and the midnight darkness, that she'd not seen for heaven knew how long—he being convinced that to be on their feet, let alone in the open, a moment after nine o'clock would be instantly fatal—and she'd cried out that she'd forgotten how lovely the night air was, and the street lights. Oh, my goodness! the street lights! And I was exactly reminded of Tom's passion when he was small for the night-darkened world and the marvellous counterstroke offered by street lighting.

Well, my mother was a child, always—that was the essence of it!

She'd been troubled, along with her amazement. 'I don't know what Daddy would say!' It was as if she had paused for a thunderbolt. And she was now more and more desperately unhappy about him during the night. Her extraordinary grief immediately following his death was now made to seem ordinary. My sister lay awake listening to the sound of mother

34

in tears that were shed for hours on end. Such a long helpless sobbing! But there was nothing, Betty sadly said, that could be done. 'Weeping is such a private business.'

The world now seemed generally out of control. Shops lit by gas became shops lit by candles. My mother's beloved street lighting flickered and went out. It was odd, our private melancholy having such a dramatically drab general setting. There were bombs in London; the army used tanks to guard Heathrow. Somehow, it seemed a not unsuitable national response to my father's death. It was in his style, I'd think. OLD MAN DIES. TANKS ON STREETS.

She was beginning to know, she said, that it had happened; she had begun to face the awful fact that she would never see him again. Never could those ashes be re-assembled and step bearishly back, grumbling, infinitely welcome, into the sitting room in the bungalow. Which *was* a sitting room, where you sat! At the end of his life, he'd achieved *that* logicality! She was imagining him, recalling him endlessly, his expressions, his movements, his voice. He was more present than when he was alive. He came to her at all ages: the thirteen-year-old, so prompt to pinch her bottom, became in a flash the eighty-year-old, so prompt to pinch her spirit. She was woken one night, she told me, by *his* tears. They had been those she'd once seen him shed as a boy—thwarted in some intention by one of his brothers; they were much given to thwarting each other. But they were also those he'd shed the night he was taken away to die—when, with the ambulance men waiting, he'd handed her his wallet, saying: 'I shan't want this'; and had then said, 'Look after Ted!'

It was—even more than the torn-up photographs—the detail I couldn't fit in anywhere, in my posthumous jigsaw. He'd not liked me, he'd longed for every other kind of son; and at the last he'd commanded her to care for me! I felt terribly aware of the inadequacy of human understanding. Perhaps even Shakespeare had got even Hamlet wrong—leaving out (because he couldn't see where to put it in) some awkward, but clearly reported, cry of the prince's: *Oh, poor Claudius!*

We ate one of the two infinitesimal Christmas puddings Mother had prepared for them. A very great maker of Christmas puddings, who'd happily have laboured seasonally on behalf of all of us, she had by his misanthropy been reduced year after year to the production of these hideously tiny, extremely tasty, individual samples. They'd been ready for 1973, and someone had to eat them. I felt ... a cannibal.

Betty said Mother had talked about what might happen after death. Well, to put it briefly, you might become a daffodil ... or a cauliflower. Dad, his ashes scattered, might well become a daffodil. The idea of his being reduced to a flower, and such a flower, made my mother giggle. It *was* an awful triumph to have reduced such a tyrant to a form so pacifically floral. 'He would like us,' said my mother, with evident terrible guilt, 'to laugh at it.' This being almost certainly a pointer to her feeling that he'd *not* have liked it. His being converted into a daffodil—as, when children, we'd been able to convert old jam-jars into windmills, toys that revolved in a breeze—would never have been his idea of a permissible joke.

My sister said she'd begun to think of hiring mother out, as a thought-provoking sort of entertainment. Well, she'd had a coffee morning, an event of a regular kind: and what was usually a meeting of rather depressed middle-aged women, *being* depressed, suddenly became an hilarious event. They'd never met anyone with my mother's philosophy: which might be described as anti-depressive. She thought being alive was amazing enough. Very well; you had a misanthropic husband; for most of your life you had to pinch and scrape; your children were scarcely ideal; and, in the end, people began to die. Still it was marvellously interesting! She had distinct recollections of things being a bit barefoot and down-at-heel ... she wouldn't go into detail, but couldn't help remembering how often her mother had had a black eye, and had claimed to have been at her old trick of coming into contact, whilst inexplicably falling, with doorknobs and the edges of tables. 'I'm thinking of hiring her out,' said Betty. 'You know, she told all those terrible jokes of hers.' Middle-class North London had wept with astonished, and thoughtful, amusement.

Well, outside there were now no lights; no trains. There'd been such a Chinese puzzle of crises that I'd concluded we were in the final stage of such things: this was the crisis crisis.

I'd not known the country so divided along simple furious social lines since before the war.

No lights.

My father entered now into my own nightmares. I was in a ... mine, it might have been. A deep darkness, that was thick and heavy—a darkness dense-packed. We were seated round a pine table, though in fact I could see nothing. I could hear only. Being able to hear without seeing was agony. Someone spoke, it was a remark that had an air of wit about it, and I woke in panic.

It was the agony of hearing—of being conscious—and yet being unable to see. I was buried under that great weight of darkness. And waking was no relief, because the night around me, as I lay in bed, was of the same black weight. I was buried in the black night. I lay there, horrified, trying not to think the thoughts that, after several repetitions of this nightmare, I knew must follow.

They were thoughts in which my whole life seemed to lie buried, gasping, fighting for breath and life, in the blackness of memory, or of time past. I did not think of precise moments, but had an impression of all my daylight existence, over all those years, entombed in my head, quite unable to extricate itself. I supposed that in this nightmare my being was murmuring to itself: You are the tomb of your own past life. Your past is buried alive inside you.

From this point my thoughts, if that is what they were, branched out in a way that deepened my terror. They deepened it because it began to seem that there was nothing I could think of that would not increase this sense of being buried alive. I thought of people I had not seen for a long time, and there seemed to be, between us, the sort of separation there might be if we were buried in different, distant areas of some dark marsh. But no, not a marsh; for this was composed of soil immensely compacted. A thick seam of coal. I lay there in the night and felt this unbearable sense of separation from people not seen for ... I began to count the years ... six months, two years, ten years. Thirty years ...

And then I turned to Kate, asleep beside me, her eyes shut on her own darkness, and I felt my intense separation from

37

someone who was visible to me, with whom I had been talking only a few hours before. ...

I did not know, for a moment, how I could live through the night: because even to turn on the light would not be to dismiss the darkness. The darkness was non-day, and everyone sealed up in the separateness of sleep.

Or of death. I thought then of my father, and he represented a separateness that words could not describe.

If this was what I felt at the death of a virtual enemy, what was it my mother felt at the death of such an extraordinary confederate?

And she came to see us at Barley Wood. She brought flowers for Kate, cigars for me. 'Now I can give instead of being told I can't,' she said. And added: 'I hope I can be a real mother, as I haven't been able to be for so long.' Again she sat among us, upright, like a little girl in her shadowy, deaf world. The promised letter had come from her doctor, and was not so obviously opposed to her return as we'd expected. Anyway, she was going back next day: Betty with her, to be replaced after a day or so by Kate. And then she must be left alone. We couldn't imagine that.

So anxious was she now to demonstrate that she was in perfect control of herself, that she had ceased to talk normally. Everything she said had about it a touch of Elizabeth I at Tilbury. She vibrated with rhetoric.

From this house built in our old garden, she looked—though looking, I thought fearfully, was not the same as seeing—towards the old house, demolished ten years before, in which we'd lived from 1952 onwards. That late-Victorian edifice, the only word for it, which we'd been strongly inclined to call The Nettles, because so many local houses were named after dominant vegetables: The Pines, The Firs. Deeply in the clutches, when we arrived, of old Mr Gristwood's glum household gods; the place where, my father's and my mother's son, I'd had to come to certain conclusions about ... being a parent, and being married.

'He said you were very brave when you first came here,' said my mother.

PART TWO

I

What my father had actually said was: 'I suppose brave is the only word!' He meant he could think of a very large number of other words and phrases: foolhardy, rash, profoundly silly. Bloody daft.

'Always been rude about *this* house,' he said in the dining-room at 10 Manor Road. Tom was trying to persuade him to do something sensible, like reading a story, but my father's mind was not, at the moment, on Goldilocks. 'Never had much time for this room! Well!' He laughed unpleasantly. 'I should think they might have difficulty in tracking each other down in that dump! ... Sorry! Mansion!'

Well ... *touché!* I suppose, yes, we were all—Ben and Marie, Charles and Amy, Kate and I—in flight from little rooms, and houses in which it was hardly adequate to say you lived in other people's pockets. The involuntary intimacy was not half as decent as that.

The word Ben and I had in our heads for the house we dreamed of sharing was 'rambling'. It had been in our vocabulary since we were in the sixth form together. When I'd visited him, as a boy, we'd had to transact our business— airily literary and political—in a corner of the Fletcher kitchen: in the company of his mother, his brother and his sister-in-law. Ben's mother had a remarkable need to read newspapers aloud to anyone who was present. 'My goodness,' she'd say, having come to the end of a silent reading of a column and a half in the *Daily Herald*. 'Now, you listen to this!' '*No*, Mum!' Ben would cry. 'First let me tell you what it's all about. It's been going on for weeks.' 'Mum!—*no!*' 'Bert wants to hear it!' I was called Bert then, for alliterative reasons. When, later, Ben was courting Marie, she took it, in her

French fashion, that he was calling me 'Bird'. That in its turn led a journalistic refugee from Vienna with whom we rambled at weekends—we then briefly being Fabians—to assume that I was called Bernard. Well, he himself would speak confusingly about a fellow-reporter at Reuters: 'A colic of mine.' It was years before I got people back to the use of a name remotely resembling the one I bore.

Mrs Fletcher's claim that I wanted to hear the newspaper story was particularly dishonest. She knew I'd smile with sickly neutrality. Ben would speak for me. 'Bert *doesn't*! Do you think he's walked all this way just to. ...' The exposition, as an approach to the reading, would remorselessly begin. 'Might as well grin and bear it,' Ben's brother Sidney would say, from his seat in the chimney corner. He worked on the railway, was scornfully at odds with the ordinary world that supposed day was day and night was night; and had a view of current affairs that—not surprisingly, in that kitchen—was a matter of nicknames. 'What's Uncle Joe up to then, Bert?' I was too young not to be dismayed by the implication that I was an expert commentator on Stalin's intentions. 'I expect you'd like to tell us what Adolf's going to do next!' Vera, his wife, would say: 'Oh, you men! It's all you talk about— politics!' She'd often address this remark at me, who'd not opened my mouth since entering the house. 'Can't keep Bert off it!' Sidney would say. Mrs Fletcher would intervene. 'Now, you all listen to this!'

I remembered taking Ben during the war to see our old English master, Williams, who'd settled after marriage in a semi-detached house in a road full of obedient geraniums in Barton-on-the-Hill. Ben was appalled to be received by this subtle man in a conventional front room: amazed to encounter those familiar volumes of the poets housed with such disgraceful tidiness on each side of a tame, porridge-coloured fireplace. 'How can he bear it?' he demanded later, and began to discuss the infamy in terms of its being imposed on Williams by his wife. Ben was much inclined to see wives as creatures who'd have their very families stowed away on shelves, alphabetically, if they didn't look out. 'I expected,' he muttered, 'something ... rambling!'

When we resorted to this word, in an attempt to crystallise

42

our ideas in respect of housing, I think what we had in mind (aside from a simple romantic image of a house difficult to take in at a glance) was that it might be possible to live where one could hold a private conversation. One might—yes, my father was right—mildly get lost. Well, we simply thought of space. Which 1 East Drive had, in the vastest, most dusty fashion.

We'd seen many large houses, mostly damp: but here suddenly was this one, tall, ugly, apparently dry, in more than an acre of garden, a great greenness, with a greater greenness of fields behind it. Though, when we first saw it, the fields were all buttercup. There'd been a battle there, five hundred years before, and it all dipped down to what was still called Dead Man's Bottom.

'Enormous potentialities,' said Ben, taking Kate and me to see the house for the first time. One was in fact immediately aware of enormous shabbiness. The three floors of it, long unpainted, climbed out of a ruff—or scruff—of wistaria grown wanton, great knees and elbows of it, imposing far too much weight on a very heavy verandah. The style was difficult to name, but something maritime came into it. The middle floor, that is, had windows curved and protruding in the manner of the rear-castles of seventeenth-century ships. Otherwise it was only possible to say ... assorted late Victorian. The top floor looked out at the world through gables; the bottom floor peered helplessly through large windows much hindered in their function by squares of coloured glass, and generally forced, by verandah and wistaria, to squint. The back of the house was a cliff of brick and ivy: for the basement, underground at the front, was here overground, there being a considerable dip between the two faces of the house. Beyond, lawn, orchard, and a great bewilderment of roses on the point of reverting to their wild form. For the house had been empty—it and the garden untended—for nearly three years, since the death of the last occupant.

It is not an adequate phrase for him—'the last occupant.' Mr Gristwood was a sort of architect. He was said, anyway, to have designed this miscellaneous house some time in the 1890s. It had been intended as the Railway Hotel, being next door to the station; but along the road lived an evangelist who was an immensely famous enemy of drink. Barley Wood had no resemblance to the districts where his war against alcohol had been waged; it is unlikely that its genteel gutters ever accommodated a single drunkard. All the same, the application for a licence was resisted, and the celebrated abstainer won the day. From the possibility of being the Railway Hotel, the house slumped to being 1 East Drive, and the home of Mr Gristwood himself.

Palace might be a better word—and elevated more fitting than slumped. For Mr Gristwood was spoken of as the uncrowned king of Barley Wood. As well as being an architect, he was a land agent and the steward for the royal duchy that owned the freehold of much of the district. He had great power. This he used in a flat, latterday fashion, so that virgins had no need to tremble, but he did exercise the *droit de seigneur* ... over flowers. If a house fell empty, Mr Gristwood would visit its gardens and bear away any plant that caught his fancy. In his upright, churchgoing fashion, he was no better, I guess, than a horticultural Fagin.

We assembled our picture of him largely from the contents of the house. On the ground floor there was little to learn. This was to be our flat—Kate's and mine. Ben and Marie would be in the middle: there being respects in which it would have seemed against nature for them to take up residence at another level. In her native France, Marie had never lived on any kind of ground floor. I had an absurd vision of her growing up in Paris as ... Maurice Chevalier's daughter, roughly: emerging now and then from aerial attics to express, in song, her appreciation of the rooftops around her. Marie said it wasn't quite like that: but certainly, being domestically lofty was in her bones. Ben had a well-known aversion to being among the boots and roots of things. Kate and I were uneasy about the half-blind character of the bottom flat, but against the background of field, looseboxes (escaped, as far as I was concerned, from Victorian fiction), an entire orchard, that was nothing much.

The ground floor said little about Mr Gristwood because it had been used as the estate office. It seemed to be saying several mysterious things about estate offices. For example,

44

that they might at times accommodate horses. In much-dented lino, some of the damage was done by horseshoes: either that, or some of Mr Gristwood's employees had been shod. There'd been widespread use of a distemper of the colour of morose cocoa, and another of that washed-out green that is never seen but on walls. Both spoke to me of the school where I taught, which was decorated as if it had been an extremely large public convenience. There was one immense room that had clearly been intended as the lounge-cum-dining room of the Railway Hotel. It seemed to have been used for rough storage: perhaps, the damage suggested, a military tank or two, and some very primitive piece of machinery, very large, with teeth. Incongruously, a chandelier hung from the centre of the ceiling, but it sagged rather than hung. It was a dilapidation of glass droplets. 'Would convert beautifully,' said Ben, indicating the entire shadowy cavern. Opening a door into an enormous, gloomy cupboard, to which very great numbers of moths seemed to have come to die, he said: 'Your bathroom, perhaps?' and hurried us to the other side of the house, where other splendid battered spaces were acclaimed as our kitchen and our living room. In the middle of it all was a kind of congress of doors, a weak point—but perhaps one should say a point of remarkable feebleness—in Mr Gristwood's original design. In short, you had only to turn through half a right angle and another door presented itself. 'A door too many,' Ben grunted, leading us through what must be the last, but wasn't.

Kate and I had mixed feelings—of dreadful alarm, and dreadful excitement. It was difficult to imagine that this sequence of ruined spaces, these high rooms that looked as if the entire British Army had been billeted in them, could ever be made into a habitable flat. On the other hand ... there was a bay window that looked out on apple trees; another that framed the showering branches of a silver birch. And the deepest excitement in us sprang from the impossibility of it all being such a *grand* impossibility. It was monstrous but ... really such a long way from the dining room at 10 Manor Road.

Little to learn down there, though, about Mr Gristwood: except for the driving mirrors screwed to one outer window-sill or another. Through these, we learned, he'd spied on the activities of his gardeners. He was as much opposed to idleness as his famous neighbour was opposed to drink.

And not much to learn about him at the top of the house—the suitability of which for Charles and Amy Hickman was genuinely beyond debate. They weren't yet married—in the style of the time, wouldn't move in until they were. Marie and Kate, each with a small child and another expected, wouldn't want to live at the top of all those stairs. The top floor was full of what were designed in 1895 as mere cupboards for maids to inhabit (my mother, not much later being a maid ten miles away, might have been among them, it would strike me), but now constituted a promising region for the Hickmans, who would certainly be able to turn the stinginess of the 1890s into the stylishness of the 1950s.

It was on the middle floor, much the closest to being immediately habitable, that Mr Gristwood had lived—and died. On the whole, it was a little universe of brass. The metal of the fatal bedstead was now dulled; but you could see how it had winked once, overseeing the departure of that ... floral thief. Somehow or other, he'd managed to spend time sitting on a corner seat with a wooden canopy, painted white, from which hung strings of coloured beads. I could never imagine this, chiefly because I couldn't see how he'd not have needed, constantly, to brush the beads aside, like rattling flies, in order to see what was going on elsewhere in the room. He'd left photographs behind: himself walled up in frock coat and cravat, his wife wearing dresses that looked like lace-trimmed straitjackets. He'd made use of an ice-box of very great antiquity; and there was an extraordinary number of chamberpots that he'd been unable to take with him. The uncertainty of our neighbours' opinion of us was later made worse by the way we used these as containers for paint. I guess there were times when most of us were to be seen simultaneously scurrying about with Mr Gristwood's chamberpots in our hands: never plain ones—for those he went in for all pretended to be wrapped in leaves and flowers. They were urinary bouquets: but unmistakable for what they primarily were, or had been. Our walking about with them in such quantity in broad daylight really didn't add up to Barley Wood as older residents had known it.

2

I think of the district as we first knew it ourselves, socially among its early post-war pollutants, in terms of an older pollutant still: the vintages of soot in which the railway station next door was soaked.

That soot! Drop-out of so much smoke! We observed, Ben and I, that as trains passed under the bridge that bore the ticket office, they went in for dramatic expulsions of steam—pungent clouds that, finding it impossible to escape upwards, rolled suffocatingly down upon us and our neighbours. The dominant male hat in Barley Wood in those days was still the bowler; and Ben held that those evil clouds constituted a response by train drivers to the positively political spectacle of the Barley Wood platform at that time of day, between eight and nine o'clock, thick with the blatantly conservative domed headgear of business men, civil servants, lawyers. In carriages pickled in soot, we'd sit, among armies of black knees, and Ben would cause copies of *The Times* to go stiff and highly polished toes to tap irritably as he outlined his view that Milton's poems were, almost without exception, absurdly long. It wasn't certain that he excluded the sonnets. 'More piss than poetry,' he once said. This was really not so much annoyance with Milton as annoyance with Miss Furlong, whose class at the Central College we attended. Miss Furlong, to Ben, was the cultural wing of the reactionary enterprise of which Barley Wood was the social wing. He had begun to attend the class in the hope of extending his knowledge of English literature; he stayed in the hope of reducing Miss Furlong to hysterics and keeping her in that condition. But the paralysis of newspapers and tattoo of feet on the 8.35 were caused not at all by Ben's view of the poet, which could have

47

been even less sympathetic without rousing the smallest interest, but by the fact that poetry was being discussed at all, and then by the saltiness of the language. Curious to think that, in the early 1950s, 'piss' was not a word commonly heard in suburban railway carriages.

Or I think of the district in 1952 in terms of the Barley Wood Stores—which still named itself in the painted-out fashion of wartime: The B----- W--- Stores. I'd try to imagine the German invasion coming to a halt while they worked that out—their sense of being hopelessly up against superior intellects. Inside, Mr Robbins managed things in the spirit of his widely circulated dictum: This is the Fortnum and Mason's of Barley Wood. Largely this spirit consisted in making the pretentious feel it was right for them to be pretentious, and the unpretentious feel that they shouldn't be in the shop at all. Mr Robbins was bullying and bland, severe and servile. At times during the fifties, when Barley Wood became, at its fringes, a preserve of writers, broadcasters and so on, he was confused. It happened once when Alec Mason entered the shop, hungrily anxious for a meat pie. Alec was in the middle of writing a script about the new multilateral schools—or comprehensives, as one or two advanced persons were calling them. He was dressed as a writer—which meant that to Mr Robbins he had every appearance of a low-paid domestic servant, c.1925. Actually, he took Alec on this occasion for someone delivering, rather than someone eager to consume, meat pies. He thought Alec was an emissary from some disgraceful if necessary lorry parked outside. 'You'll have to wait, my man!' Mr Robbins cried. 'You can see I'm busy!' Even when Alec made a lively response to this remark, Mr Robbins was not greatly abashed. Well, there had been a time, and nothing but a world war separated us from it, when it would never have occurred to a resident to make himself indistinguishable from a delivery man.

And there was the general shop next door, where Miss Fluster presided under her bunting of outmoded underwear. Can she really have found herself often required, when she was not selling sweets or bottles of ink, to accommodate the gentlewomen of Barley Wood with bloomers? There they hung, anyway, on a line of string above the counter. In due course, our small sons would find it difficult to address her soberly under that line, so evocatively vacant: there being an air of bottoms that had only recently gone absent. *Bum!* said Miss Fluster's shop to every child that entered it, and to some adults too.

Down the road lived gentle Mr Stutters, who had been alone since his parent, for mortal reasons, had quietly quit, in the early 1930s, and who remembered how his mother had been disgraced on the arrival of the family in Barley Wood in 1912. She had been looked down upon—witty, odd Mr Stutters remembered—as the first local mother personally to push her child's perambulator. ...

And Mrs Shelley, the vicar's widow. I hadn't been living in East Drive more than a week when, a gloved hand raised, she commanded me to halt. 'Oxford or Cambridge?' she demanded. I thought in my astonishment that this was the old playground question, once common exchange between children who hadn't the smallest idea what a university was. It was a challenge as to which side you supported in the Boat Race, and was offered even if you were wearing your favour, the silver boat with a silky tuft growing out of it, light blue or dark blue according to your allegiance. You could be encased in such favours and the question would still have been asked. 'Cambridge,' I informed Mrs Shelley, naming my own infantile fixation: and only when I was dismissed with one of her freezing nods did I realise she was inquiring about my education.

I'm sure in any case she thought I was lying. Well, I was one of those living in the Co-op, and had probably not even had the benefit of primary schooling.

The Co-op was the name they gave to 1 East Drive when we moved into it. This was an attempt to place us by reference to a kind of shop taken to be at the other end of the world from Fortnum and Mason's—or its local embodiment, the B-----W--- Stores. It's difficult now to believe that in 1952, in Barley Wood, Co-op was regarded as perhaps the only hyphenated four-letter word.

As far as the district was concerned, our names might have been Marx, Lenin and Trotsky. If that's what they had been, our venture could not have led to a more censorious crop of rumours. We had our wives in common—that was probably the least of it—and were observably forgetful of the origin of any particular child. There seemed to be only two children, male and female, but this was almost certainly an illusion. Given such indifference to marital boundaries, the products might well be of an indistinguishable character. Some inevitable difference as between boy and girl might be as much as could be achieved.

It was obvious, anyway, that Kate and Marie were both pregnant. Probably never much else.

'Bookish fellow, eh?' grunted Mr Ryall-Musk, from across the road, peering through a window as I disconsolately freed my library from the sacking in which it had travelled to East Drive. That had been in a disreputable van of which, and of whose tatty owner, Kate and I were deeply fond, since it was with their assistance that the dramatic society to which we'd belonged had travelled from one festival to another. It was to them—the society, the van—that we owed the accident of our marriage—which was beginning to look a very substantial accident indeed. Life seemed to be filling up with examples of the wildest chance solidifying into the most adamant reality. Perhaps, I sometimes thought, *that's* what life was, altogether—the accidental becoming the immutable. ... Our arrival in Barley Wood with our legs dangling over the tailboard of this van must have made many of its residents try to remember the year in which it all began ... 1789? Oh, the fearful decline in the style of removal itself! Once it had been Harrods throughout, and your child's least considerable toy, forgotten in some corner of the least important room, wrapped for transport in careful tissue paper!

Later that day I went to fetch Tom from his refuge with Kate's parents in nearby Barton-on-the-Hill. He, at that stage when you're like a tiny announcer, interrupted programmes with a news-flash: 'I going painting with Daddy!' For weeks, 1 East Drive had been a place being painted. Tom was much taken with the notion of painting, and had enormous plans for varying the coloration of the entire world as soon as he had half the command over affairs exhibited by his amazing parents. I pushed him to East Drive in his pram, wondering again to find myself a man pushing a pram. By what curious

50

drifts of chance and intention had I put myself into the position of having to propel this odd vehicle, so oddly loaded? There, in it, was my son, my dear ridiculous son, myself all over again, but a portion of my existence that was obstinately busy with creating an existence of his own! This small, delicious, rebellious, exhausting branch of myself, who was at the same time an entirely comic fusion of Kate and me. It was like one of the *New Statesman* competitions Ben and I went in for. A four-line epigram in the style of. . . . A hundred words of prose in the manner of. . . . The usual prizes are offered for the invention of a tiny, vivid creature, with the gift of converting a perambulator into an empire, in the combined style of Kate and her accidental, still profoundly astonished mate. . . .

We sat in 1 East Drive, that first night, under those remote ceilings that were characteristic of the bottom floor, and felt like brutal soldiery, uneasily billeted. Well, it had been an aspect of our feeling about the move, from the beginning. There'd been that furtive sense of social promotion. The orchard and the looseboxes . . . innumerable trees . . . a front drive, and *two* front gates, both double . . . and a basement . . . an open-fronted garden shelter of metal painted sombre pink, containing a wooden bench of a superior kind, the whole being known to us as the Lovers' Seat. . . . And this was only the beginning of the inventory. These were all props of the middle-class stories of my lower-middle-class childhood: I had moved into a modified version of The Grange, The Hall, The Manor. I had definitely moved out of that stifling world of the semi-detached. . . .

Was I perhaps not wholly displeased, for the oddity of it, to have a Mr Ryall-Musk as my entirely displeased neighbour?

Kate said: 'Do you think living under such high ceilings will change our characters?'

It didn't seem unlikely. All the domestic ceilings we'd ever known were eight feet up, at most: and these were half as high again. And there was the possible effect on our natures of being able to stride about the place. I'd leave the kitchen, our one strictly habitable room, and make my way into our bedroom, a set out of a mild horror film, its floor heaped with books, and be amazed by the amount of time it took me to get there. Through the tall uncurtained windows, round-arched, streetlight came, and the shadows of leaves danced in it, turned into little creatures that dashed madly about the floor or streaked up the walls and down again. To this flickering strangeness was added the effect of a revolving light from the next-door policebox. The corners of the room were obviously thick with vampires. I was glad Kate would be sleeping there with me: our two timidities would, as usual, add up to a single quiet heroism. Meanwhile, unaccountably, Tom was fast asleep in his own bed, his face scuttled over by shadows. I thought this was the house, all right, for his latest obsession: which was with blood. Given power, he'd have made it a matter of law that, if blood were sighted anywhere, he should be instantly summoned, to watch trembling as it formed a shocking pinhead on the site of some scratch. . . .

Then I walked the other way, through the insanity of doors that connected the two arms of the flat, and returned exhausted to Kate. She wasn't big, yet, with half the time to go before the birth of our next child: but already, in that huge shadowy kitchen, I saw her as she'd been just before Tom came: presiding over her large lap, looking like a cellist who'd swallowed her cello.

And the silence upstairs was the silence of my oldest friend and his wife. Here we were! together, as we'd dreamed, in this dusty and chilly Utopia, ready to drive out Mr Gristwood's glum household gods and replace them with our own: which should be bright, foolish ('Life's a poor thing if we can't be foolish,' Ben had said) . . . and literary.

3

It was winter when we moved in, and icy air gave a curious edge to everything that happened. At weekends Ben and I went out to dig at the plots we'd chosen for ourselves at the end of the garden—a plausible background, as we took it to be, for our discussion of the *New Statesman* competitions. Day after day we felt on our skin faint touches of unrealised snow. Then it came, together with a gale, that kept a strong spray of it leaping for hours over a courtyard wall below one of our windows. It was a constantly renewed bride's train without a bride. Tom, having never before seen snow whilst capable of similes, made a pioneering claim to the view that it was like sugar.

Our digging became a less plausible battering at frozen clay.

We were using the weekend competitions, we thought, as a form of literary limbering up. This was a term from our schooldays. Having an all-rounder who was not only able but happy to sprint faster than anyone else and leap further in all directions, the school had won a national schoolboys' games: and that, athletically, had unhinged it. For a while we were all required to run, leap and throw things. I ought to have been safely incapable, but turned out to have the gift of running. I was, to my dismay, naturally fleet. Again and again I was named in the fervid notices requiring us to go out on the field at inconvenient times—after school, usually—and limber up. The phrase did not connect in any way with my idea of myself. It had emerged that Ben also had winged feet; but he seemed to take them seriously. Ordered to limber up, he limbered up. I would hurry away down the school drive, trying to add touches of dignity and determination to the act of sneaking off. But then, across the suddenly hushed field, Ben's cry would ring out, studiously treacherous: 'Going home?'

'Five times round the field at a moderate pace,' those curt notices would say. 'Then once full out. Follow with cold shower and brisk rub-down.' The *New Statesman* issued mellower instructions. 'The usual prizes are offered for an inscription—one rhymed couplet—for the collar of a dog belonging to any famous person.' I'd worked out a perfect two-liner for a renowned mountaineer's pet:

> Robinson owns me: for he seeks,
> At times, a change from larger Pekes.

But I couldn't think of the name of a renowned mountaineer—Robinson was merely holding the place for him. And
Ben doubted if a mountaineer would favour a Pekinese. A
Great Dane, perhaps. But I'd found another use for that
breed:

> I'm Gielgud's dog. It's useless to be vain!
> I am a Great, but he's a Greater Dane!

Well—not the best of couplets, either of them, said Ben. I'd
expected him to say so. He had what he called his instinct to
spurn; and on top of that, as he freely admitted, he found it
difficult to praise rivals. He'd always been given to tearing off
epaulettes before anyone else came forward with laurel
wreaths. To his mind, his own couplet, designed for the
spaniel belonging to a well-known archaeologist, was far
sharper. 'You're always patting the people you disparage on
the head,' said Ben. I protested that I didn't see the
competition as an exercise in disparagement. In any case, *his*
couplet was surely extraordinarily libellous. I meant that it
might easily form the basis of a straightforward action in the
courts, as a result of which Ben's career would not mildly be
nipped, but savagely be severed, in the bud. Ben said he'd
observed that his essentially anti-establishment viewpoint
threw people into disarray. He'd noticed it at work. 'People
like me up to a point, and then ... my goodness, they smell the
honest guttersnipe in me, and they *don't*!' From where Ben
stood, this meant that he would be acclaimed long after the
rest of us—smooth non-guttersnipes, making of the literary
gift a means of pleasing the powerful—had been totally dis-
credited. Posterity would rush back in the direction of Ben's
tomb and redirect the award of the *New Statesman*'s guinea
from me (dead and disgraced) to Ben (dead but rehabilitated).

We smiled at each other, and demonstrated the absence of
all personal feeling by attacking with particular energy the
frozen earth under our spades. Then Ben said: 'My finding
your couplets lousy, you know, isn't incompatible with my
enjoying them.'

It was curious, I thought, as between Ben and me: his
aggression, and my failure to be aggressive.

Ben's instinct in any situation was to smell out the attempt to down him, and quench it at once. If a ticket collector on Barley Wood station asked to see his ticket, Ben immediately suspected that he was in danger of being made to look small. I'd been with him on such an occasion when he'd certainly shown his ticket, but only with such growls of dissent and distaste as (from his point of view) meant that the ticket was virtually undisplayed.

Ben bristled: surrounded by sycophants, creeps, rivals for various virile crowns, who would certainly pounce if Ben didn't pounce first.

So he was afraid (I'd sometimes think) of eschewing aggression; and I was afraid of exhibiting it. He always bristled outwardly; I, of course, did quite a bit of inward bristling. How odd that, so absolutely different, we were so close!

My own dread of behaving in a hostile fashion sprang from having a belligerent father, and a pacific mother. My father had never let any irritation pass, ever: he'd been from birth at war with his enemies—at a rough stock-taking, the rest of the human race. It struck me early that if one got through some typical passage of human existence—lasting, say, twenty minutes—with nothing worse than having one's toes trodden on, one's ribs bruised and one's susceptibilities generally ruffled, one could count oneself lucky. Well, there were so many of us, and, poor creatures, we were endowed with only the most rough-and-ready apparatus for making our way through the infinite sensitivity of things: no wonder we blundered into each other, small wonder that we'd have been better designed without elbows—or if, in general, we'd been in size about ...two inches by two inches, and smooth all round. ... It was balls of angora wool, I'd decided recently, that I thought human beings would best resemble. Look at the human shape as it was!—a travesty of good design: well, knees ... well, ankles ... well, *elbows*. ...

And think of the human nervous system! My God, we were crawling with nerves! Touch us anywhere, and there was such a response from inner warning systems as if each of us had been a consortium of fifty major fire stations! I didn't know how we avoided spending the whole of our lives dancing up and down on the spot, every one a little tragedy of overstimulation!

I'd thought, on one or two agitated occasions since we'd moved into 1 East Drive: the only tolerable motto was, *As amiably as possible.*

I felt all this because, besides being shrinkingly my father's son, I was expandingly my mother's son, too. If one of my main aims in life was *not* to report waiters, cinema ushers, ticket collectors in my father's manner (it would have simplified his life if he'd been able to lay a complaint against everyone in those professions at once, submitting to the authorities an exhaustive list), another aim was to smile on such persons, in Lizzie Pye's manner. Her marriage with my father could be described as a protracted attempt on the part of her mollifying smile to make up for the damage done by his exacerbating scowl. ...

Well, there it was. Ben, with *his* father—in a plain working class family—dead early, and his mother, in the sexual terms of the time, four or five times a father, had grown up embattled. I, with a father of (in the sexual terms of the time) exceptional masculinity, and a mother gently unconvinced of the value of being disagreeable, had grown up with the strongest possible impression of the pleasure of being pleasant. And here we were, Ben and I, together in Barley Wood, pursuing a dream which drew on common ground between us: a dream of being persons of a little literary achievement (well, *huge*, actually) ... and of living brightly—and foolishly.

It was suddenly, amid all that iciness, shining. The crooked branches of the fruit-trees in the orchard made nets in which sunlight was caught. Brightnesses thrashed inside those nets like captured fish. The sun shone full on our horseboxes: on the brilliant spines of the poplars. And none of us had ever lived in such a place! None of us had ever before owned a square foot, let alone an entire acre, of winter sunshine!

Or rather—I'd remember Mr Gristwood—had had this brief illusion of ownership!

Ben said, warningly: 'We mustn't be maudlin about this place, you know!' And his face broke into a rather beautiful, maudlin smile.

4

My father visited us from time to time, brisk with discouragement. 'My goodness,' he cried, in front of Mr Gristwood's
greenhouse, which had taken advantage of its owner's old age
and death to deviate from the true. Its essential angles had
become 45° instead of 90°. Tom would morbidly come and
contemplate it: at the moment, a tiny connoisseur of disaster.
I'd think how sad it was that he'd missed Samson's treatment
of the palace at Gaza. 'Poor broken greenhouse!' he'd sigh, in
the tone in which he was accustomed to commiserate with the
moon if it was anything but full: 'Poor broken moon!' My
father allowed himself no such spasms of pity. 'My God!' he
groaned. 'You'll never get that right in fifty years!' I realised
that he was trying to be cheerful: thus the refusal to name the
period he usually favoured when making such prophecies—a
century. Workmen arrived to convert the house into three
flats. 'They won't be out,' he cried, 'before Christmas.' He
asked me what I was painting. A door or two, I said. 'Not
painting doors!' he cried. 'Well, I think you are *very* foolish! It
takes years of experience to paint a door!' I decided not to ask
him how to reconcile such an apprenticeship with the urgent
need that such of our umpteen doors as survived the
conversion should bear some other colour than the excremen-
tal brown universally affected by Mr Gristwood. ...

My mother in those days, I now see, was as far from Lizzie
Pye as she'd ever be. My father had settled down in the Tithe
Redemption Commission: a leisurely enterprise, designed to
unpick the ancient fabric of religious economics. It was
enormously a matter of old maps; any step you took raised the
documentary dust, and my father seemed officially comfortable, half-hidden in the antiquity of it all. My sister and I,

from being serious problems at home, were now serious problems at some distance: which was a much more relaxed way of having problems. We were both very much like Mr Gristwood's greenhouse—our getting married had brought about instant, and deeply interesting, collapse. You'd never get us right in ... a hundred years. We had no illusions about our father's favourite activity. It was to discuss us in terms of the disasters we were. Tom might have sympathised—except that his small child's morbid interest in things going wrong was rooted in pity. My father's certainty that my sister and I, once we'd moved out from under his roof, had taken one false step after another, had its roots, alas, in satisfaction.

My mother didn't agree with a word of it—but she was now cut off from the seditious influence that Betty and I had provided. She—who was to end life as a bone or two—was now all puzzled flesh. Among the more curious views that she took over from my father was that the enterprise at East Drive was a kind of ... resigned triple acceptance of shoddiness. Of course, any of us would have been far happier to live in some prim box like 10 Manor Road. Our venture in Barley Wood was that of a gaggle of young unfortunates for whom the alternative to trim semi-detached was some corner in a ruin.

Talking to Kate, my mother confessed that they'd kept painful news from us. Betty and Brian had found a house in a North London suburb that was everything that could be wished, in terms of trimness, and of it not being necessary to share with anyone. 'He told me not to tell you, but. ...' I stared at her hard, and she giggled. Well, there was never a moment when *that* vital element of Lizzie Pye was absent: her giggle, which represented her fundamental understanding that beneath almost everything that happened, comedy was prancing about, exposing its impertinent drawers ... in some cases, and this was probably one of them, proving that it hadn't bothered with drawers at all. ... You tended to discover that what life was saying, like Miss Fluster's shop, was '*Bum!*'

But in this strange stretch of her existence, she lost for the moment a number of her gifts. Or perhaps it was simply that her instinct was thrown askew by her knowledge of my father's ungenerous feelings about us all. He had such feelings even about Tom—whom he loved as much as he loved anyone: and who was adamantly determined to love him. Early on, Tom had decided that my father worked in the garden largely for his benefit, so that, for example, he could turn up wet and wriggling worms. For a long time Tom was simply amazed that the earth contained such creatures, animated by some principle so remote from that which lay behind the existence of most other living things: well, no head, no arms, no legs. Spectacularly, no face. And my father in one corner of himself acceded to the idea that he was in the garden only to turn up these amazing worms. I'd come across them together staring down at one, gripped by a single primitive amazement. Tom appreciated much of what, at his age, I'd appreciated in my father: especially the sandpaper of his occasionally unshaven, weekend face. But at the same time as being a tiny creature who gained my father's love by taking it for granted that my father himself was loveable, Tom was also an aspect of us: of Kate and me; and therefore, inevitably, an instance of serious mismanagement. Knowing that I was tender, my father delighted in moments when Kate was severe: believing this must be a strain between us. When *I* was severe, he held that this was because Kate required me to be so. He frowned at any of a small child's inescapable petu-lances or tired angers; launched into homilies that made Tom worse. He speculated unpleasantly on the reasons for these things. 'We think you keep him out too late!' 'Oh, my goodness! Your mother and father have been overfeeding you, I expect!' Wrath would boil up in Kate and me; suddenly we'd all be Toms.

And if there was no anger, then there'd be what we'd learned to dread, in our short experience of parenthood: the elders sitting round the small child, observing him, and the small child becoming furious, or unhappily uppish, because he was unable to escape from that ring of grown-up eyes.

The dining room at 10 Manor Road, I'd think, strikes again!

And it was this nervous atmosphere, perhaps, that made Lizzie Pye so unlike herself; made her snatch at Tom, or bring her face suddenly close to his and laugh in a strange and unexplained fashion. She'd make him jump and even cry with some abruptness of the kind, and then would be sulkily and miserably puzzled herself: not having meant this sort of thing, at all. ...

Lizzie Pye at sixty: a compass thrown quite out of true.

5

Two pieces of learning at Barley Wood: one more slow than the other. The slower one was that nothing constitutes so private a style, so difficult to mix with anyone else's style, than the fashion in which you bring up children. Or—not to use a tidy phrase for a great untidiness—the style in which, somehow, you come to terms with the impossibility of being parents, which springs directly from the impossibility of being children.

Ben and Marie—Kate and I—the Hickmans—were all to turn out to have different philosophies in this distracting matter. To attempt to accommodate them in a single house and garden was like pretending that you could lock together unmatching pieces of a jigsaw puzzle. What happened in the end was that the shape of each piece became sadly battered, forced out of true.

It was all—amid enchantments, pleasures, many real moments of neighbourliness—a disorientation like Lizzie Pye's. It took ages to understand why our dream of happy comradeship in an atmosphere of buttercups turned out to have other, sourer elements.

And the quicker piece of learning was an addition to discoveries we'd already made: and it was simply that children and parents were doomed to find each other both adorable and damnable. There were times when I'd walk about growling to myself the confession that *now* I knew why people who could have nannies (despicable upper-class people) ... had nannies. I'd come home from school, on that hideous railway—it was like travelling in the bowels of a very old boiler—and would feel at once the unfairness of it: that, having been in another world all day, I was looking forward to the change to a small, domestic scene; and Kate, who'd been inextricably engaged in that scene since Tom's first waking cry, would be exhausted, full of the most indigestible mixture of delight and fury ... rather angry, somewhere in her dishevelled soul, that I *had* been out, at liberty, able to loll back (as anger would have suggested to her that I did) in those sooty vehicles of escape, the local trains, and talk to Ben with airy unreality of ... oh, damn it ... even more ostentatious escapers like John Donne, Robert Browning. ...

My love, Kate, and I, her love, would find ourselves at astounding war.

My father watched over all this, I now see, with the mischievous passion of a man who'd had a dissatisfied son, and now saw this son in a situation where he was, surely, finding it difficult to be a satisfying father. He watched unkindly for any awkwardness between Tom and me. It was another odd feature of that early experience of parenthood, when we were trying to understand the baffling politics of the connection between adults and children: that one prominent observer had his money on things going very badly indeed. ...

Tom, between two and three when we arrived in Barley Wood, was essentially a delight, an item of magic in our daily life. The possibility of conversation was his latest discovery, and it erupted in him ... an immense boiling. He reminded me of the traction engine, bearing the name Winston on its boilerplate, that I'd worked with during the war, threshing. Tom and it were of the same boiling nature; and what the governor was to Winston, those whirling brass balls that regulated the function of the engine, Tom's hands were to his verbal function. They fluttered enchantingly while he tried to make a propulsive steam out of the parts of speech.

Here was a creature who believed his favourite treat was 'a nice cream', and who, much taken with Kate's habit of calling him 'sweetheart', enthusiastically made the term his own; so that even Mr Robbins in the B----- W--- Stores was welcomed with a genial cry of "Allo, *sea-pup!*' An alternative form of address of which Tom was fond involved the warmest possible

61

use of the mere surname: ''Allo, *Robbins!*' All of it was ascribed, one guessed, to the morally vague atmosphere of the Co-op. A long way, the B----- W--- Stores would have muttered, from the traditional local habit of addressing an elder as 'Sir'.

There was no moment when Tom's pockets did not bulge with treasures, always including considerable stocks of leaden cattle. Many of these had lost their legs: he had the largest herd of crippled cows in the world. And these had to be supported ... made to lean against a skirting-board, a table leg. He said they had to ''gainsted up.' I was entranced by this example of the unorthodox inventiveness of a child's approach to language. (Ugh!—'approach to language', I'd think! My damned schoolmaster's ... approach to language!)

And Tom was passionate, always, for stories: pleading, with a kind of steely cajolery: 'About Goldilocks' or 'About a monkey'; sometimes adding anxious hints as to plot: 'About Jack and the Beanstalk ... he hid in the gasmeter.' Or he would approach you backwards, a book under his arm: the backwardness being designed to limit the loss of reading time involved in lifting him on to your lap. His trembling intensity would sometimes set me laughing with love and delight—an irrelevance that appalled him; he'd seize my chin and tug it round to the correct position for reading, and his small face would be swamped with his displeasure.

He accepted the new amazing world of house and garden as if it was an addition to all that fiction. Following his custom, where new words were too unlikely, of making do with old ones, he spoke of the looseboxes as 'larders.' There were suddenly real animals around, amazing horses, astonishing actual cows. Out of this green sleeve the world even produced a donkey, owned by a retired tradesman who'd built himself, round the corner from East Drive, a house that must have come straight out of his own childhood reading. It was made of bricks and timber, but looked as if it might be made of sweetmeats. Old Mr Herring had created a successful chain of shops, but it seemed he'd always really wanted to be a pixie. The donkey was clearly part of this fantasy, and looked over any hedge it was currently chewing with its owner's expression of, as it were, contented disquietude. It seemed to Tom essential that he should provide the donkey, and as many other animals as possible, together with a random menagerie of insects, with lumps of sugar, carrots or blades of grass. He was always asking to be accompanied on some kindly errand. No animal, insect or bird he encountered went unaddressed: he had for them a special voice, so thrillingly gentle that you'd have thought they were all in the depths of nervous break-down.

The pleasantest creature! Spied as he scampered about the flat—or made his grave, excited way from place to place with half a library of tattered books under his arm—or lay on the floor, muttering a world into existence out of scraps of wood and his items of legless agriculture—he filled us with love and amazement. Sometimes I could say what I felt about him only in a kind of kitchen-verse—as I'd done a year or so before:

A little lad, he tucks his vital cuddler
Under his chin (a violin gesture) and sinks
Into the large abstraction of his eyes,
Which both abjure their right to indulge in blinks.
His small version of a hand is on the rail,
Where negligently it clings, what time his legs
(Down which his trousers drop, like an upside-down
Vision of a garment fixed to a line by pegs),
Move up and down, to the motion of his thoughts,
Or whatever it is that goes on deep in his eyes ...
If you think that he'll stay like that for long, you're in
(And so is he) for a remarkable surprise.
For deep in the pool of his perfect introspection,
The still pool whose rippling his flexing knees repeat,
Lives a frog of fury, that suddenly leaps to the surface and
Makes him sway on his six-inch-long-shoe-covered feet.
And the frog shouts in his throat, and shakes in his chest,
And casts off the cuddler, and flurries the pool of his eyes ...
And the moment of thought is over, and he bends to attempt
Once again to fit together cups of incompatible size.

Yet how, at times, could we endure him? Waking at some ludicrous hour, he found it impossible to understand why active life should not be instantly resumed. We'd cling to sleep, trying not to hear his cries: firm at first, and then becoming dejected, incredulous, furious—and finally sly: 'Pottie, truly!' The formula 'Pottie, truly!' was based on the idea that there might be some other formula ... 'Pottie, falsely!', in fact—a phrase he never used, though he might often have done so. We'd now be hopelessly trying not to consider the possibility that the fervent sincerity of this cry indicated that he was ... fervently sincere ... On such a morning, in a rage that would have been suitable for the last scene of a Shakespearian tragedy, I shot myself across our room and into his as if I'd been a bullet I was firing, and launched an attack, violently weak, on his bottom. He was aghast. The good brave world had turned bad and cowardly, and had sunk its teeth into him. Kate rushed in at once to redress the balance. She was of the excellent opinion that he should never have more than one enemy at a time. I snarled inwardly at the ease with which she now became the most popular mother ever known.

Not that Kate had any hope of hanging on to this position. She might have remained eligible if it had merely been a matter of enduring anxious poverty; or trying to make a home in a nest of dusty barns; or if I'd been more dependably worldly; or if she hadn't been pregnant; or if Ben and Marie, drawing on larger resources, had not always been several steps ahead of us. Well, another piece of learning: that in Utopia, all incomes must be equal, or all the natives extraordinarily tactful in the deployment of their wealth. The sound of that amazing thing, a washing machine, as it made itself heard from the floor above while Kate wrestled with a rudimentary wringer, would have soured the sweetest nature. But added to all this was the torment inflicted by this tiny St Francis, our son, loved by animals with the facile enthusiasm of those not even marginally involved in being his mother. Kate said that holding that position was rather like sitting for a non-stop primitive examination. There was no answer she could think of to the question 'Why?' that would nip in the bud infinite repetitions of that question.

We'd all said how good it would be for Tom and Sally, Ben and Marie's little daughter, to have each other to play with. In fact, Ben had suggested out of his habit of vague

64

opportunism that one of the advantages of living together was that each would have the benefits of a large family without being obliged to produce one. I think he had some notion of children taking entire responsibility for children: giving, perhaps, some annual account of themselves. ... The naïvety of such a view, as it turned out, was abysmal. The first effect of Tom and Sally coming together in that generous acre was that they became unrecognisably uppish. A kind of mad arrogance seized them. They laughed wildly and falsely, addressing each other in streams of gibberish that caused them very coarse delight indeed. Had their knees been big enough to make it worthwhile, they'd have slapped them.

They also dared each other to do things neither would have done alone: achievements that appalled even them. This person who was not Tom or Sally, this little wrecker who almost certainly sported what Tom regarded as the sure sign of a villain, a 'Miss Marsh'—'A Miss Marsh and a beard,' he'd shudder—made merry with paintpots: and spent a disastrous hour transferring coal from the cellar in the basement to the main hall of the house.

And several times they were found in the depth of hedges with their pants round their ankles. I thought how deep-rooted was the human sense of unnecessary shame when, blundering on a tableau of this sort, I noticed that Tom leapt in the air with alarm, and became horribly pale. They accounted for their dishevelments with stories about ... seeking to be cool, or simple simultaneous failures of elastic. Alas, these occasions brought about one of the first of those little conflicts of style between the different ways of rearing children. Ben and Marie were not able entirely to avoid suspecting that our tiny son had some ... oh, most oblique element of the rapist, the male brute, about him. I thought, remembering childhood hedges of my own, that it was all part of the secret life of children: a world that adults stumbling upon it should pretend not to have seen.

Oh, Tom was our delight. 'It's nice when you find there's companionship coming from a child,' said Kate, one aston-ished day, when Tom had wanted an apple, and had said: 'I get it for you.' Kate said it wasn't possible, but he'd climbed on a chair and pulled the fruit bowl towards him, and carried

65

the apple across to her. 'Then he got his stool and we sat together and ate apples.' Kate was awestruck. Well, it was the first time she'd realised that in that totally dependent Tom were the seeds of a Tom who would one day manage his own existence—and become a friendly element in hers.

Backing towards me with a book of rhymes, he said: 'Not poetry ... *Poems*!' At this stage he was made furious by the adult carelessness that offered more than one word for the same thing.

And in public, at times, *impossible*! Going anywhere with a small child, we'd already decided, was like never visiting a china-shop without having carefully engaged the services of a bull.

6

Buying the house had not been easy. The figures involved had for me, poorly versed in such things, a kind of black poetry. It had cost us £3,750: of which we'd paid £250 in what I believed to be cash. Raising a proportion of this, since neither Kate nor I *had* cash, was a nightmare. Ben had plunderable relatives, Charles seemed to experience little difficulty. But we were left with appeals to two of the last people on earth anyone with any sense would have turned to: my father and Kate's.

Ben had put the task to me in a form so terrifying that I'd goggled at him. 'Ask your father to deposit the deeds of his own house with our building society, as a guarantee. Perfectly safe. That will do it,' said Ben. 'I'll have a word with him myself, if you like.'

My father was in possession of the deeds of 10 Manor Road after a quarter of a century of weekly payments, at times very difficult to raise. I think if he could have afforded to hire a guard to watch over them perpetually, he'd have done so. I imagine yet another use of that dining room: in a corner, the deeds, and their armed guardian. I suppose he might have yielded them to ... a saint, able to present cast-iron credentials: Winston Churchill: the film actress Madeleine Carroll, for whom he'd always had a famous longing. He might have been induced to give them up at gunpoint, though I'd not be entirely sure of that. What is certain is that he'd not put them in the mildest jeopardy at the behest of his son, in order that that wretched boy might inhabit a corner of a broken-down house in a district in which he'd be socially out of his depth. Putting such a request to him would be like going up to a lion and asking him to deposit with you, on trust, his zebra steak.

As for Ben having a word with him ... 'Young Fletcher', as my father would continue to call him long after youth had deserted Ben's long clever face, was a less suitable petitioner even than I was. Like my father, a civil servant; but unlike him, already showing signs of upwardness, in contrast with the dreary levels along which most of my father's career had trudged. Ben was already earning £1,000 a year! That such a young cock should come smiling up with the impertinent suggestion that an older man might, under whatever conditions, surrender the very rock on which his painful fortunes were based!

Of course, I did understand why he'd be reluctant—or uneasy: it being much of what he had, and hard-won. And left to myself I'd never have asked him to do it. Partly because I knew he wouldn't discuss the matter in a kindly, open fashion, but also because it didn't seem to me—looking at the proposal in terms of the special value these particular deeds had for this particular man of property—to be fair to do so. On the other hand, when Ben and Charles were raising their part of the money needed—and Ben at least by appeals to relatives— Kate and I could not squeamishly refuse to make our own appeals, even if they seemed perfectly hopeless.

On a visit to Manor Road, I spoke to my father. He listened, expressionless, and changed the subject. Later he rang, his voice bitterly cold. 'I've been thinking over your request in respect of the deeds of this house,' he said, from an ice-floe somewhere in the north Atlantic, 'and I thought I would let you know at once that the answer is No.' 'Well, Dad

...' I said. 'Yes. Goodnight,' he said. I sometimes thought that particular sound of the telephone being put down, though it must have been exactly the same as the sound of any other telephone being put down, *was* different. In other cases one surely didn't have quite the same sensation of being shot?

So we tried Kate's father, Jim. Her mother acted as a sort of softener, talking to Jim in a very general way about the plight of the young, the need to look nasty proposals in the eye and to discern the niceness that would turn out to be their eventual quality. 'I don't think there's much hope,' she told us. She warned against a direct plea from either Kate or me. 'I might just manage it myself,' she said, nervously. In a general atmosphere of watches being synchronised, we went to look for Jim in his workshop in the garden. 'Would you,' Dorothy asked, 'care to invest in the building society that's—?' 'No: I wouldn't,' said Jim: and for a long time had nothing to add. Later it turned out that he'd been put against borrowing within a family by the example of a younger brother, who made enormous inroads on the savings accumulated by his siblings and then disappeared, being identified by Jim himself many years later as a face in a row of upper-class faces in a photograph in *The Tatler*. 'Sir James Day', said the caption—which was not Jim's errant brother's name or title, but an amalgam of names from various quarters of the family. ...

In the end we were lent the money we needed by Kate's grandmother, who was aged ninety-nine, and thought she could spare it for a year or two. Not longer: Kate's parents, with whom she lived, could not go on for ever, and she might at any moment need to support herself.

One of the problems of the purchase was that it was three-fold. Building societies seemed to recoil from the complexity of it. Among other things, they needed to be sure that if one of the three failed to keep up instalments, they could intervene in some manner that made sense. Given a single mortgagee, they'd sell the house over his defaulting head. What could they do in the case of one disastrous borrower alongside two undisastrous ones? The answer was that they'd let the defaulter's flat at a rent that would cover a third of the whole mortgage. But here were three people who, in order to convert the house into flats, were anxious to claim an improvement

68

grant from the local council. If such a grant were made, the council would impose a notional rent on each of the flats that, in the event of someone defaulting, would quite hideously fail to repay the mortgage. ...

Helping hands from every side, some belonging to private and some to public enterprise, threatened to get together and throttle us, horribly. 'We don't want,' said one anxious building society, 'to slam the door.' 'You're creating a pretty good draught,' Ben reported himself as grunting.

Ben and I would meet every morning on the Barley Wood platform, wistful about leaving house and garden; and he would tell me of the latest move. It was still cruelly cold, but bright, day after day, the trees falsely leaved with light. We'd look up to the tunnel from the north, and down to the tunnel to the south; and the morning light would lie silky on the foam of smoke out of the nearer tunnel, towards London. There'd be this general foamy smokiness punctuated by the bowler hats of our neighbours, the very white oblongs of their quality newspapers. And we'd look towards the house, a lofty end-on view of it, dominated by a bay window that gave Kate and me our kitchen glimpse of things: mostly a matter, just now, of the usually trembling twigginess of the orchard. And behind that window there'd be Kate with that pain under her ribs so sharp that she woke in the night to weep over it. What fierce changes a woman's body had to endure, when a child was in the making! It was as if Kate had become a thing of clay, to be baked and baked again: a mould, dubiously elastic, here and there cracking with the effect of rapid expansions.

Ben might have something to tell me about ... our fire escape. The local authority had demanded that one of these be erected: a metal zigzag running down some face of the house. We were against that, on aesthetic grounds and on grounds of cost. For a while, Ben and Charles, who both had a great taste for being legally up against it, worked furiously on a double front. First: If it had to be built, how could it be built in a tolerable form, and with the smallest expense? Ben, in need of such information, never trawled for it in shallow waters. He went at once to the expert depths. So he'd ring, and command the attention of, the editor of some magazine devoted to ... well, if not specifically fire escapes, then some general theme of domestic security. *The Safe Homes Quarterly*, perhaps. Curious about costs, he'd ring and capture stray blacksmiths. When Ben was engaged in some mission of the kind, he'd drum up an army of advisers in a matter of days. Strange important persons—editors, blacksmiths—would arrive actually at the house, agog, having come substantial distances. It was a glimpse of the skills that were to transform my old schoolfriend into a senior bureaucrat. It was part also of a manipulative sense of drama he'd had even as a boy.

A second line of approach to—or rather, retreat from—the fire escape was to discover, somehow, that there was after all no statutory requirement that we construct one. And that Ben managed. He was able to demonstrate that the Act laying down the regulation had been anxious to protect vulnerable tenants from callous landlords. In our case, we were our own landlords, and so free to be as callous towards ourselves as we wished. Astonished officials confessed that they had no answer to this argument. Ben, who'd burrowed for it (incidentally ringing up the man who'd drafted the Act), and Charles, who'd expertly held Ben's ankles during the burrowing process, were delighted. So was I, of course; but never being at home in these tangled legalities—having absolutely no head for them—I was also astonished, more so even than the local officials. But then, I believe, this amazement was shared by Norman Lock, our solicitor, who was no mere spectator, like me, but often, I'd feel, was quietly startled by the confusions in and out of which our affairs were constantly slipping.

I had the strangest enjoyment of our frequent visits to Norman's office, slightly marred by the guilt of feeling it. Surely I should not be deriving entertainment from these momentous discussions? But, being at sea myself, I was amused by the behaviour of my companions, which was that of persons quite insolently at home on the stormiest legal waters. We'd sit in that quiet room that had been quiet in precisely the same way since the days of Norman's grandfather, and one of the others would see some great wave coming—a matter perhaps of a very minor provision of some terribly small but stupendously important Act of Parliament—and they'd rise together on the swell of it, laughing as it rolled on to crash harmlessly against a funereal row of files,

70

many bearing hyphenated Barley Wood names. At once the presence of a series of follow-up breakers would be remarked by Ben, Charles and Norman in enormously swift succession: somewhere around this point they'd get drenched, but would emerge blinking, laughing, undrowned. 'They won't get us with any of those,' Norman would cry. At other times the passage of our cause through fearful weather was apparent to me only from a rapid sequence of nods, stifled laughs, eyebrows raised and eyebrows lowered, and the like: for whole stretches they needed only to hang on, exchanging these signals—usually expressive of amusement. When it was genuine alarm that was expressed, my complacency would remain: for I'd be certain that some new, very large explosion of triumph and pleasure could not be far behind. ...

Norman regarded life itself as a piece of very serious cosmic misdrafting. It really wasn't on, he thought—that is, as an intellectual model. The loopholes that had been left for cruelty, pain, hypocrisy and savage sorts of misunderstanding were quite unacceptable—appallingly careless.

Large, witty, exceedingly pleasant, Norman would often round off one of our meetings with an attack on existence itself. 'Oh you know, it's extremely silly,' he'd say, as if this was the tangle that had brought us into the room in the first place. As I suppose it was. ...

Yet there was something about Norman's pessimism that would send me home smiling. Perhaps it was because physically he was such a very large and beaming pessimist.

7

The affection Ben and I felt for Norman was very much a matter of his being the only lawyer we knew with a passion for Keats. That was really, I'd think, because Keats had been concerned with so many things that men had found it difficult to be contentious about: mists, nightingales and globed peonies. Norman was passionately fond of flowers, as being rarely seen in witness boxes ... or indeed, in that quiet office of his, where they'd not long have survived the documentary dustiness.

Norman was literary; and so, helplessly, were Ben and I.

We'd longed to be writers from our schooldays onwards. Williams, the English teacher we had in common, would read out Ben's essays to the class I belonged to; and my essays to the class Ben belonged to. It was our first encounter before we came together in the sixth form. We knew each other from the start as rivals whose work tended to be read out. Side by side, as sixth formers, exploratorily friendly, we'd written experienced stories of the kind written by inexperienced adolescents.

Oh, that being on the stylishly ignorant, literary end of experience! It had long produced an imbalance between one sort of reality, under our noses, and another palpably under the noses of the writers we admired. But such a dizzying distance between the two sets of noses! I was, after all, perfectly at home with the works of Aldous Huxley, and felt extremely companionable towards him; in some sense or other, there were these notable cronies, A. Huxley and E. Blishen. I was part of a whole crowd of remote intimates of the kind. Yet Huxley described an order of existence that could not have been further from my own had it been situated in quite another planet. Dammit, it *was* another planet! To put it briefly, characters in Huxley were always in Florence, or Siena, or Venice. My family, go back as far as you like, had only that association with Italy that resulted from the melancholy requirement that British troops should, every now and then, be belligerently present. ... I felt on elbowing terms with Huxley: but in another sense he was ... a Martian educated at Eton, which, to be frank, *was* on Mars, anyway.

Ben said we were *déclassé*. It was like playing a team game without really knowing which team you belonged to. It meant we were always in danger of scoring through our own goal. To foster a more confident idea of the colours we were playing under—that might have been a reason why Ben and I attended Miss Furlong's class in English literature.

Actually, I attended her class because I had to: as an emergency-trained teacher, I was required to provide evidence of studious stamina, and had elected to do so by way of Miss Furlong. Ben had joined so that we could spend an evening a week together.

Miss Furlong's approach to literature was characterised by immense disdain for the explicit. To her, literature was a thrilling vagueness. She greatly approved of Blake, on the grounds that it was difficult to be sure of his meaning. I'd reflect that Blake, that exact man, would have been astonished to find himself among Miss Furlong's favourites.

Sometimes I'd imagine the presence among us in that dingy room in the Central College of the great writers on whom Miss Furlong pronounced. Some kind of dock—or stocks—would have been necessary for many of them. Several would have been heavily manacled and under close guard: William Godwin, for example, who was responsible, in Miss Furlong's view, for the entire modern world. There had been until about 1790 all those persons of sensitivity, engaged single-mindedly in keeping egalitarianism at bay: and then Shelley's wretched father-in-law had opened the gates and let it in. This had led directly to the crowded London Underground by means of which Miss Furlong every Thursday made her way to the Central. It had led also to popular education and the existence of huge numbers of human beings quite blatantly uninterested in literature. They included, Miss Furlong made it clear, not a few who attended the Central for literary instruction. Their most conspicuous representative in our class was a nice, bothered man, Mr Pink. When she felt like airing her desperate view of modernity, Miss Furlong would address a question to him. As once when she asked: 'And what conclusion have *you* come to, Mr Pink, about Crashaw as one of the last of the metaphysicals?'

Mr Pink visibly jumped on hearing the poet so categorised. He had not realised that Crashaw *was* one of the last of the metaphysicals. It was not his habit to think even of poets in such terms. The vague idea that clung to the phrase of something tribal, as with 'the last of the Mohicans', made Mr

Pink squeak with miserable astonishment and perplexity. 'I've been reading everybody I can lay hands on about Crashaw,' he lamented, 'like mad'—feeling, I guess, that an affirmation of sanity abandoned would put him right with Miss Furlong—'but not one of them said. ...' He was going to finish this course, Mr Pink, with an impression of the critics as persons who *never* prepared him to satisfy Miss Furlong's sudden thrusts of questioning. 'Oh come, Mr Pink!' cried our instructress. 'This *will* not do! Your own first-hand examination of the text....!' Mr Pink, who would never have dreamed of being so bold as to examine the text at first hand, added a groan to his shriek. 'I really have been doing nothing all the week but reading,' he cried. 'Not good enough,' Miss Furlong pronounced. 'Really not good enough, Mr Pink! You must *hone* your *critical faculties*!' 'Oh, I shall,' averred Mr Pink with bewildered passion: 'I shall!' His fervour was clearly related rather to relief at sensing that the questions were at an end than to a realistic assessment of this new obligation. 'Sometimes,' he'd confided over coffees in the Central canteen, 'I wonder what she's driving at.' It was towards a diploma in understanding Miss Furlong that Mr Pink was hopelessly working, rather than towards one in understanding Crashaw, Godwin, Blake *et al*.

I used to call for Ben on Thursday evenings at the government office where he worked. It was one of the handsomest eighteenth-century buildings in London, and I was always surprised to find him, under those ceilings, in his familiar drab twentieth-century grey suiting. There were often other young men present who, like him, were working their way into the habit of being officially powerful. There was one, tattily elegant, whose Cambridge face—on the basis of that old Boat Race attachment of mine, I thought that's what it was—prepared for any remark he made with little twitches and early signals of his finding himself amusing. Nothing I heard him say was ever cast in the form of a common sentence. 'He farts in copperplate,' said Ben. Being addressed by him was rather—I thought—like being pelted with fabergé eggs. ...

It was a high-powered civil service nursery, and Ben, who longed to be a poet, verging on a novelist, would die if taken away from that world of power. He needed to be an arranger

... or a dramatiser, as I used to think when we were boys. Then, he'd always been in the middle of some human scene, influencing it, causing it to move in some particular direction: making exciting theatre out of it. If someone was in trouble, Ben would be there, clearing paths, removing obstacles; often, confronting minor officials, his eyes coldly bright with anger, challenging bureaucratic habits and inertias. The Civil Service promised that he might do on a large scale what he'd done on that small one. I'd often tried to imagine that preferred world of my friend's, and could not. Again, we were so close, and so vastly distant. ...

We'd go along, then, to the nearest public baths, before joining Miss Furlong at the Central.

For builders had moved into 1 East Drive, and one of us— we were not sure which, but it might have been both—stank.

Deprived of the improvement grant, we'd been obliged to economise drastically. One effect was that, instead of making our living room and kitchen on the side we now inhabited— the one that had started as two rooms—Kate and I would have to make ourselves at home, when all was done, on the other side, consisting, now, largely of that single immense and dark room. *That* would have to be partitioned, pared down, and the cupboard in which it culminated, in which any Mother Hubbard might have looked for the bones of a mastodon, converted unbelievably into our bathroom.

Effect number two: Ben and Marie would be living and sleeping directly above us. It was an arrangement we'd all aimed to avoid. Kate and I had special reasons to wish it otherwise. Ben, Marie and Sally were tall persons (Sally was, so to speak, a tall person in the making) who trod the earth— and floorboards—with most positive treads. They confessed that they would not have enjoyed living under themselves. We were also furiously aware of an example of Ben's incapacity to adjust his habits. All his life, it seemed, he had removed his shoes while sitting on the edge of the bed, and allowed them to fall to the floor. This had, for us below, very much the effect of a drumroll. He then removed his trousers and turned them upside down, matching crease to crease. What followed next was a cascade of coins. It could obviously have been avoided if

75

Ben had schooled himself to adopt a different, but still simple, routine: if he'd removed the coins first, and *then* turned upside down, and folded, the trousers.

I sometimes thought that one of the aspects of his character that made him a gifted official was that he was incorrigible.

And a last effect of our losing the grant—because the only building society that would finance us simply wouldn't allow us to take it up—was that we had to have the least expensive conversion possible. In our discussions with the builders we sank from the position of honoured clients to persons for whom they were doing acts of barely profitable kindness. They came, but in small, erratic numbers, as to workmen; and intermittently. We were low down on their list of labours. So they'd arrive to rip yet another quarter of the house apart, and then go off to please someone with real money to spend.

The bathing arrangements in the house were removed altogether, so that at any moment only a single wash basin, on this floor or that, was on offer. And so it was that at one of Miss Furlong's lectures Ben and I sniffed anxiously, wondering which of us smelt rancid. It seemed a good idea to use the public baths round the corner from the Central; and visiting them became an element in those evenings oddly idyllic. We'd sit in a line on benches, waiting for cubicles to empty. The place had a toxic smell, as of generations of human poison. The first evening I sat next to a man who growled: 'Time every bloody house had a bloody bathroom! Bloody country!' 'Bloody right!' I said, suddenly wistful for my wartime days on the land, and all those simple companionable furies of opinion. 'I'm a bloody bus conductor,' he said. 'I'm a bloody teacher,' I said. The water thumping into the bath in steaming torrents was hotter than any I'd ever encountered. Using the cold tap, one knew one couldn't temper it. I'd cry out as I lowered myself into that cruel liquid, and my whole body would become at once a fixed flush. I'd lie there under the hollowly shouting, giggling, cursing cloud of steam that spread beneath the syrup-coloured ceiling. ...

Boiled, we'd go on to be amazed by Miss Furlong's views on ... Wordsworth. Like other poets he had, it seemed, a psychology. Miss Furlong spoke of people's psychologies as if they were limbs. Wordsworth's psychology was inferior to ...

76

boiled, we dozed ... Dante's. We woke to hear her cry: 'Why did Wordsworth fail where Dante succeeded?': and add, 'I would like the answer that T. S. Eliot would give to that question.' Instead she received the answer Ben would give— and gave. Perhaps, said Ben, Wordsworth hadn't enough devil in him. 'In the Blakean sense, you mean?' cried Miss Furlong, unable to believe that Ben could mean it in some quite common or garden sense. And then, her voice rising a jubilant octave: 'Would you dislodge him from among the immortals?' It was so far from being the sort of task to which Ben would turn his hand at the end of a Thursday evening that we burst out laughing. Miss Furlong always had a front row of ladies who—what can one say?—fed out of her hand. This fringe now turned and frowned. Ben murmured in my ear: 'What's the use of being intellectually trained if you can't come to a quick opinion on insufficient evidence?' ... and fell again into his boiled sleep.

To our dismay we were now inclined to feel, off and on, tender towards Miss Furlong. 'I wish,' said Ben, 'I could make up my mind between thinking "What a rash creature!" and "She's rather a dear!"'

8

It was now that we became, on an immense scale, painters.

Inside, the house was gashed and gaping. The off-and-on nature of the operation meant that a wall would begin to rear itself from the basement up through the centre, the basis of those divisions that would give us our own front doors: and stop half-way. We'd grown accustomed to living in a ruin; now, for a while, it was a ruin that was being, in some perfectly haphazard way, ruined. Kate and Marie grew pale and vexed.

Charles and Amy had joined us. Their wedding had concluded with the singing of 'The Lord is my shepherd.' When it came to the lines: 'And in God's House for ever more My dwelling place shall be', Ben murmured: 'So they're not coming to East Drive, after all!' However, there may have been mortgage problems: because here they were. Charles began at once to paint his gables: constructing for the purpose ingenious platforms that enabled him to work outside— thrillingly in mid-air. We'd have held our breath, but had become deadened to that particular danger when Ben tumbled from the top of a ladder.

This had been placed against the towering back wall of the house. There'd been alternative views of ivy, in which 1 East Drive was virtually wrapped: the view that it preserved the brickwork, and the other view that it destroyed it. The building society that backed our three-fold purchase was of the latter faith. So Ben was up there, hacking away at the topmost level of that immense green mat; and something happened that I suppose we should have foreseen. That is, that after he'd loosened a certain amount of the mat, the weight of free ivy would begin to tear away the rooted ivy below—so that that vegetable continent, that great green mass full of many summers of dust and old nests, would become self-detaching.

From the ground I worked it out, late as usual, as it occurred. The ladder was forced away from the wall, and Ben went flying. In his hand he had a bill hook. Drawing rather conceitedly on experience gained during the Second World War, I'd sharpened this until you could have scalped with it (as we said at the time) a building society manager in charge of the department that has views about ivy. Ben spun through the air, characteristically silent; though words meant as much to him as to me, I couldn't imagine him at bad moments, *however* bad, wasting time on speech, or even cries of despair. When we got drunk, as youngsters, it was I who'd babble away, confessional torrents, while Ben remained guarded, rather sergeant-major-like, very stern. So now he gave his attention to falling; landed on his back (which he should logically have broken) on the bannister of an iron staircase— still holding aloft the billhook (with which he should logically

78

have cut himself to pieces); slid down the bannister, headfirst; did a thoughtful somersault on the grass: and leapt to his feet, pale, mildly angry and anxious that there should be no great discussion of the event. Especially by Marie—who ran towards him, uttering mixed words of loving horror and sheer displeasure: as usual, that appreciation of Ben on which their marriage had been based only just balancing the fury he was always causing her with his clumsiness.

Well, if there was anything to fall from, Ben fell from it. Had falling upwards been possible, the air would have been full of him. . . .

Now he and I painted together lower down: verandahs, balconies, those immense windows. Ben would be dabbing in his former sailor's fashion at some hungry stretch of wood-work. Dabbing—tickling—was his style. With him, this was wartime learning, too: he'd been trained to *appear* to be painting a destroyer in mid-Atlantic. In the Navy you called any area you missed—any old grey you failed to cover with new grey—a 'holiday'. Ben's painting of 1 East Drive was full of holidays; and, helplessly conscientious, I'd travel behind him, closing them up. I hardly noticed I did it, as he hardly noticed it was done, for we'd be talking. It was what we'd had in mind, when we thought of sharing a house—that there'd be opportunities for talk, usefully but not oppressively connected with practical activities.

We talked much about what united us: the love of—and hunger for—writing. 'Why does it matter so much?' Ben would murmur. Well, it was partly a business of that . . . ravishing pleasure, putting words together. Jeweller's work, I'd think. But it was also a need not merely to accept life, but to make a return for it. Failure to write—to make that sort of response to things—made us edgy, guilty. And I'd feel that if I didn't write, after a drab day's teaching, then there was nothing to put up against that dullness.

And sometimes we'd be writing about what had been drab—for Ben, in his minor Ministry: for me, in my essentially dejected school—and the drabness would come alive, be kicking.

Well, at this moment, there was for me that colourless creature, Cr Mrs Hogg, chairman of the school governors. If I'd not brought my attention to bear on her, through the business of trying to find words for her, she'd have remained colourless. That was it: writing was our way of paying attention! Oh, Cr Mrs Hogg! it made one yawn to think of her! Difficult to take her seriously as an educational figure! She was fervently attached to the school, and often visited it; but the effect was that of a housewife coming to inspect a rather bizarre kitchen that happened to fall within her province. She'd enter a classroom and urge the teacher not to notice her. 'Don't bother about me, Mr. ...' Names were not her strong suit. It was difficult not to bother about Cr Mrs Hogg, wandering round the room: examining whatever happened to be hanging on the walls, and sometimes uttering little yelps or moans. These, in fact, were not expressions of dismay: they were expressions of nothing whatever. She yelped and moaned as other people clear their throats. She'd stand over a boy and seem to be assessing him for some unimaginable use that might be made of him, smiling or frowning as she did so. Her smiles and frowns were also without particular significance: they helped to keep her face busy, a councillor's face. What she said, then, was always kindly, general—bland, but with a touch of sternness in it. 'Your teachers work very hard for you, and I hope you work very hard for them,' she'd say, in her very local voice, making her face fearfully grave; but I noticed that boys tended to smile when she spoke in this vein. Not, as they might have done, with irony; not with scorn. I guessed it was with pleasure—for this was granny's voice, its undertone of severity only increasing the comfort of it. I found myself oddly fond of Cr Mrs Hogg; for I was quite certain that the person visiting my classroom wasn't Cr Mrs Hogg at all, but little Alice Hogg (except that of course she wouldn't have been called Hogg then), member of some far-off standard Seven in this very parish, startling herself now by being important in a setting where, then, she been so *un*important ...

Cr Mrs Hogg transformed! by the act of close attention involved in writing! Only by writing about her did I discover what I knew about her.

So Ben and I talked about writing—plying our absent-minded paint on ladders and verandahs poised above the orchard or the lawn. The only flaw: a guilty secret. I'd sent a piece to the *Manchester Guardian*, a sketch about a boy I taught whose natural exclamatoriness—increased by the noisiness of his home—caused him to be every teacher's target. He was discussed in the staffroom in terms of a deliberate wish to deafen, and I was certain he was the often wretched victim of his own lungs, modelled on his father's. The sketch had been accepted. I'd walked round for a day or so crushed by the thought of it—as if I'd had some inordinate laurel wreath imposed upon me, which came down over my eyes, so I could barely see where I was going. I dared not mention it to Ben, who would certainly take it badly. That is to say, I'd have to find the right moment to tell him. It was bad enough, our little discomforts and ungenerous twinges when one, and not the other, was rewarded by the *New Statesman*, *Spectator*, *Time and Tide*. . . .

But much of what we talked about was an exploration of our differences. Ben said he demanded logic: things going 'click' together. I thought I liked things going together with a silky sound. He attacked the habit of wide reading. 'I hate it because of the rubbish you accumulate.' I understood his dread of mental and emotional overcrowding; but it seemed to me that, in this respect, literature was no different from life. Life made the accumulation of rubbish a certainty. Was not the important operation, both in life and literature, a sifting one? Could you ever in advance preserve yourself from rubbish?

But then we disagreed, too, about fashion. This argument had centred particularly round the new modes introduced the year before by the Festival of Britain. The characteristic use of light woods, in narrow strips; the crispness of new designs of fabric and carpeting; all the new lines and curves of things established on the South Bank. Kate and I, on the only visit we could afford to that bright scene, found there was an afternoon concert at the Festival Hall. When, after the astonishments of the foyers and staircases, and the great glass views up and down the river, we stood in the hall itself and saw those black boxes that seemed rather to be flying alongside the walls than to be attached to them, Kate burst into tears. Well, it was the first totally fresh public exercise of the desire to give delight to others that we'd known for more than a decade. Easy now to forget how those novelties of design and fabric and construction amazed us in 1951: being, not simply what they were, but also exhilarating statements of the very opposite principles to those that, for so long, we'd lived by. Since 1939 it had been a dreadful sombre gravity, joined to a dreadful austerity: but here were lightheartedness and a luxurious acceptance of the possibility of style, beauty!

Ben said: 'It will be everywhere! You will grow tired of it! It will be degraded by imitation!' And I knew he was right, yet it seemed to me he was also wrong. The fact that any new style would in time be coarsened and become a tiresome *old* style seemed no reason for refusing to feel pleasure in the novelty as it emerged. Again, how could men ever hope to escape from this cycle, except by altogether outlawing innovation? Becoming extremely subject to fashion was a source of much human folly, but was it not foolish also to suppose human beings could ever simply shake fashion off?

Would Ben himself walk about with trousers without turn-ups? And would he refuse to conform if turn-ups were ... unimaginably, as it seemed in 1952 ... turned down?

He accused me of being over-polite, and wrote, partly for my benefit, an essay entitled: 'Manners Masketh man.' He also found me guilty of a longing for stability. He himself wished to live amid perpetual storms, shocks and surprises. Behind the longing for continuous and steady relationships, he held, lay a dread of independence—a frightened conservatism. The philosophy he preferred was that of methodically rocking the boat. ...

Oh hell, I said, I'd been in boats being rocked, methodically and otherwise, throughout my childhood and adolescence. Well, my father had rocked the family boat, no end. I'd spent many nights on the stairs at home, listening to the sounds from below as, in that shaky craft, my belated father retorted to Lizzie Pye's miserable rages! I'd hated that rocking boat, and such kinds of storm and shock! I had no desire for torpidity and complacency and all those terrible words that were on the tip of Ben's tongue, but I couldn't see that wanting to keep your domestic craft steady meant you'd surrendered to boredom, hypocrisy, uxoriousness (other words that I knew Ben had in reserve). Ben said yes, it was probably a matter of your adolescent experience: some emerged from it *self-reliant*, and some did not.

I thought, as we painted busily and happily on, that alongside a dictionary of true, we needed another dictionary of false, synonyms. Was a desire to rock boats truly the equivalent of self-reliance: a desire that boats should sail steadily, the equivalent of helpless dependence? Was ship-wreck the only excitement the sea had to offer?

And we were happy, all these discussions of difference were reasons for happiness, as Ben made his holidays and I unmade them. Well, we really had never in our lives lived in such a place! It seemed to me like possessing a large living picture, that changed from day to day. Now, in this first of our Barley Wood springs, there'd be mornings when I'd draw the curtains (we now had curtains) and there, close up under my startled eyes, was the richest fruit of colour—it was leaves and twigs and the beginning of apples and pears and plums, all smeared with sunlight—burning daubs of gold, yellow, red: and, a few yards further back, dull silver mist. And a half an hour later the mist would have gone, and the table we sat at for breakfast, in our bay window over the orchard (which, alas, was to become the window of a bedroom instead of that of our kitchen), would be spread with sunlight, and sun in our emptied tea-cups winked like golden water!

And sometimes in a room that had been gloomy, almost in Mr Gristwood's old style, the sunlight would suddenly well, like water into a glass tank, silently, smoothly. ...

Ben recklessly let literature have its head and said it was like living in a house in a play by Chekhov.

9

'I wouldn't have missed having a baby for anything,' said Lizzie Pye, peeping out from behind my large, barely happy sixty-year-old mother. 'I liked having you, dear. It's like a

flower opening! It was such a lovely feeling!' She darkened.
'But I wish you and Kate had a little more money. I'd like him
to give you some, but ... Oh, my dear, I know how it can' (she
made balls of her fists) 'clench you up, make you. ...' She
finished the sentence with a grimace. Then my father entered
the room, and Lizzie Pye vanished. ...

Well, years before, reading one of the earliest Penguins, I'd
been struck by a comment made by its author. It was Richard
Aldington's *Death of a Hero*, and he'd pointed out how rarely a
novelist mentioned how much his characters had in their
pockets, or in the bank. Every one of us walks about every day
having, perhaps, stirring adventures, physical and spiritual:
but being perfectly conscious, the whole thrilling time, of the
exact amount of money he commands. And nothing much *is*
said about that, in most novels; nothing, that is, about this
very precise daily awareness of how much we have to dispose
of.

In Barley Wood, at that time, I seemed largely to have the
disposition of minus quantities of money. Nothing at all for
little, unexpected things—like half a crown towards a colleague's leaving gift. Paying for the appalling tea we drank three
or four times a day in the staffroom—its very appallingness
now and then becoming desirable, as a mark of our being
momentarily in that tawdry refuge—was an expected outlay:
but even so, I had to defer the weekly payment until it built up
into a formidable debt. There were several moments during
the early 1950s when I was in danger of being ruined by my
unresolved obligation to the Stonehill Street Staff Tea Fund.
As for smoking, I could keep this going only by constant small
borrowings from colleagues. I'd feel an unhealthy excitement
when I caught sight of casual coins in the possession of the
boys I taught. Contriving that they passed from them to me
would hardly amount to theft. Rectification of unbearable
injustice. Little family, the Blishens, deserving of better
subventions. Case dismissed. Costs awarded against the
Department of Education and Science.

There were clothes, too ... bad enough in my case, but
worse in Kate's. Extraordinary to think that in those days we
wore braces: those oddly unattractive means by which the
trousers were prevented from falling. Primitive sartorial

technology. The day of the adjustable waist band had not arrived; and the belt was reserved, in most men's mind—and practice—for weekends, and holidays. The essence of braces was elasticity. This was something they simply lost, over the years. I had braces, one set only, that had a flaccidity that qualified them for ... oh, that other word in the Blake epigram. How wounded Miss Furlong would have been if she'd known that her favourite student (I confess I was that) was ready to think of Blake's utterance in terms of what held up his (the student's) trousers. 'Damn braces, bless relaxes.' My braces had simply become relaxes. I spent much of my time trying to remain basically decent.

And my shoes split and I could not replace them. ...

But it was hideously worse for Kate. That is to say—again in the philosophy of the time—a man looking shabby was one thing: a woman, something else. I thought Kate would look marvellous in, oh, some old bright scrap of cloth. I couldn't keep my hands off her when she wore a certain tattered smock. But then our relationship was such, you could say, that certain kinds of dilapidation came into their own. For public purposes Kate clearly required a daily succession of clothing that did some justice to her feeling about herself, and her natural wish to be admired rather than deplored. And there wasn't a hope of its being provided. I couldn't have guessed what grief this would cause. You were unable—oh, it had been a phrase of my father's—to make the best of yourself. Withdrawing slowly from the lofty principles of scruffiness that I'd established for myself under his soldierly eye, I saw the force of the phrase. Of course, there *were* aids—which had their price—that could bring out the attractiveness of any human being who so easily might otherwise lapse into bedragglement.

What I meant was that it was deeply demoralising to a young woman to be unable to cultivate herself ... oh, as any plant in the garden might expect to be cultivated, with prunings, weedings, waterings, supportings with sticks, and sprayings.

My poor, unweeded Kate!

We were invited to the wedding of one of my colleagues. A wedding, my God! Kate found it necessary to borrow a hat;

and a dress; and shoes. I remember with aching vividness the morning on which we set off for the event—Kate this uncomfortable anthology of other women's clothes and accessories. Alongside the impossibility of my giving her a present of any kind on her thirty-third birthday, this ranks as my most painful memory of the thorniness, the miserable stings and humiliating pangs, of poverty.

Years before, working on the land during the war, I'd been yoked as a digger of ditches with an older man who'd only recently married, and talked of his wife in tremulous, loving terms. Would her sweetness, he'd muse, survive the struggle to feed them, house them—provide them with the occasional modest extravagance (the relax as a change from the brace) that might make all the difference between sweetness enduring, and sweetness sinking stage by stage into sourness?

Now I understood Bob's gentle alarms. Even more intensely on the day of that wedding when drink flowed, and I took it with the thirst of someone not accustomed to unlimited whisky and wine in abundance; and became totally, eloquently helpless. ... So that Kate in her borrowed scraps of dress had to steer homewards her companion in his startled, talkative cups. ...

And that evening Charles appeared at the door with a bill for £11.12s.6d.

Unkind to suggest that Charles, or anyone else, was ... unkind. It was the gulf between one bank account and another. And I was struck by the way both Charles and Ben sought to show that I wasn't, after all, the worst off. Well, dammit, I understood why they did that—I hated to be the chap at the bottom, so could see how one would hate to be a chap at the top. The wry little comedies of poverty ... and the extraordinarily difficult role it is to play, that of the financially limping man among companions with perfect ankles. ...

Poor Charles!—who had no idea why his absolutely honest little communal bill asking £11.12s.6d from each of us caused such pallor at the newly-installed door of the bottom flat.

A methodical man, Charles, given to thoroughness in anything he did: a man with the soundest practical flair.

86

There came a time when he painted the great double front doors of the house, anxiously making sure that Ben and I were kept at a distance. We'd have given them the usual undercoat and topcoat, talking the while, and perhaps not quite bringing ourselves to dismantle, first, the fixtures and fittings; so that brass doorknobs and letter box would have had their brightness spoiled with splashes of paint. . . . Charles took the doors off their hinges; carried them into the basement; undercoated, and rubbed down; undercoated, and rubbed down; reported from time to time on his progress; topcoated, and rubbed down; topcoated, and rubbed down (I am simplifying severely); and mounted them again, many weeks later, armoured in paint that you could have fired shot at and barely scratched.

Hard for Charles, at times, to be linked in any enterprise with slapdash clowns like Ben and me.

IO

Ben said he was glad to have heard shouts, screams, a child's tears coming from our flat. He'd have been appalled had he heard only a serene silence. It made him feel less awful about the shouts, screams and child's tears to be heard coming from upstairs.

Well, Tom was in trouble for doing what he must do: which weren't, indeed, bad things to do: but impossible when done on the heels, always on the heels, of an exhausted and pregnant woman. He was given to sudden shouts, nerve-shattering dances. In no way was he to be warned against suddenness—because in that, clearly, lay the whole point of it. An elated violence rose within him, as abrupt and dazzling as the sun emerging from a cloud: he had to cry out, he had to perform one of his clattering jigs. And then Kate would shout;

and I would shout. And I'd try to continue with a piece of writing; and Kate with some aspect of her endless struggle with dust. We thought there was something scientifically queer about the way dust driven from the flat became instantly dust returned to it.

And Tom wept for the sheer mystery of our distemper.

I worried away at the problem of trying to write simply—contending with the corrupt desire to overload and strain. But what did I mean by simplicity? I thought of some of the highlights of the reading Miss Furlong's class had led to: Chaucer's *Troilus and Criseyde*: Spenser's *Faerie Queene*. I wanted a simplicity that both of them had—and the notion that either had simplicity would have made Miss Furlong herself laugh. (Who had begun lately to talk of being aware of people 'at the electro-magnetic level'. It had suggested to Ben and me a whole range of kinds of awareness—'at the hydraulic level' was Ben's bawdy favourite.) But what both Chaucer and Spenser had was a story-telling drive; and somehow, at their best, the marvellous gift that kept idle, though not glorious, words at bay. ...

Words enchanted Tom; talking of a clown of whom he'd seen a picture, he said: 'He had red hair—like a red-setter dog—a red-setter clown!' Kate and I said how tired we both looked—well, it had been a long, unrestful winter and tumultuous spring. Tom said: 'We ought to change our faces.' His energies sprouted as ours failed. Now he had a passionate curiosity about number. 'How many toys have I in my toy-box, Mummy?' And when Kate turned out to have no answer: 'Why don't you tell me?' And when she could not explain why she could not tell him: 'Why don't you know?' He tried to mortify her by suggesting she was not his only resource. 'I'll ask Daddy when he comes in.' At the end of such a sequence Kate spanked him. It merely filled his head with a new range of questions. 'Why did you spank me? I don't know why you spanked me.' When I came in, he told me about it, as though hoping for fresh light or a new opinion. He wanted instant satisfaction in respect of the number of legs possessed by the following long list of animals and pieces of furniture. Kate shouted. I shouted.

'If we had half a moment to spare, he'd entrance us,' sighed

Kate.

At times we'd laugh, having caught ourselves being bored to death by our own groans, shouts, sometimes ridiculously overlapping furies. And I thought what a fantastically broken quality domestic existence had.

Our scurrying lives were Aprillish ... pettish outbursts and rueful laughter. And kind people did kind things to make it worse. As when Kate's mother presented us with a flight of ceramic ducks for a wall of our new sitting room. Kate was caught, horrified, between detestation of the ducks, and detestation of the idea of hurting her mother's feelings. She accepted that the ducks couldn't be admitted to the sitting room. But she thought they might be hung in a corridor. 'Oh Teddy ... they're terrible, but she doesn't know it, and it *is* meant as a kindness ...' It was the perfect prig's dilemma, and we glowered at each other. We both knew the ducks would not be hung anywhere. It was too much; though neither would have cared to produce a public statement explaining our position. The quarrel was silent and sullen, and lasted for two days. Then, not having kissed or embraced during that time, we longed for each other, and began to giggle when we met; and at last it became an ache simply not to be borne. Hurrah, I'd think, for the senses! Their needs, thank God, and their appraisals, whatever the obstinacies of the spirit, always brought such quarrels to a tender end.

The quarrels were very often financial. For having smoked an ounce of tobacco in twenty-four hours, I was *hauled* by Kate *over the coals*—or *taken to task*. (I'd turn over such phrases in my mind, astonished: we'd not married in order to visit such severities upon each other—but then we'd not married so that Kate could enter into a lifelong dust-up ... with dust). I *dressed her down* for not having been above being superior ... an awkward accusation, as I saw, but all the same. ... It turned out that Ben had been, at the same time, in similar trouble. Stalking out of the house after a financial dispute with Marie, he'd found he had only sixpence in his pocket, and went lunchless. ...

We'd gone on painting outdoors, and now that the conversion was over, we painted indoors as well; became painting machines; in fine weather, turned out with Charles to paint the looseboxes. White and green. On the white doors I insisted on painting green the bolts and hinges. 'Bloody Blishen!' said Ben and Charles. There seemed no end to the abuse of my name by facile alliterations.

Ben said: 'What shall we do when we've painted everything?'

The great lawn at the back of the house, mown, turned out to have an Edwardian splendour. If merely two or three of us appeared on it, with diffident deckchairs, it began to have the air of one of those early photographs: our rough-and-ready dress seemed gingham and bustle and parasol. There were tiny abrasions. Ben was inclined to wish the children elsewhere. He proposed, in a manner only half-fantastic, a barbed-wire enclosure at the bottom of the garden. He turned out to be at odds with Jesus. 'He should have said, "Suffer little children to bugger off!"' Ben growled, on a sunny Sunday afternoon that had turned weepy. Kate glowed with dissent. Dogs and neighbours arrived—a deckchair collapsed. All was forgotten—especially since the neighbour was Peter Trumpet, who caused agonies that made other agonies seem nothing. But Ben's advocacy of exile for children—Kate's glare—were hints of friction to come. . . .

Peter Trumpet was a prep. school teacher who had the most extraordinary capacity to take some obvious idea and expound it at length and without mercy. It was impossible to interrupt him.

It might strike him—lying back in one of our Sunday deckchairs—as useful to remark that it was better for a class to be attentive than not. 'Because, when you come to think of it,' he'd begin, 'if a class is—er—making a noise, then—er—things are very difficult for the teacher. They're—um—difficult for him because, you see, no one can—er—really hear what he's—um—saying. It just is very difficult to—um—make out what a teacher has to say when the children are noisy. Then it's bad for *them*.' He'd lean down and savagely tear grass out of our treasured lawn. 'I mean, it's ... you know, it's—um—bad for them, you see, because—er—really, if they—er—can't hear what the teacher's—um—saying, they—er—don't learn anything. In those circumstances, they simply can't learn—er—anything, you see. . . .' And so on.

Perhaps because he'd realised that people were always trying to silence him, he talked in the manner of someone who was walling himself in with speech. It was a high castle wall, you simply couldn't climb over it—couldn't get at him and scream: '*I see*! Yes, I *do* see what you mean! I saw it at once— five minutes ago! Oh, *please* stop!'

People paced up and down, outside the wall. They smiled nervously in his direction, rose from their seats and sat down again, made desperate attempts to persuade Trumpet that they saw his point, could see the next point coming, minutes away, and all the points to follow. But if anyone, maddened by it all, leapt at the wall and seemed about to secure a foothold on it, then Trumpet would pour down on them, relentlessly, the boiling oil of his 'ers' and 'ums'.

He was a kind, dull man who caused enormous social pain.

I I

I was obsessed with coal and paraffin. We made, in a local store, after agonised thought, hushed arrangements for the purchase of a carpet: £12 horribly down, and the rest of £40 over six months. Bills constantly arrived: for £8.13s.6d, largely. I think of that as the sum by which we were, for so long, tormented. My attempts at weekend competitions turned from frivolities to grim activities. If I were successful, I'd be delighted in a frantic way that would have astonished the staff of the *New Statesman*: but success, too, could lead to despairs. Well, sometimes, in relation to the feelings I had when a victory of mine was a defeat of Ben's, I'd remember wryly a dreadful verse of John Greenleaf Whittier's that I'd been much moved by when nine or ten; the pretty schoolgirl speaks to the crestfallen schoolboy:

'I'm sorry that I spelt the word—
'I hate to go above you:
'Because'—the blue eyes lower fell—
'Because, you see, I love you!'

'Imagine Ben in a state because he'd beaten *you*!' Kate would cry. The fact is that I did not care to be the instrument of Ben's dejection. Well, I'd have won a guinea, and he'd have gone unmentioned: but he'd recover quickly by way of an attack on literary success of any kind, which was the invariable mark of a disgusting eagerness to please. Adding a hostile comment or two on my prose style, he'd become sunny again.

Soon after we'd buried the last of Mr Gristwood's baubles in a great pit in a corner of the garden—such a mass of old glass and bottles and tiles and gewgaws as would have made us a fortune a few years later, when the fashion for Victoriana began—the weather became enormously hot; and Kate simply became enormous. We had, day after day, a very nasty sense of being made up of old cotton wool. It seemed that at any moment the long riddle—'What exactly has Kate got wrapped up in that great parcel of a belly?'—would be answered. Her doctor and friend, Nancy Trevellick, thought for a while it might be twins.

'I believe we've got something out of the usual run,' she said, appalling Kate, who longed for the most conventional issue.

It was characteristic of Nancy to speak of Kate's burden as if it had been, if not quite her own, at least one she shared with her patient. She was the briskest of women: advancing on any statement she had to make too rapidly to notice ambiguities. In the early days of our marrige she'd responded to Kate's request for contraceptive advice by handing her an immense jar of pessaries, looking very much like a jar of sweets. 'Pop one of those in before you have relations,' she rattled: as if the peril guarded against was the arrival of a mother or aunt for tea. 'People,' she once memorably told us, 'do like to die at home': and she seemed to be describing some macabre new craze. She was *deeply* medical, cheerfully seeing almost everything in clinical or morbid terms. We went to dinner with her soon after our arrival in Barley Wood, and she described the melon that she'd decided against buying as a starter for our meal. Its size was for or against it, I forget which. 'Big as a new-born baby's head!' she cried. We admired a reproduction of Botticelli's *Primavera* hanging in the dining room, and remembered that another hung in her surgery. Well, she loved the painting—and was much drawn to La Primavera herself. 'Quite obviously in the early stages of TB!' We saw that Botticelli's floating lady was, for Nancy Trevellick, the patient that got away. She'd have liked to have her not only on her walls but on her books.

So fast did she bustle through life, and such was the tenderness under her outward appearance of stout sensible professional woman, that I'd wonder what she was fleeing from. Whatever it was, it involved her in identifying herself totally, not only with the subject-matter of great paintings, but with her patients. Kate's father Jim had once managed a garage in Barton-on-the-Hill, and Nancy was a customer. 'I must have my car, Mr Brown,' she was given to crying: 'I'm expecting a baby at any moment.' 'Fill me up, Mr Brown, will you—it sounds very much as though I've got appendicitis.' She also identified with her car. 'What's the chance of your giving me a good going-over at the end of the week, Mr Brown?'

She was wrong, mercifully, about Kate's contents.

It was a day of great heat, under the thickest hood of cloud. I arrived home to find Kate in pain. It might be wind, she thought. The spasms became more frequent: we decided it was not wind. I rang the hospital. Tom gathered together his currently essential oddments, a toy attaché case full of them—books, farm animals, crayons, paper, drawing pins to cover the possibility that he might produce work imperatively requiring to be exhibited, and fragments of narcotic fluff—for he had this curious habit of rolling balls of wool from anything that offered and sniffing at them, in a depraved fashion—and then gravely transferred himself to the care of the Hickmans.

I gave Kate, pale and cheerful, into the custody of a nurse, black and cheerful.

And close to midnight, Ben joined me in the Lovers' Seat. I

93

was thinking how extraordinary it was that I should be waiting for the birth of our second child in such a setting: in Mr Gristwood's old garden, now so curiously ours; under a full moon; on a night profoundly still, stuffed with scent; with, down there towards the fields, pyramids of flowers in the chestnut-trees chalked on the air: and in that other direction the orchard, riddled with moonlight and shadow, all weeds and grass and gorse, and apples and plums and pears making themselves ready for great pickings; and, though neither air nor leaves seemed even faintly to move, the tops of the poplars making the slightest possible shivering music.

Ben said it was working out all right, wasn't it? And we mustn't let anything spoil it—lack of money, or absurd differences of opinion on anything whatever. And perhaps we should think of turning that old paint-shed in the courtyard into a den for writing in! Because we ought really to move on, oughtn't we, from weekend competitions—and even pieces in the *Manchester Guardian* (where Ben too had appeared, so I didn't have to slink about guiltily)? Well, what about books? We could write a novel together! A novel about life at 1 East Drive! Why invent characters when they were on comic duty all round us! ... Well, perhaps it might be an idea to try ringing the hospital again.

It was a boy. About a hundred years old, I discovered next day. The world's very smallest scholar. You could see the marks where his pince-nez rubbed against his nose. He wore boxing gloves of lint, because he was given to ripping up his own skin. He was a very ancient, very small scholar with a tremendous leaning towards fisticuffs. We appraised each other for the first time and then he invented the yawn, and yawned enormously, as if this was what he might devote himself to, without ever actually stopping.

I put up no resistance at all to Kate's suggestion that we call him Daniel.

PART THREE

I

Dan played 'Greensleeves'. It was a piece my mother particularly liked, because I'd made attempts at it on the piano when I was a boy. There were a score of snatches of music—bits of Chopin, Schubert, Beethoven—that she recognised from those days, and that to her were like distantly remembered sounds of battle to an old soldier. In general my playing the piano had been to my father like my going to the grammar school: an idea that he'd initiated, and deeply regretted. 'There he goes with that bloody funeral march!' I very rarely played funeral marches, but he felt almost everything I did try my hand at was sombre if not morbid. Mother partly shared this feeling: which was based on the view that the arts in general were symptoms of ill-health in those who professed them, and causes of ill-health in those who paid heed to them. Beethoven was a man who'd been rendered incapable, by a depressed and sickly outlook, from writing 'Tea for Two' or 'Underneath the Arches.' But the Lizzie Pye part of my mother was grieved on my behalf. 'Let him be, Dick. It settles his nerves.' She'd always vaguely believed that he might be in favour of anything that had that effect. But all it did was to enable him to say: 'I don't give a damn for *his* nerves! What about *mine*!'

And over the years the musical scraps that had been the cause of that old disagreeableness became, by a process peculiar to her, a reason for being happy.

Not that she really minded what Dan played to her: feeling as she did that having a grandson who could conjure anything at all from a guitar separated her by a great distance from the common mob of grandmothers. 'I told Dr Mackenzie how you played,' she informed Dan. 'He said it sounded super.'

97

Almost certainly that grave Scotsman had not used this word. It was one my mother had picked up since my father's death during those visits to London that he'd never have allowed her to undertake. My sister Betty had said: 'I keep thinking that he must be turning in his grave, and then I think ... poor chap, he can't!' And we wondered what substitute activity was available to the cremated. ...

Early on my mother had consulted me about that usage. 'Mrs Bruce next door said she'd had a good holiday, and I said "Super!" Was that right?' She sat bolt upright, tiny skeletal thing, a schoolgirl risking all with a direct question to teacher. 'Fine, Mum!' She leaned forward: 'I was going to say—*you* always say "Fine!"' The schoolgirl's expression remained respectful, but only just. If she'd had a fan she might well have tapped me on the nose with it.

The making of observations of this sort—'You often wave your hands about when you're talking,' she'd told Kate a moment or so ago (in the middle of Kate's talking)—was one of the marks of the new woman who'd appeared out of the shadows of that long marriage. I again found myself thinking of political parallels. If my father's death had reminded me of the fall of an unpopular government, my mother's existence since then had not been unlike the breathtakingly innovatory first hundred days of some eagerly welcomed new administration. She'd made changes in all directions: or—it's sadly truer to say—she'd attempted such changes. Many had failed because her local world there on the south coast simply did not understand that my father's bungalow, which might well have borne on its gate the name Cold Shoulder, was now my mother's bungalow, for which the name might be Open Arms.

She was now very nearly blind; and her dreams of convivial afternoons, and tea parties, and perhaps shared evenings here and elsewhere, had come to nothing. No one was remotely interested.

2

We'd come down together, Kate and Tom and Dan and I—a rare occasion on which we'd managed to be in the same spot, at the same time, with the same intentions. Dan had driven, and Tom had sat in front with him; and I'd been reminded of perhaps the last time we'd all been together in a car.

It was on a family holiday, in the Lake District. Tom was fifteen, Dan two years younger. I remembered it partly in terms of the photographs that had been taken. The boys, however you looked at it, appeared always faintly satirical; amiably mocking elements in each recorded scene. ... And Tom and I on Striding Edge, in mist. I remember my amazement when we reached that high spur. Kate and I had been shortly before to a Giacometti exhibition—coming away from the Tate, we'd met nothing but elongated people in his style: and now, here was this huge run of ragged Giacometti metal, and, slow and tiny, Giacometti-thin climbers labouring, infinitely slowly, along it. I'd been giddy the whole way across that long razor of rock—past the memorials that spoke of people spinning in quantities to their death throughout the nineteenth century, or so my vertiginous imagination read them. And how unsympathetic Tom had been! These revelations of paternal instability made it irresistible for him to adopt a posture of the coolest superiority. What a demonstration of the essential shakiness of one's elders, and their inability to cut the smallest dash! In every field they inched along, complaining of dizziness! He neglected the obvious handholds in order to stress the difference between my alarmed crawl across steep places, and his own careless agility. For him this really was Striding Edge: for me, it was Crawling and Creeping Edge. 'You're a son of low quality,' I

99

groaned. 'A fascist, too. This is how brutes are made: early practice in mocking the weakness of others!' Oh, how we irritated each other!—and oh, how difficult irritation was to sustain, at times, if I looked into Tom's mischievous face!

But it was a painful holiday. The journey to Keswick in the cramped intimacy of the car—the dining room at 10 Manor Road or Ben's boyhood kitchen on wheels!—at a time when the boys specialised in low-level Rabelaisianisms, uttered in voices in which Cockney and Liverpudlian were raucously mixed! Poor Kate—who was specially sensitive about clarity of speech—or rather, easily maddened by demonstrations of scorn for it! They thought our dislike of the endless stream of hideous sounds sprang from a despicable middle-class desire that our children should speak like ... Barley Woodians. 'For God's sake!' I was rash enough to storm. 'It's like being at a conference of inferior pornographers!' 'Inferior, note,' said Tom. 'Again we fail our parents, Dan! Failure in Pornography!' It was impossible to win because we had nothing to say that was not too complex, and Tom (of whom Dan was a faithful if sometimes absent-minded echo) had nothing to say that was not too simple.

He had tremendous power: being full of certainties, and simple, sharp ways of expressing them!

And the terrible words of which he'd lately come into possession! Like 'paranoia.' At Scale Force he'd said he rather not conceal the truth: such a trickle could not move him! I deplored this readiness to be unenchanted, so young. He said that was the statement of a paranoiac—dashed because an expedition he'd planned, with some trumpeting, had failed to excite a captive member of that expedition. ... But on the way back to the farm where we were staying, there'd been a drift into discussion of the future, and Tom had said: 'What will I be? Just someone who's cruel to people, I suppose!' And he made a tragic clown's face ... and I wanted to hug this exhausting enemy!

And sitting in the car again, the rain tumbling, and all of us reacting against the sandwiches that we'd lunched on day after day: most of them jam sandwiches, *wet* with jam. Sodden sandwiches! That had been an outing devised and lovingly prepared for by Kate, and what she'd had in mind was an experience of Ullswater in the brightest sunshine. As we sat there in a darkness that was all descending water, hating these sandwiches, Tom said: 'You must have sat up all night planning this, Mum!' And our dog Sally, whose first summer it was, barked furiously ... never to be at home with the spectacle of human beings bent double, hooting.

Such a painful and comic mythology that had accumulated over that last of our family fortnights! When I said Tom was *less witty, advanced and important* than he thought—into the mythology it went! I blew blazing ash out of my pipe as Dan was rowing us across Derwentwater, and burnt a hole in Tom's jeans—into the mythology with it! Middle-aged men cannot control their own dottles! And into the mythology went the phrase Tom used when we picked them up after they'd watched a football match in Carlisle. 'You mustn't mind,' he said, cruelly delicate, 'if we find returning to your dom-esticated atmosphere rather dull.' Oh God, another of those words he'd picked up to beat us round the head with! And we were humbly aware, of course, of the respect in which, as companions, we were no match at all for his fifth-form friends—who were invisibly present throughout the holiday, sneering, shrugging and tittering as we spoke. How could our mild chatter, among these soaking fells, vie with the mordan-cies Tom was accustomed to exchange with boys we knew as Pod, Riff, Crack and other sharp names.

'A rather painful stage,' panted my diary, 'in the process by which the boys disengage from us.' And we agreed that really, it would never work again—a shared holiday.

And ten years later, driving down to New Chilton to see that valiant creature, my mother, I said to Kate—suddenly aware of the great reversal of things: us where they'd always been in the back, they where we'd always been in the front: 'Let's have our revenge! Let *us* play *them* up!'

But we couldn't think of anything to do.

3

One habit my mother hadn't lost, and wouldn't, was that of giving a little polish of her own to any civil thing that had been said to her. Mrs Bruce next door had ventured to remark that she was not only brave beyond precedent but also—for her age—lovely beyond words. Enid, the strange young woman who came in to dust the place for her, had asked if, without offence, she might comment on Mother's personal fastidiousness. My mother had seen no reason why permission for this comment should be refused. And Dr Mackenzie was so moved when he came to see her that he'd hardly known where to put himself. This notion of people rushing about blindly trying to find somewhere, anywhere, to stow themselves when overcome by the feelings she roused in them, was one she'd always had. As a small child I'd sometimes had a picture of the house full of highly emotional people in search of what I thought of as dark cupboards.

But the truth was that Dr Mackenzie hadn't been the admirer she'd hoped for. His being the kindly and gentle man he was, and Scots—and my mother having picked up from television the idea of a connection between being Scots and being a good doctor—meant that she attached an extraordinary importance to him. It was as if he were a very much improved version of my father. She wore rather often a kilt they'd bought once on a coach tour of the Highlands: and admitted to dreaming at times that she was Mrs Mackenzie. But he had been severe with her; she might fall, she might burn herself, she might have . . . trouble with her heart. Well, she was plucky, of course: but foolhardy, too. There were ways in which she could be looked after. A flat of her own in a home for the . . . partially sighted. She uttered little whimpers when people talked like this. It was as if they were carelessly opening doors to admit all the scuttling terrors she was so busy keeping at bay.

And she was deeply hurt by what Dr Mackenzie had said; as she was to be by every one of this decent man's expressions of disapproval. Here was a quarter from which she had the most desperate need of encouragement and praise, and it was refused. It took the spirit out of her, for the moment. What was the good, then, of her having mastered the telephone? She'd taught herself to count the fingerholes on the dial. At first the process had been so slow that by the time she'd completed a number the apparatus seemed to have lost interest. Her first success had come one evening when she was trying to ring me. There suddenly was her voice; 'I did it! I did it! Aren't I clever!' And then she talked very loudly—for her, very fast: intent on giving an impression of firm control, laced with light, amused laughter.

It was always, when she rang, like someone phoning in a brisk, jocular voice from a distant dungeon—for the bungalow was as dark as that to her; as lonely; and as full of tiny scaring sounds. She made much use of radio and television to keep those sounds at a distance. She'd sit very close to the television set, peering at the dim wash of colour she knew to be people— faces—and ... joining in. 'I join in, dear,' she told me over the phone. 'I joined in Panorama just now.' And I tried to imagine it—my mother adding a word or two, perhaps, on some crisis in the Middle East. Or ticking off a politician. 'Politeness never cost anyone anything.' Or she'd get someone wrong, and see she'd done so, and apologise. It must have sounded like a kind of aural graffiti ... the radio or television going its steady, indifferent way, and my mother scribbling her remarks all over it.

My sister pointed out that it was only an extension of what had always been her practice. Well, she'd always talked to herself. As children we'd been accustomed to hearing her doing so. There was Lizzie Pye I, who had an optimistic view of things: and Lizzie Pye II, who thought things were bad, on the whole, and that Lizzie Pye I was a fool. We'd never made much of it, as children—assuming, I guess, that all mothers talked to themselves. She also talked in this way to other people: my father, neighbours—providing them with nothing much more by way of reply than a feeble kind of bluster. It must have gone back a long way, this habit: to the days when she felt so different from her father and her sisters—and the day, a little later, when she'd run away from home. Her father had called her, for that very fastidiousness people now praised, a 'snob.' A little thirteen-year-old snob! 'He said he never wanted to see me again. And he didn't!' She must have had an enormous need to talk him down before she could vanish from her angry home.

She was telling Tom about it now, as we sat in that living room in which my father's absence still made itself felt like a presence. That reminded me of a time when Kate had gone to visit cousins in Canada, and I'd missed her badly, and found phrases for it: that I'd felt myself to be sitting there with her absence, and that she was not there all round me, over the whole house. My father was not present in the same powerful fashion.

'We were very poor, Tom,' my mother was saying, in words that had not varied as long as I could remember, 'but we were very clean.' It was her retort to the worst that life could offer: that she'd been rooted in unavoidable poverty, but that (thanks to her mother) this had been countered by chosen cleanliness. They'd been clean together, she and her mother, until her father's drunken brutality had led to her mother's collapse into what they called melancholia—'melon ...', as Lizzie Pye had always called it, letting the rest of the difficult word trail away ... and her spending the last quarter of a century of her life in Colney Hatch.

My mother was talking to Tom about this because Tom had been telling her about the people—and especially the children—of Salford, where he was working with a street theatre group. It fired her wonderfully, the idea of this much-loved grandson being at work among children very much like Lizzie Pye and Dickie Blishen, c.1900. 'I had the gift for learning,' she was telling Tom, 'but I was always kept at home to look after the baby.' She told him how, having left school at twelve, she'd walked five or six miles every morning to work—'Mr and Mrs Wren, grocers.' Oh, Mr and Mrs Wren! characters out of my childhood! With Mr Stickley, who she'd got on to now, and who'd courted her passionately, desperately, hopelessly. 'You didn't think much of him, Gran?' asked Tom. 'Too stiff,' said my mother; and peered with blind confidence in Tom's direction, knowing he'd understand. 'Not like Dick?' Tom hinted. She snorted. 'A bit on the simple side,' she said.

Poor Mr Stickley! Another character out of my childhood! Stiff, simple Mr Stickley—so unlike my supple, tricky father— who'd adored Lizzie Pye from his uninspiring headquarters in the railway ticket office at Wembley Hill! The defeat of Mr Stickley, despite an outing to Great Mistletoe!—and my father's triumph!—were part of the living folklore of my childhood. I felt my mother's young warmth now as my old mother told the story again, to my sons. And I thought how it was a sort of damage I could have done without, to be told not long ago by a mildly scornful cousin of my mother's that Great Mistletoe had been Great Missenden, and that Mr Stickley (a tadpole of a man floating hopelessly in the futureless pond of Wembley Hill) was really a Mr Strickland.

'Very classy,' she was saying now. That was Mr Chunnel (no one had ever put us right about *that* name), whose father owned a string of butcher's shops, and whose own passion for my mother was never mentioned, that of his parents being more a feature of the case. 'They wanted me to have him very badly.' As a child I'd always imagined the Chunnels queuing up for my mum impatiently, with immense pointless anxiety. How could they not know that my dad would win, in the end? They'd wanted my mum, as someone might want a particularly appetising cut of beef or pork: and they'd jolly well not been able to have her!

A favourite stretch of Lizzie Pye's history! The boring if impressive suitors who swarmed when my father went away ... to the war, which I'd vaguely think of as the cause of his absence from the story; but also to the arms of other women, as even my mother's telling of the story when we were small made ... mysteriously clear. There'd been this gap—which morality could not cover ... a very symbol for the absence of morality ... before he returned to his senses, and to her. Meanwhile, there'd been Mr Stickley, Mr Chunnel, and a certain Mr Matthews—who was not quite my mother's type.

Well, it seemed that he too had parents who were dreadfully keen on capturing my mother for their son's benefit, which, even as a child, I thought of as a matter of socks, shirts, sheets, laundry in general.

It was an early root of my own feeling about such things— that you turned against the stiff, the simple, even the classy, if it was their laundry they were largely concerned with, and turned instead to someone awkward, handsome, regrettable, like my father.

Well, laundry! My mother was now telling Tom and Dan about Uncle George, and how close he and my father had been, and how sultry that closeness had become, at times, and how very much it was a matter of laundry. That is, of Uncle George's laundry. He and my father, among those quarrelling brothers, had been close when they were young. George was the bright, enterprising one, who'd charmed his way from telegraph boy's uniform to double-breasted suits and the whitest of white collars. And there'd been that time, another chapter in the lore of my childhood, when he'd retained a room in a London hotel, as a base for adventure, and my father had been summoned there, from time to time, to sit with his brother while George changed from the common underwear in which he'd arrived, into the silken underwear in which he meant to depart. Overhearing this tale again and again as a child, I'd made pictures of it in my head that would last for ever: my father sitting amazed, disapproving, envious in one of the fat armchairs I thought a hotel bedroom would be full of, while Uncle George attired himself for adventure in blinding white silk.

In later years Uncle George and my father had drifted apart ... my uncle becoming amiably grander and grander, less and less inclined to admit that he had any ordinary blood in him: with a sort of marvellously chummy hauteur that wouldn't have excluded my father, if that angry man hadn't objected to being ribbed for lacking style, dash, swagger. Uncle George was swagger itself, and accumulated the outward signs of it: including a collection of snuffboxes, French miniatures, medals, eighteenth-century pottery, that was housed in a room my father called 'the bloody museum.' 'This,' said Uncle George, taking me into it once, 'is what your father had the bloody cheek to call my museum.' Later he'd tried to explain to one of my cousins how his brother Dick lived. 'They're little houses joined together, two by two,' he said, as if describing some rare architectural freak. 'I remember visiting my brother Dick one Sunday; and, to my surprise, there were men on ladders, painting. Workmen at it on a Sunday! Strange, I thought! But it turned out that they were painting their own houses!'

It struck me now, remembering this, that Uncle George had been set on escaping from the world of the semi-detached, too. Except that what he'd been intent on putting behind him was the world of the slum terrace. Barfett Street, Paddington, where they'd begun. Standing in his roomy garden on a southern hillside, with his roomier house behind him, on that visit when I was introduced to the bloody museum, he said: 'Well, it's a long way from Barfett Street, Teddy!'

'Had a Christmas card from my brother George,' my father would rap towards the end of his life. 'Sent it straight back, unopened.'

And now my mother was telling us how she'd phoned Uncle George ... and he'd said he'd call in and see her. She was looking forward to being fondly candid with him. 'Well, we've known each other since we were sixteen. I knew him when he hadn't any fluff on his—' She couldn't remember whether 'fluff' was the word, and if so, what you had it on. She giggled in the uncertainty of it. 'Would my dear husband be very angry, do you think?' 'No, Gran!' said Tom, very loudly for us all.

She wanted to make it clear, she said, since she might have seemed to be crying up Uncle George's underwear at the expense of that of other members of the family, that my father had always been particular, too, about what he wore *underneath*. Not silk, ever. But always good of its kind, and meticulously clean. 'Your grandfather never suffered from body odeon,' she invited Tom and Dan to note.

But if only he'd been a little more adventurous in Uncle George's style! Well, the occasional weekend in some comfortable hotel a few miles along the coast wouldn't have hurt them!

I followed her into the kitchen and watched her aim a saucepan of water indecisively in the direction of a wildly flaring gas ring. Kate came in and said 'What a nice saucepan!' and took it from her as if to admire it. I wondered as I lowered the flame why my mother didn't hear the roar of it, and realised she was getting much deafer, too.

She was worried about the young woman, Enid, who did the dusting. My mother had taken her to her bosom, at once: ready, as always, to hail a newcomer, uninvestigated, in ideal terms. Enid was sweet, considerate, and had become fond of my mother in some fairly delirious fashion, which meant that it was by way of a series of hurts and sadnesses that Enid was discovered to be sour, thoughtless, and fond only of herself. I thought uneasily she might also be malicious. Some of my mother's favourite and vital certainties, contributing to her belief that she could manage by herself, began to seem less secure: she was here and there a little bewildered where she had always been positive. And there'd been the matter of her eighty-fourth birthday, when it became clear that her dream of a party attended by a substantial fraction of New Chilton's population had no hope of being realised, and she clung to the promise of (what it came down to in the end) Enid's company. The highest of high teas had been lovingly and, I guess, dangerously prepared: and then, instead of Enid, Enid's mother arrived, with some imprecise excuse from her daughter. And she'd turned out to be absolutely the kind of woman even my tolerant mother could not tolerate. 'So moaning! In the end I almost had to tell her to go!' Her not crying as she told me this on the phone sounded terribly like crying. 'Well, it was the first time he wasn't there to fuss over me. But I won't say any more about that!'

I'd think at times that it was as if, having for so long taken my father to contain much of the cruelty of things, she'd been exposed, now he'd gone, to small stabs and pinches and stray kicks that took her quite by surprise: she having thought that when her beloved darkness had moved away, there'd be nothing but sunshine!

4

She asked about Ben—a favourite of hers since our schooldays, when in the dining room at 10 Manor Road he would sit
in the armchair opposite the one to which my father said I
threatened to become rooted ('That boy and his bloody books
are never anywhere else'). She'd appeal to Ben: 'Shouldn't he
get out and about like other boys?' 'Well,' Ben would say.
'You wouldn't want him to be like Brian Cook?' *He* was a
schoolmate of ours quite odiously active: whose hatred of the
opposite principle was such that whenever he caught sight of
me a snarling cry of 'Professor!' was wrenched out of him. 'He
always looks so . . . spit and spam,' said my mother, who never
got that right. 'I suppose Bert could do with a spring clean,'
Ben would say. 'There you are!' She'd train on me the bright
lights of her triumph. 'I *am* glad you said that, Ben!' And she'd
clap her hands, and caper a little. I think she was always
aware that she was being teased: but Ben's dry courtesies
charmed her. She worried over him greatly during the war,
when he was serving in destroyers on the Atlantic run. His
appearance during one leave was greeted with a naval hint
she'd worked up from information given to her by Mr
Folkestone, the ex-sailor who lived next door. 'You must be
very careful to scrape your bottom,' she cried, before Ben had
stepped into the house. 'Valuable advice,' he murmured.
'Thank you, Mrs B.'

I told her my old friend was now somewhere near the
Himalayas, straightening things out. He'd made in a recent
brief letter a laconic reference to the mountains, assuring me
that they were not what he was levelling. Some educational
matter, 5,000 feet above the sea. Ben was still glaring at other
officials: he'd been doing it now for more than thirty years,

and had glared the pusillanimous into corners all over the world. 'I've met here,' he'd written, 'the little Welsh boy who was the brother of the very tempting little Welsh girl we knew at Swansea, before the war. He's not little any more, and is even balder than I am. It seems *she* is a grandmother. Ah, the sadness of it all!'

That had been ... in 1937, when Ben was about to enter the Civil Service as a clerical officer, and I was waiting, wholly without hope, for the results of the Higher School Certificate examination. Our English master, Williams, had asked if we'd care to spend a fortnight at a summer school near his home in Swansea. He could arrange it. Mostly unemployed miners, it would be. Politics, a bit of simple philosophy ... and there'd be music, of course. 'It might help you through an awkward time,' he said. So we went. It was a big house on a hill, with a great bay of the sea round every corner. The miners were mostly young, and we thought it was the dreadful idleness that had been imposed upon them that made them so ... lascivious. But perhaps it was us, feeling our own sexual longings expressed in those strong unemployed bodies. They stretched and yawned and talked about the girls on the beaches. One of those was the daughter of the house ... of whom Ben was to hear again nearly forty years later. The miners undressed behind rocks, and so did she, and there was a dark guffawing, sudden excitements of song, and laughter again. I was aware of the way my direct and honest friend, Ben, became a little secret, looked sideways—at curious moments wasn't to be talked to. I guess he was aware of the same things in me. Our hearts thundered together whenever she emerged from her rock and went running, so white, so slim and yet so thrillingly substantial, down to the sea. ...

I was inclined to suggest, at the time, that I might commit suicide. Everything I was and did had tightened itself into the most dreadful knot, and there wasn't a hope I'd ever be disentangled. Wherever I turned myself, my father stood athwart the path, bitterly opposed to what I was and to what I sought. Ben said people who talked about killing themselves never did. I thought he was cruelly cool, and was glad of it.

And there was Ruth, a refugee from Germany, scholarly, with greying hair worn heaped up but falling gradually into

ruin whenever she was involved in argument: so that at the
end of any severe period of discussion she was busy shovelling
it back on to the top of her head, only to have it fall down
again.... And I fell in love with her for the helplessness of her
hair, and because she was part of that terrible Europe
suddenly present, to hand—someone who'd fled from Hitler
and whose very dishevelment seemed to rebuke us all ...

And up from Swansea a grand thin lady came, a patron of
the place, the only woman around with whom I didn't fall in
love. She was given to a sort of didactic stateliness, much
moved by the thought that we were all becoming steadily
more educated as we sat there ... which was true of the miners
only if you subtracted from the attention they gave to the
lectures, the attention given to a scheme for collectively
marrying the grand lady. That is, they thought they'd form a
committee: elect a suitor from among them: support his
courtship: and, when the marriage had taken place, share out
her fortune. I was wishing that *I* could marry the Welsh girl
with, in some fashion I wasn't clear about, the scholarly
German intervening. ...

And up from Swansea too came a pianist who ... well, one
can only say he subjected the school's unready upright to
Chopin, especially the Revolutionary Study and the A Flat
Polonaise, and the astonished instrument shook, cringed, and
then gave out such stirring clamours that I enlarged my
dream of marriage, I wooed and won white-skinned grey-
haired slim young scholars in very great quantities. ...

And we returned to London—Ben to the Civil Service, I to
the collapse of the hopes I'd already abandoned (for I'd
known that reading novels was not the way to prepare for the
Higher School Certificate): and shortly afterwards Ben wrote
saying how miserable he was, and we must get together and
cheer each other. Although, being Ben, he'd actually written:

'You can see my state of mind, you can feel my desperation.
Balance has left me, humour is fled. Write to me quickly,
comfort me, cheer me: pour your lyrical syrup on the rough
palate of my soul.'

'I'm glad you still hear from Ben,' said my mother.

5

It had dawned on her as the day wore on that we were all there: and she didn't want us to go. She wouldn't say this, but she held Dan's hand in a tight grip, and then Tom's, and worked through us all and started again.

She'd mastered the experience now, she said. Now she did know that he had gone. It wasn't some long black dream. What she wasn't yet on top of were the simple terrible incidents of the night he'd been taken away, to die in the morning. He'd sobbed so hard. And she kept remembering how he'd say to her, during those last months: 'I've been very cruel and bad to you.' 'Well,' she said, 'I wasn't going to soothe his conscience for him. So I'd say, "You didn't think I was as green as I was painted?"' And now she worried about it, because that was why he was so scared of dying, and had wept so bitterly that last night. He'd been so bad, and he thought he'd have to pay for it. Perhaps *she* should have been kinder to *him*!

But then she told how a neighbour had asked if he might borrow one of my father's paintbrushes. 'Yes,' my mother reported herself as saying. 'But only if you think nicely of him when you use it. My dear husband was not as bad as he was painted!'

So much painting! Well, now she was painting him in the colours of canonisation! The hurtful truth was for inside the family, and then only alongside a proper recognition of his charm, and the cheekiness that had become increasingly rare but was always irresistible. For the outer world, there was to be this resolute story about his being the victim of a campaign of defamation. With himself—she'd have agreed if she'd gone so far—as the chief campaigner.

Someone had angered her by suggesting that the funeral bill, for £200 or so, was excessive. 'I don't want to talk that way about it,' she cried. 'I almost kissed the cheque. I wouldn't care if it was £2,000!' For over fifty years she had bought his food, much of his clothing, his medicines, most of the household goods he needed. There was for her a holiness about that last purchase of all, and she was not going to allow any sordid quibble to spoil it.

And I wondered afresh how she'd survived in a family that would cheerfully squabble all the way to the gates of Heaven, and beyond. . . .

Then she was telling Tom and Dan about her earliest memories—in which the Salvation Army had featured, playing its 'tangerines'—and she moved at once to a very recent experience, when she'd actually gone to sea with my sister and brother-in-law in a cabin cruiser owned by a friend of theirs. My mother's being absolutely incapable of travelling anywhere on water had been an article of faith during my childhood, one of the facts on which the world rested. Now, there she was, insisting on staying at the very lowest level: sitting, intense, concentrating on the avoidance of drowning. 'And,' said my sister, 'obviously enjoying every moment of it.'

What she herself felt was that by follies of her own she'd set limits to her pleasure in things. Fastening on my hand, she said: 'I'm such a silly! If only I had my sight now, I could enjoy myself much more!' It was Lizzie Pye I once again telling Lizzie Pye II that she was a fool!

And when it became clear that the day would end, we would go; nothing could prevent it; she made me look in her handbag for five pounds carefully secured for the occasion: one for each of us—oh, for sheet music for Dan, for beer for Tom, for . . . anything we liked, for any of us! 'Please don't argue—you'd spoil it.' Dear Lizzie Pye!—you'd have thought she was showering the world with fivers! 'He'd have said, "What do you want to do that for?"' And she gave that little jab of a thumb upwards. 'I want to do it because I've always wanted to do it.'

And, not happily, we went—leaving that frail figure at a window, peering out into an almost invisible world, blindly waving.

Seeing her at that window reminded me of her in wartime, when the dining room at 10 Manor Road had been a flimsy refuge from fire and high explosive. An evening in the middle of that long torment of air raids, in 1940. My father coming home; and my mother bursting with the stored-up emotion of the day; all that brooding, mixed with a deep general sense of injustice—and topped with a simple terror of the night to come.

Seizing, as she always did, on the first thing she thought of as a trigger for her necessary explosion. It was a neighbour's saying that we'd shown a chink of light during the air raid of the night before. 'Mrs Folkestone said if we knew what we suffered in this room last night—the light was showing. ...' 'Suffered?' cried my father. 'What do you mean by "suffered"? I'm afraid I don't understand what you—or bloody Mrs Folkestone—are getting at.' It was always the same: her onrush meeting that harsh, heavy obstacle, my father, in one of his most damnable roles: that of the man of soothing common sense. 'Let's try to get this straight. We showed a little bit of light last night—according to Mrs Folkestone. What the hell was Mrs Folkestone doing, noticing whether we were showing a little bit of light or not? If I know anything about that old bag—'—'Oh, Dick!'—'—she was probably peeping through her own curtains and showing a lot more bloody light herself.' 'No, Dick, she—' 'Well, put that to one side. Let's try to find out what you mean by "suffered."'' Oh, such a formula! My mother always saw it as meaning that she'd be taken down to the dungeons by my father's henchmen, who would subject her, on this matter, to forms of interrogation that would unavoidably be lacking in comfort.

Why did my father never understand that his common sense failed to soothe?

And she'd protest—why couldn't he ever take her worries seriously?—and then they each set out to deepen the other's wildness. Her bid for simple reassurance and comfort would become more fantastic; and his refusal to provide them would disguise itself in more and more absurd forms of 'common sense.' Her poor frenzy grew; his reasonableness became more grotesque—his assertions seeming after a time like actual detonations. He *bombed* her with his denials of sym-

114

pathy. It seemed to be the air raid anticipated. There was her nervous, shaking attempt to state she knew not what; and his brutality that turned upon its own fear embodied in another.

'This pitiful, furious parody of a marriage,' I wrote in my diary. Well, it was another grotesque element in the scene: the son with the incurable itch to write, the obsessed reporter, sitting scribbling in a corner of that angry room. And I was consumed with a longing, that began to seem terrible in its simplicity, that they would merely set out to understand each other. . . .

There'd been, I remember, a battle in the air, in the afternoon. Its mutter had come before it, drums before a feast, and Manor Road had emptied. But from my bedroom window I saw the Irish nurse who lodged in the house opposite, standing in the side entrance in her blue scrap of a dressing gown. I was deeply familiar with *that*, from much secret staring, but had never seen it publicly exhibited before. I remember the sense of shock, as if some private dream had elected to shout itself from a rooftop. Then suddenly in that general mutter there was a sterner, more intent note; and then a perfectly majestic cloud of German planes appeared directly overhead, wide silver spots in the blue sky, their concerted engines drumming; their progress the slow one of a queen with her train flowing. . . . And there'd come a snarling, leaping note, a little ball of black smoke had suddenly vaulted into the sky and stuck there; and silver Spitfires swept over the house. Somehow one German plane became detached; there was the hammer of machine-guns, like stone being ripped, and suddenly the snarl and roar of pursuit, as a tiny crucifix, trailing smoke, spun and curved at the tail of a larger one. They moved faster than what seemed the likely speed of any human intention. Up and down, amazingly rapid drops of mercury, running in battle over the sky above Barton-on-the-Hill. . . . It seemed so odd, such a battle over a town so profoundly undramatic. . . . And then the battle disappeared into the blue. Then they'd all gone: and the Irish nurse had gone: and I looked back on it and saw there'd only been a few particularly brief moments of hammering, howling and anger, and those tiny silver crosses precipitately falling, precipitately climbing. ...

And Lizzie Pye, longing for Dick to come home and anchor her again in some kind of bearable reality; and knowing, I guess, that this would never happen. For somehow he'd made himself incapable of providing comfort.

And the air raid that night had been punctual. The bombs fell; and we lay in angular torture, on the dining room floor, molested by ungainly dreams. There was constantly that persecuting hum, like the sound of a man gasping for breath; and the sudden jolt of guns. And at last I gave up the attempt at sleep and wrote in my diary:

'When my sister was brought down, cross-eyed with tiredness, with a sleepy smile, I hated the things that dared to menace her. And now as she and Mother lie on the floor, I want to invent some unfailing protection for them, anything against that unbearable blast of steel that tears the flesh to bits and fills the blood with powdered brick and breaks the head from the body or stabs into the stomach or twists off a limb— horror you can't think of.

'I want you to be amazed, future reader, to be amazed at these air raids. I long for someone so innocent that I could enjoy his astonishment at the outrageousness of this unremitting aerial siege.'

6

As my mother grew blinder, her face grew tighter. It became a prison door. And behind it, I sensed, her spirit, frightened and appalled, paced the small room of her head. Well, it must have been a black space, no larger than her head, where her shrunk life must walk up and down. And inches beyond that blinded mask, the endless liberty of the sighted began—that boundless space in which our inner selves were able to spread.

No matter what panic was set going inside us, it could be thinned out and made so much less fearful in the huge territory provided by sight.

But my mother's eyes looked fogged, futile. She had, of course, her own word for it: 'It's all a kind of hazel,' she said. I longed to know what she was suffering—and hopelessly wished I could be of help.

When I rang her I'd hear her assume a sturdy briskness: the intention of being cheerful proclaimed itself. Well, it had been a good week: she'd got Enid to read out to her three bills ... and then she'd paid them. No, no neighbour had actually come to see her. But I'd remember how she'd told me about losing the lid of the teapot. Well, she'd found it—and I'd never guess where. Under the bed! And her little girl's giggle. 'I like losing things. You never know where you'll find them!'

And yes, she'd seen Uncle George. He'd called in—and sounded just as he'd always sounded. 'You're a wonderful little woman, Lizzie,' he'd said, as the first instalment in a fairly giddy, spread-out speech of praise, which had glanced at her splendid memory, the marvellous way she'd looked after Dick, and the justice of such criticism as she was now directing at him, George. She'd told him he should have stopped teasing his brother. 'It was very wicked of you, George, to take the monkey out of him for being a civil servant,' she claimed to have said. (When it came to 'taking the mickey', she'd always assumed that the rest of the world had got it wrong.) Uncle George had more or less broken down and blubbered. 'You're amazing, Lizzie,' he'd concluded, hastily. He'd also confessed that he'd been going about for years claiming to be older than her. She sternly invited him to revise this claim. He did so, and praised the cakes she'd baked for him. He'd never encountered anything like them before, and would be glad to have a name he could use in describing them to his family and friends, as he confidently expected to be doing for some time to come. 'Little gutter cakes,' she explained; having always secretly wondered what the devil the world was talking about when it spoke of 'gateaux.'

Once she was delighted because I'd written her a letter. She said she'd like me to do that—Enid would read it, or she'd call in Mrs Bruce from next door. It was nice talking on the phone, as we did every other night, but she missed having letters. But what really pleased her was that I addressed her on the envelope as Elizabeth. She'd always felt that Eliza was a sawn-off, reach-me-down form—as if her parents had tired halfway through the business of naming her. She was as thrilled as if I'd made her a Dame.

But there were times when no one had come, she'd not rediscovered anything in amusing circumstances—there'd not even been any bills to pay. She'd been there in the prison of her head inside the prison of the house. I wasn't to think she was unhappy; she certainly wasn't. (I could imagine her standing to attention as she said it. Being on the telephone was always a full-dress matter for her, but when she was telling her occasional valiant lie the need to be soldierly would have been greater than ever.) But if driven very hard she might admit—but mustn't be taken seriously—that she was pretty lonely.

And always she signed off in the same way; apology for taking your time vying with gratitude for the extraordinary good nature which had caused you to ring in the first place. 'Goodnight, my dear. I won't keep you, my dear. Thank you for ringing, my dear.' Well, she was going off at once to laugh, dance, and take things pretty lightly. Which meant that she was going off to cry, angrily: the anger being directed against herself, for being such a sickly, cowardly creature.

I remembered her again at his funeral—when, contrary to all her intentions, she'd wept: or rather, her face had been flooded, her small body shaken like a child's, and through it all she'd stood as upright as she could, respectful, on duty. What she'd desperately hoped was to remain dry and stoical—not to make a scene. And as she stood weeping there, I'd touched her elbow only most lightly, taking care not to make it a recognition that some breakdown had taken place.

Because she was so intent on ignoring her own tears, thinking them a kind of disgrace. They made it more difficult for others to get through things.

7

And I went down alone to see her; and she was standing at the
window, peering out. I waved, and walked in through the
doors she'd unlocked for me; and when I entered the front
room, she was still staring out, and leapt with fright when I
spoke from behind her.

I'd walked up the path a few feet distant and she'd not
known it.

And then it was as if some lover had arrived. We thought
(and she was frightfully merry about it) that we might fry an
egg or two for our lunch. Had she ever shown me her own
special way of frying an egg? We cracked eggs in the scarred
kitchen and while she threw them round in her wildly
flourished frying pan, I turned down great bursts of flame.
She'd incorporated the flourish, which must have been
designed to cover the approximate nature of the way she
aimed eggs at frying pans, into her techniques as a cook. And
those, most of her life, had been great techniques. When she
wanted something to be light, it was light; when she wanted
something crisp, it was crisp. She'd always been a kitchen-
slave, but a kitchen-slave of immense style. ...

We must go arm-in-arm into the garden, she said, because
she had a little problem she'd saved up for me. She didn't
want to make it sound in the least desperate; but when she got
on to the lawn, *his* lawn, his *beloved* lawn—which the gardener
he'd hired in his last days was continuing to tend as he would
have wished—she at once didn't know where she was. It was a
desert of dimly-seen greenness. Was there any way that, once
in the middle of it, she could school herself to turn in such a
direction as would bring her at last back to the bungalow?
'Help me, Ted,' she said. But when we stood together in that

green centre, we had to laugh. Because her sense of being lost had transferred itself to me: we were both marooned. She hugged me furiously. 'There isn't any answer,' she said.

And would I mind doing something rather odd? But she didn't think I would. It was to look through her wardrobe and tell her frankly what dresses were stained and in need of laundering, and what were not. Well, she was always asking Enid about this, but no longer trusted her answers.

I wished, as I always did, that I was Kate; or my sister; or Tom. All three had a gift, talking to my deaf mother. They could penetrate her deafness; and Kate and Betty had the ability to say the loose extravagant things my mother enjoyed hearing. It had always been a problem between her and me: my lack of zestful small talk. She'd typically chided me for it when I was younger: 'Oh, you're boring!' And yet, equally typically, she'd had respect for it. 'I know you don't like to talk for the sake of talking'. (Untrue: but her subjects weren't my subjects.) I'd have been glad, that day, to have the gift of promiscuous gossip, a flow of the sort of oddities of information she enjoyed.

But then, she was so eager herself. A thrilling excitement seized her. Looking back, I understand that this was because she was at last on the brink of breaking down. She could not have borne much longer the loneliness to which she turned out to have condemned herself. Even if I'd sat there dumb and glum, I'd still have been enormously welcome.

And she went over old ground, making it vivid all over again. How, to her relatives, my father had been the perfect embodiment of what they meant by 'rotter'. She'd often used this word of him, but now we looked at it together, astonished. Well, of course, he *was* a rotter! But she'd always known it. And it was really why she'd clung to him instead of seeking some mate as modest and amiable as herself. She'd always been consistent, never having anything but a double view of him: as the hard man ('He *was* a hard man'), cause of so many tears, and as the marvellous lad she'd hung on to despite all warnings, from outside and from within herself.

And she remembered again his last weeks. How he'd said, 'You know, I've been thinking. I've been very bad to you. I've a lot to be sorry for.' And she'd thought he wanted her to say:

'It doesn't matter.' But she didn't say it. 'I thought it was right, what he said, so I didn't answer him.'

And I imagined my father, longing to be excused, forgiven, absolved: tormented by the thought of the bad opinions he'd leave behind. Feeling for a forgiveness he wouldn't know what to do with—since it belonged to the order of human feelings he didn't really believe in.

And his faithlessness. All those women. Even one from the office who'd visited the bungalow, a few years before; and he'd locked them together into the living room. 'She was a good bed-mate. She gave me some fun,' he'd suddenly said: one of those occasions the memory of which caused those terrified tears on his last night alive. Well, said my mother, what she remembered was fearing she was pregnant and knowing it would make their barely possible existence quite impossible. So she'd stood outside The Rising Sun in Barton-on-the-Hill, screwing up the courage to go in and buy half a bottle of gin. How could you be a good bed-mate when you were terrified of the consequences of being one?

'But I can understand,' she said, 'that a man might want a change.' And I wondered if he'd ever divined that her love was as deep as *that*. ...

She'd delighted in having children. It was terrible to be forced to be frightened of having them. She remembered how my knees had protruded when she was carrying me. She'd greatly enjoyed carrying Betty and me and our brother who'd died on his first birthday. 'I don't know,' she said again, 'how anyone can say they don't want a baby.'

But it was all tied up with ... sex. Which you ought to be able to enjoy. But she remembered notes my father used to scribble and press into her hand, when they were together at his mother's house in New Barton, before they were married. Mrs Blishen Senior—how often I'd heard my mother use that strange form in talking of her mother-in-law!—hadn't approved of 'goings-on', even between the engaged. So in those notes my father had begged Lizzie Pye not to sit too close to him, because he couldn't bear it. He wanted to hug her, he wanted to have her, and he mustn't.

'Poor darling,' she said: referring, obviously, in some great obituary bundle, to his old loving frustrations, nearly sixty years before, and to his being dead; and also to those later frustrations, when he'd turned to this or that woman at the office. She must tell me that she suspected ('I wouldn't be so wicked as to say I'm sure') that he'd hoped she might go first, so that he could have a little time by himself ... with a creature she always referred to with police-court delicacy as Miss B.

Which somehow made her remember how, in her first job as a between-maid, she was discovered by her mistress on her knees, cleaning a grate whilst wearing a pretty white frock with a frilly white apron—both made for her by her mother: and her mistress had said she was too charming and clean for such work ... promoting her instantly upstairs. ...

And tomorrow the eye specialist was coming, to see if anything could be done for her. She didn't want to talk about this—and desperately longed to talk about it.

At some stage during the night, sleeping in my father's old bed, I discovered I had a cold. It didn't feel like an ordinary one: a stunning headache, followed by a general sensation of having been brutally flogged. ... I prayed it wouldn't have carried to her: and when I left next day, kissed her as glancingly as I could. And it was the first time she'd cried at parting. She'd been talking about how you missed the companionship of a husband, and how she'd often wished they could have gone together—'and been cremated together, or whatever you do.' (She'd always shied away from specific statements about that, her vague references suggesting it was some kind of silly behaviour indulged in by the dead.) Of course, it wouldn't work if we were always together—Betty and me and her. She saw that! 'Goodbye then, my dear,' she said, for we'd reached the door; and the tears spilled themselves out of her blind eyes as if something had broken inside her head. And I walked away spilling tears of my own, and looked back to see her in the living room window, waving to the absent world.

And when I rang her next day, taking care not to sound like a man who'd just got out of bed and meant to go straight back, she said, in her briskest and most healthy voice: 'I'm sorry I seemed a bit sad when you went. But we'd had such a good time, hadn't we?' And then she talked about the eye specialist, who'd diagnosed the worst cataract he'd ever seen. ('A cat-rack?' she asked, exploringly. 'Yes, Mum—I know what you mean.') But he was very confident. He had a long queue, but of course at her age she would jump it. Well, there was no question of her deciding whether or not to have it done. He'd already booked it. And she was looking forward to it as if it had been a wedding, or Christmas. She could confess now that she was virtually blind. Well, she couldn't actually any longer see the stove.

Could she really endure such an operation? I wondered. Could she even endure the expectation of it? Or the hideous disappointment of a failure. ... I'd been aware of her hands during that visit—always on the move, feeling for the world. They were small hands, the skin permanently wrinkled from so many decades of household water. They were, I thought, not merely monstrously anxious—they were actually trying to *see*. They were trying to establish the existence of things outside that small black space in which she was trapped. ...

But anyway, she did not seem to have picked up this violent influenza.

8

But she had.

When I rang again, Mrs Bruce from next door answered. My mother had one of her 'chests', and would tell me about it herself. This she did, trying desperately to sound like someone whose hideous rawness of voice, and cruel cough, were libels on her actual condition, which was one of almost perfect health. It was evident at once that she could not be left alone, and since my sister had the 'flu, without benefit of contact with me, Kate drove down to take charge. She rang to say she'd found my mother on her feet, but only in honour of

Kate's arrival: that achieved, she'd wept copiously with guilt and relief and fallen into bed, Kate's hand in hers. It was much later that Kate was able to recover this hand.

Next day she was her dogged self, and took care to point out that her appearance of alarming illness was a particularly foolish illusion. 'I still have my facilities.' She made no reference, and expected no reference to be made, to her continuing need to have her hand held. At once there was a terrifying transformation; she seemed, Kate said, about to die, much in the fashion of some small, barely fledged bird. Her mouth was wide open and she stared desperately. Kate rang Dr Mackenzie, who made in no time one of his comfortingly sober appearances, and said my mother was enduring a little series of coronaries. There was a fifty per cent chance that she'd recover: and if she failed to do so, the end would be sudden and merciful. He prescribed pills to drain the fluids from her chest.

Excellent Dr Mackenzie! His field was life and death, but I'd have been as much impressed if it had been, say, weather forecasting, or something perfectly plain and abstract like ... moral philosophy. He policed these hideous frontier regions, unarmed, drily gentle; and I thought the Greeks must have known him—as perhaps the most sympathetically prosaic of fatal ferrymen. ...

For a woman showing so many signs of final illness, my mother was oddly talkative. And as so often since my father's death, her topic was the future. She had to admit that small flaws had made themselves apparent in her grand scheme of living alone, and she proposed to retreat (in some fashion that did not involve her in turning her back) to a secondary scheme of barely reduced grandeur, which might involve living in some pleasant home not more than, say, ten minutes drive from Betty and me.

At this point I joined them, and was startled by the change in her. She had black hollows for eyes, and looked like nothing so much as a Hallowe'en mask. She was being given large doses of morphine, and was sinking down through layer after layer of memory. Dr Mackenzie, arriving as I did, said a peaceful end must be hoped for. If she did recover, it could only be to undergo again exactly the same agonies. Her heart was ... on its last legs. He'd always been astonished that it had lasted so long. 'For half my lifetime we seem to have been giving her digitalis.' Her thinness and weightlessness were partly responsible for her unlikely survival. But she was close to such a congestive condition as must end in heart failure. It was not possible to go on walking the tightrope between too little moisture and too much. If her distress became extreme, and beyond the power of thirty drops of morphine to remedy, we were to call him, and he would see that ... intolerable agony had an end.

We said we could perhaps continue to nurse her for another week. My sister, recovering from her 'flu, would relieve Kate and me for a day or so. ... Yes, a week. He said he'd put out feelers in respect of a local nursing home. There were several round about, all much the same—not brilliant, but kind enough: except one, which he'd steer us away from, expensive and *not* very kind.

At once we decided that if the end seemed close and another week beyond the first was involved, we'd of course hang on. Kate and I remembered Nancy Trevellick: 'People do like to die at home!' Then, from this hangman's conference, we went in to see her: who, on the point of death, was anxious to categorise Kate's role in her recent adventures. 'I don't know what I'd have done without her. I'd have died.'

And so she lay there, groaning, a little sharp ('Don't treat me like an invalid') and full of odd memories. From the excess of some drugs and the absence of others she cried out with the effect of astonishments that were eighty years old. So she remembered how her Uncle Bill used to bring home for the night children from bad homes. And once it had been a little girl who, said my mother in her mortal excitement, 'was ready for sex.' And this meant, it seemed—she fell back swooning into drugged sleep—that she'd been encouraged 'to play with her father.'

It rained. We paced the bungalow, monstrously separated from our daily routines. ...

Kate went home, and my sister took her place. I'd meant to go with Kate—my professional life was falling to pieces—but could not bring myself to leave Betty alone in such an emergency. There were moments when my mother seemed in such distress, so close to an end; and others when her obstinate positive interest in everything, her shrewdness and the impossibility of deceiving her, made it seem that we were contriving the end of something quite heroically persistent. We were acquiescing in the overthrow of a champion. The excellent, gentle, nearly eighty-five-year-old Lizzie Pye was, on the most sympathetic grounds, to be eradicated.

And she cried out in the night, not for Dick, my father, but for Arthur, his brother. I'd always suspected that in the end, by some margin of emotion long ago engendered, it was Arthur she loved. He was my father, simplified. Physically he was his brother, darkly handsome; but in some obstreperous fashion he was gentler, that one of the brothers whose violence was largely good-natured. I'd always thought of him as a sort of gypsy. He'd kept pigs, was a vegetable gardener who seemed himself to have some of the character of a tomato, a marrow: squeeze him and there'd be pips, and healthy green juice. Among my earliest memories: sitting under the horn of his gramophone, a mouth that seemed to be formed out of great green leaves. The pips and juice *that* yielded were rowdily musical: on the whole, brass bands being skittish. He had sons who were cornettists almost from birth. They blew enormously; and we marched round their small living room, while Uncle Arthur laughed in a manner, richly suggestive, that I later associated with the *News of the World*, copies of which were to be found all over the house: in mounds in the kitchen and under the stairs, and in frustrating fragments on a nail in the lavatory. I see, looking back, that to me in some fashion Uncle Arthur seemed a more genuine member of our family than my father, reading a somehow more suitable newspaper, letting himself go in respect of a music more appropriate, alongside a whole order of more honest domestic stenches. Well, his house smelt of damp and of layer after layer of old cooking and stored fruit: whereas ours smelt of polish and presumption. I'd loved as a child the sense of sweat Uncle Arthur engendered: all that cackling inclination to make out of his home a sort of smelly warehouse. (He *had* worked once as a Covent Garden porter.) Sitting there, as a boy, I'd felt quite thrillingly the disgrace of being from Manor Road with its spruceness—the world of the *Daily Express* and, hideously conclusive, of the grammar school courted and the grammar school achieved. It had been a salty excitement, living on the frontier between these worlds. For me, pale promising child, Uncle Arthur was an alternative existence: his shirt sleeves always rolled up, his forehead always brown and shining. Of all the brothers he made the coarsest jokes about my father being a civil servant: that bowler hat, that umbrella! Flexing his springy gardener's legs, he'd pretend to believe that my father spent his working life perched on a high stool. I could see very well why, behind rash love for my father, my mother had concealed even rasher love for Uncle Arthur.

9

Oddly, out of all the incoherence and distress, she said: 'It's been an enjoyable week. Like a holiday!' And that, I supposed, was because we were all there, and fussing over her. All the same, to see the business of dying in such terms! It seemed to me that if she *were* bound for immense hereafters, Heaven or Hell, she'd throw them into confusion at once with her capacity to construct the sensible and prosaic out of the most dramatic material: or small domestic pleasures out of ecstasies or agonies.

Not that she had any difficulty in grasping the dangerous nature of her illness. 'What causes all this?' she asked me. 'You caught a chill . . .' I said. And she snorted. Of course, it was easily possible to be *too* sensible, *too* prosaic! A chill!

I wanted to tell her of Flamineo's cry at the end of Webster's *The White Devil*: 'I have caught an everlasting cold!' Given any sort of literary preparation, she'd have liked that!

Perpetually she raised her left arm in the air—and let it fall, with a sigh of the most profound weariness. It helped the heart, I guess: forming the weak handle of a hopelessly weakening pump. At her worst, in between the effects of doses of morphine, she pleaded with her pain: '*Don't!*' And her body being all bone, there was no comfort for her however she lay.

But the remorseless observer turned out again and again to be offering a comment. 'One thing I've noticed: no one wants to wash your feet!' And five minutes later: 'When I have a bath, I shall have the time of my life!' And again: 'Longest time I've ever had Kate stay in my house.' A long struggling pause: then, 'Marvellous person!'

There was even a sensation of ... seminar. 'I think we've come to a very nice time,' she said. 'We can sit down and talk nicely about it.' Her pitiful arm rose and fell, following which, the lecturer gained a croaking strength. 'In Circus Road,' she said, referring to her West London past. 'Little old-fashioned house, divided out into flats. There was two little children. This is Gospel! I can remember it as if it was yesterday. My poor dear mother looking out of the window, and my father looking at a book—not that he could read it. ... There was a little girl lived next door and ... this little boy, only three years old, he pushed her on her back and started jumping up and down on top of her. "God," said my father, "they've started young!" Probably didn't know what they were doing. Didn't even know the meaning of it ...'

She gasped for breath, fell vacant, then said; 'I'm very happy. Do you know why I'm happy? Because of my three children. They're what I call these sex-fairies. I've been thinking—I'd like all children—and after they've grown up—I'd like to see them in the nude. Not being dirty. Natural. They could wear a towel or carry one ... Son should speak to mother, mother should speak to son, son should speak to father. ...' And then, her voice becoming several degrees more Cockney, as well as amazingly magisterial: 'I would like a book wrote about it, to say his mother believed this.' She glared at me from her suffering rostrum.

And I wondered what on earth my mother's childhood had really been like. It was as if deep pools, of something like the strangest hot mud, were bubbling, old steams arising. My mother's sexual visions, based on some notion of universal candid availability, were suddenly present, turning much that

I'd known about her into disguise and façade.

And yet, even as I thought this, I thought also that in some deep fashion I'd always known these things about her: in her kisses, her sudden reachings out, her small soft hand once holding my smaller hand. And, of course, the narcissus in her. ... All those warm self-praises. In these last years you'd so often catch her holding her hands in front of her failing, and then partly recovered, and then again failing sight: astonished and pleased by her own neatness, by such deft flesh and able bones. ... So many of the flurries of feeling I'd known in her, and that had embarrassed me when I was not quite a child any more—those excitements that seemed comic and so often brought a flow of words gone wrong, the attempt to be impressive verbally as in other confused fashions—so many of those sudden passionate pomposities that had so irritated and even enraged my father ... well, *passions* is what they were: sudden deep boilings. ...

There'd been that unmanageable early experience, a matter of children imitating the adults in whose company they slept: and so the destruction of all taboos as between child and grown-up. ... But even that, surely, was a merely bashful way of looking at it. Among the desperately poor there'd been from the beginning few of the fences and warning notices of the world of sexuality made respectable. There'd been agencies, like the nonconformist church my mother belonged to, that had talked about the world in terms of that other kind of sexual topography, in which fences were obediently skirted, forbidden fields avoided. But life had begun in a landscape quite different, where small children copied closely observed adults: and might be encouraged to ... play with their fathers.

And out of it all my mother had formed a vision of sexuality that had no sleaziness about it, nothing of the guffaw. To Betty she said: 'Sex is lovely. Sex isn't dirty.' And then: 'I came into the world like it, and I shall leave the world like it. That makes me very happy.' And suddenly, a few moments later: 'The gates of heaven are always open!'

If I was ordinarily employed, I thought, I should not be able to be here. But then I *wasn't* ordinarily employed—and I wouldn't want to be anywhere else.

IO

'It's a strange world when you're ill,' she said. She was weak, dry, hardly able to take her heart pill. Her head itched, and she believed she'd been colonised by fleas. She didn't know day from night. She startled my sister with an exclamation: 'I love you all!' Kate came, with my brother-in-law. I returned home, to apply patches to my life as a freelance writer. Kate reported on the phone that she had now barely the strength to take a single sip of tea. In the night she had suddenly said: 'If I was young, I'd go to Turkey.' 'Why Turkey, dear?' Betty had asked. 'Because it's warm.' A long pause. 'Or Cyprus.'

My mother's grasp of geography had always been uncertain; and I thought how she must have lain there searching through an atlas she did not believe in for the names of places she vaguely connected with heat. Cyprus I understood; but where had Turkey come from?

Dr Mackenzie, reported by Kate, had been surprised to find she was still there. It couldn't be much longer, if only because she was now eating nothing. No longer did a little belch follow each of the few sips of tea she was still able to take. She had momentary changes of personality: became briefly tyrannical, cantankerous, a bully. The touch of the preacher increased; she was in full canonicals; and at once was the plainest Lizzie Pye again. Then she had a dream about gravy. For the first time I could remember, she used the word 'bloody.' It was in Notting Hill, there was a great party, attended by Lady Taylor, to whom my great-aunt Ada had been a companion. None of us had ever met Lady Taylor, but once for us all she'd been a more substantial acquaintance than many mere everyday neighbours. There'd been royalty, too, of an inexplicit kind: and then suddenly gravy flowing everywhere—

130

'this damned bloody gravy.' My mother struggled hopelessly to sit up in bed, the better to utter these enjoyably frightful words. And on surges and swells of this damned bloody gravy she had been going in and out of the bedroom window and up and down the respectable road the bungalow stood in. 'Whoops,' she cried, to indicate that she was leaving again, and 'Whoops', to indicate that she was returning. Her giggle was girlish.

And there, my God, was my ancient mother, in the West London world in which she lived in the 1890s, floating in and out of a window in New Chilton in the 1970s, buoyed up on a glorious scandalous flood of gravy. . . .

I met Tom at Waterloo, a bottle of champagne in my travelling bag. The next day would be her eighty-fifth— clearly, her last—birthday. Dr Mackenzie had suggested that champagne might be in order. It was made for my mother's terminal mood.

She greeted Tom with a ringing affirmation: 'We were poor, but we were clean,' before making of her weak arm an astonishingly strong hoop to draw him to her.

On the morning of her birthday, her good melancholy doctor appeared to say that the trouble with morphine, and such care as she'd had, was that the strain was almost removed, and dying must take longer. She was lucky to have her family round her. In many cases, he said drily, there was no sign of sons or daughters until it was time for the will to be read. 'We have to act as *locum filii*.'

And I found that hard simply to take in—that so many could leave their old people to die alone.

We opened the champagne, drank; and she fell asleep.

11

And next morning she was clearly better. She'd talked to
Betty during the night about the enormous meal we were all to
have together when she'd recovered. To bring herself to name
the courses, however splendid, would reduce the feast to
banality. Oh, we were going to eat as never before!

Dr Mackenzie arrived: was baffled. The congestion had
gone, he said; the crisis was over. Her heart had nothing more
to offer, but there was now virtually no strain upon it: her
pulse was strong. A few days ago one would have said it was
impossible she could be alive. But now. ... He shook his
scientific head.

Betty talked of being unwilling to go home for fear that
something might happen in her absence. I spoke of an
engagement I'd cancelled. Dr Mackenzie again shook his
head. We had it badly, he said; as if it had been some dubious
and slightly unhealthy enthusiasm. She really ought to go
away, to some home. Even his dry tenderness thought that
was a fair fate for her. Well, with our care and good nursing
we had pickled a rod for our own backs. And he went off,
sighing.

And Tom went: after a ceremony of temporary goodbyes.
My mother always found her grandchildren difficult to
dispense with, and Tom had her special affection because she
felt that in Salford, by some sort of time-defying proxy, he was
tending her and the children she'd grown up among, between
1890 and 1900. She commanded him to fetch her handbag,
and gave him money. 'For you and Mary-Ram,' she said,
getting his girl-friend's name hopelessly wrong. 'For wine.'

She slept ... an afternoon, an entire evening. She then woke
crisply and took me to task. 'I don't know how you can spend

so much time down here,' she said, as if I'd been sensationally malingering. She fixed me with a black and blind eye. 'Haven't you got any work to do?' she asked.

The unmistakable sign of recovery was that she began to piece a story together, based on the happenings of the fortnight during which, against the grain of professional advice, she'd decided to remain alive. She examined witnesses at all hours, and made her usual deft rearrangements of the material supplied. She'd always treated actual events as a sort of rough draft, and did so now.

To life in an old people's home she was resigned, and was already idealising it. There would be all these brisk kindly people, a little multitude of nurses backed by a small squad of matrons, who would both tend and admire her. But as the vision grew brighter, the reality it was meant to dazzle out of existence became quietly more difficult to deal with. She was leaving the bungalow. She was abandoning *his* home, and hers. 'I've been wondering if I'm a coward,' she suddenly said.

She sat, a curiously pretty skeleton, in her armchair facing his; and the conflicting Lizzie Pyes talked it out. Finger rubbing on finger, they allowed each other no mercy. The dreamer ('I'm looking forward to it') acknowledged the arguments of the realist ('The thing is, I can't expect to get used to it at once'). ...

As for us, we ran about, making arrangements; and I thought of the valiant helplessness life could come to—this tiny scrap of suffering talking to herself in the midst of all these dispositions. Kate had found a home in the exact spot my mother had dreamed of, ten minutes from us and from my sister. It was for retired gentlefolk, and my mother, I thought, was retired roughfolk. But it seemed likely to be kind, and to provide something more than basic care.

Dr Mackenzie paid what she luckily didn't realise was his last visit, and so the last time she'd see this attendant, so complicatedly loved. (One of her latest embroideries was that she was widely mistaken for Mrs Mackenzie.) 'I don't think,' he said to us, 'that I've been very clever about this.' To her he said: 'You are immortal!' The word was over her head. 'Oh,' she politely murmured: 'You always say that!'

And so we drove away from the bungalow, grateful for once for her blindness; and she dozed most of the way to London, except when she stirred to say, 'You can't think what it's like to be out in the daylight again'; and, anxiously, 'I'll be all right—if I have a friend. I've always been unfortunate—I've always seemed to be isolated.'

And then she was in the narrow bright room that was to be her home—much impressed by the telephone beside her bed with which she could at any moment make her needs known. I was certain that part of the increased activity of her hands, as they added their element of Lizzie Pye III to her internal debate, sprang from the existence of this phone; she was throbbing with schemes for its employment. Sometimes she would require a cup of tea; but sometimes she would make demands that amounted to a wish to be hugged. At the other end of the line would be the friend she'd never had in the setting provided by my father, that rigorous opponent of friendship.

'Are you happy?' she asked me: reversing our roles as so often she'd done. It seemed that the real heroes of the hour were Kate, Betty and I, who'd managed this move for her. It did not strike her that the question of her own happiness might be held to occupy some fairly central position.

'Are *you*?' I asked.

She smiled in a surprised fashion, and touched my hand: before taking up the cup of tea they'd brought her—the first of an astonishing series of cups of tea she could hardly wait to begin lifting the phone to command.

PART FOUR

I

'You'll like this,' said my mother, handing Kate a cup of tea. 'It's Typhoid.'

We'd called in at Manor Road on our way home from court, where we'd spent yet another day defending the case brought against us by an amiable electrician. This had followed from the bill for the conversion of 1 East Drive being for several hundred pounds more than the sum to which the original estimate had been sternly pared. Well, said persons suddenly knowledgeable, it should have been expected. This was a building firm that owed its existence to war-work. It had been used to going carelessly ahead, knowing bills were never questioned. But, we said, we'd made it clear that wherever more expense seemed necessary than had been allowed for, there should be consultation! Ah yes, said our belated advisers: but bad habits died hard. Scoundrels, all of them! Lucky to get away so lightly!

Our first reaction was that we couldn't pay, and clearly were not bound to do so. A firm and final estimate was a firm and final estimate—that was how we saw it, unaware that, before all was over, this apparently watertight statement would be held to be no better than a verbal sieve. But since it did appear that some of the work responsible for the excess was work we might in any case have felt compelled to agree to, we decided we might propose a compromise. We'd offer to pay half of the difference between the final estimate and the bill.

When we went through the details with our lawyer, Norman Lock—who seemed more than ever convinced that, in some rather jolly way, life was not worth living—he took exception to almost every item. 'Oh,' he cried, 'he can't have that!' He couldn't have this, either—or the other. 'Always ruining themselves by under-estimating, builders,' said Norman with the satisfaction of a man describing one of the few sound features of an ill-made universe. Given his head, he would have reduced the excess to something like the figure by which Kate and I were accustomed to being tormented: £8.13s.6d. But no—fair (or fairly fair), we said, was fair. We'd stick to our offer.

From the builder there were shocked cries and grumbles, converted into what Ben said might fittingly be called the wooden language of the trade: and then ... surrender. We paid our cheque in full and final settlement; he delivered his receipt, employing the same reassuring phrase.

Weeks later we were visited by the sub-contracting electrician. Had we paid the builder? Because he himself had not received a penny. And his bill was a large part of the total, for his own estimate had always been tentative, subject to change when he got to grips with the old wiring of the house; and *that* had turned out to be in need of almost complete renewal. Had we not been warned of the uncertain character of his work?

He was a plain, honest, baffled man, and we were not surprised to learn a little later that he was suing the builder. But our poise *was* disturbed by a further development: as a precaution, he was joining us to the case. It seemed the builder was preparing to allege that much of the excess sprang from careless, capricious, unrecorded orders for extra work placed by us: or, to be exact, by our wives. Falling back on some notion of women as creatures given to making intemperate demands of any workmen who happened to be around was, it seemed, a familiar move in such a case. The point was that builders were heavily handicapped by innocence and gallantry, so that to the difficulty of believing that a wife's expressed wishes might not coincide with her husband's was added the impossibility of ever causing a woman distress by saying No to her. And so on.

Our wives, having acted on the nervous warning we'd all been given—never to make the idlest of proposals to anyone resembling a builder—were furious. The question was: Should we pay up, or take the risk of the case going against us—which might mean we'd have to pay anyway, and meet everybody's costs as well? It would be ruin. Well, for Kate and me, certainly. We were half-ruined all the time: step up that familiar demand by merely sixpence to £8.14s.od. and we'd be done for. Lately, it was true, I'd been getting more pieces in the *Manchester Guardian*: but, gratifying though this was, it provided no armour against a savage stroke of civil law. Then there was the publisher who'd written to ask if I'd think of writing a book based on my teaching experiences. I'd gladly thought of it; and had been doing so for six months or more. The trouble was that being asked to write a book was to me an event so marvellous that I had no real wish to top it. It had been thought, by a publisher of repute, that I had a book in me. He'd written in his own hand to say so. I felt no need to stir myself further. In my reckoning, this was the utmost reach of fame.

So literature did not stand between me and ruin: instead it took up a distant position, sympathetic but keenly interested, clearly not at all averse to recording the final disaster ... in my own diary.

But in the end it became clear to us that we couldn't bear the builder to be victorious. So we'd had these two days in court, at long intervals; the first sober and dull; but this one, hideously stirring. The builder had been giving evidence, and it was a mass of fiction. The concept of perjury did not meet the case. This was casual invention on oath. Kate and Marie and Amy Hickman, hearing themselves traduced, could not remain silent. They gasped, groaned and turned to look at each other with eyes huge with horror. The judge, his long clever face bisected by half-glasses, glared at them; at one point, groaned himself; and at last said: 'I really may have to take steps against these ladies. ...'

Amy felt the falsehoods so keenly that she'd been taken ill, and Charles had to lead her out of court. The case halted while this happened. The judge's glasses slipped lower down the intellectual pylon that was his nose. I felt Amy's honest sickness, on top of the transparently helpless shock all three women had exhibited, must work in our favour. Surely the judge must think that he had never witnessed so moving a display of innocence.

Ben said: 'Beware of believing that the law ever has much of a heart!'

I was rash enough now to quote this in my father's hearing. In allowing ourselves to be taken to court, he believed, we were on the way to besmirching the family name in some quite final fashion. Henceforth, Blishen would be synonymous with the bilking of electricians. Blishening would go into the dictionaries as the term for a particularly disgusting civil offence. 'That young Fletcher. . . .' my father groaned. He'd managed to conclude that Ben was marching to legal war, holding me in front of him as a shield. Well, Ben came originally from East Barton, rather than Barton-on-the-Hill, and so had no local reputation to lose. To have one's roots in East Barton was to start *without* reputation. It sometimes seemed that my father had forgotten that he himself came from East Barton. Oh, the intricacies of local snobbery, in these few square miles covered by Bartons of various kinds! Barley Wood, of course, though not strictly one of them, was that district that made them all humble, as a Rolls-Royce made any other car seem not much of a car. It caused my poor father complicated anguish, to have me living in Barley Wood with the financial status and outlook of an East Barnetonian. It was part of my being, on the draughtsboard of things, always in the wrong square—perpetually huffable.

2

Occupying the wrong square, I often thought, was turning out to be a characteristic of most of us at 1 East Drive.

The house was in one sense very much the right square. Now that it was painted and settled, it seemed most of the time as desirable a residence as any of us had imagined. Odd, of course; especially as to colour. Confronted by the blank shell of our own flat, we'd thought for some months of little but shades and tints. Colours, not in their everyday obvious truth, but as they were slyly defined in commercial colour cards. So we'd allowed ourselves to be much agitated as between nuances of some pink pallor announced here as mushroom and elsewhere as June Sunset. And having decided between them—after debate that seemed astonishing at the time and in retrospect seems perfectly amazing—I smeared large areas with the chosen paint, for weeks on end. There was this period of my life when, having till then been nothing much but a reader and writer, I became nothing much but an interior decorator. With Ben it had been almost the same, but with the difference that he had quite another approach to painting. This went deeper than his wartime training in leaving gaps. He was hasty, and did not recognise the existence of the straight line. He would never draw a paintbrush patiently along the precise edge of anything.

Oh, it didn't matter! How could it be of consequence to Ben and me—any difference between his philosophy as a painter, which might be called Slapdashism: and mine, for which the name might be Carefulism? I couldn't help aiming at precision. I laboured to avoid the wavering line, the overlap. Often I raged at myself, finding I was caught in this temperamental trap. Could I really be looking forward to one obsessively finicky weekend of painting after another? Could I be angry with Ben for simply being different? But I was: I quietly hated his complacent incompetence as, I realised, he secretly detested my insistent efficiency.

It was one of those wrong squares. Ben and I, living and working side by side, were made sore by some of the very differences that had drawn us together. For instance, I now saw that he was an overwhelmer, and I an underwhelmer.

Well, as much as anything this was a matter of the couples we made. Marie and Ben were natural centre-stagers. If we were all together, with others, Ben and Marie talked marvellously of themselves. It wasn't egotism. They were genuinely captivated by their own adventures, and made grand narrative out of them. Marie would astonish the company with a tale about Ben, and Ben would retort with some amazing witty history in which Marie was the chief character. Together they would describe astounding persons they'd met, and the dramatic circumstances in which these meetings had

141

occurred.

Kate and I, by comparison, had a damnable demureness. Added to this was an uncertainty we both felt about the actual outlines of anything that happened to us, and of anyone we met. Doubt was our nature: and so we were marked out as those who listened, rather than those who were listened to. We also became aware of Ben as the deliberately bad audience. His talent was not so much for booing, as for creating a poor atmosphere for any performance you entered upon. It was much as if a company of actors were to observe, as the curtain went up, that the audience were all deeply engaged in reading their newspapers. Ben made an art out of being inattentive.

It was, again, a difference of styles. Ben and Marie steamed steadily forward, flags and bunting flying from every mast. Kate and I were in this little dinghy with the ripped and sordid sails. It was not a difference that went to the heart of our relationship: still, together, without others, much of the time, we were happy and at ease. But oh, there was this conflict of style!—which spread to other areas of our shared life.

The matter, for example, of the *au pair*.

When Ben and Marie announced that they were acquiring an *au pair*, I was not at all sure what was involved. I'd picked up the edges of a meaning that suggested ... some order of pretty slave.

In this case the slave turned out to be French. 'Pretty', however, didn't seem to be the word. Caroline, as we perceived during a shy encounter on the evening of her arrival, was a fourteen-year-old of pleasant plainness, with plaits and a circular hat of a childish kind. I was amazed that anyone so young and so simple should be allowed to yield herself up for employment so ambiguous. True, my sense of its ambiguity was beginning to fade, and I saw that I'd been perhaps unduly influenced by the term being French. There was, however still some sense about it of sleazy servitude. ... Anyway, must it be taken that Ben and Marie meant to employ this unworldly schoolchild as a mixture of housemaid and nanny?

Next morning I was puzzled by an exotic presence in the

front drive. Walking out in the direction of the B----- W---
Stores was a young woman of astounding beauty in her late
teens. Her hair was up in an enchanting ... oh, to call it 'bun'
must be wrong: it was a meringue composed of pure honey.
Her face had clearly been made a little more vivid by art, but
had no need of it. She wore a dress of startling simplicity ...
and I felt there was not much need of that, either. Who she
was I could not imagine. Kate's less dazzled eyes were not
long deceived. 'My goodness!' she cried. 'It's the *au pair*! It's
Caroline!'

And it was.

She was a charmer. She amazed that summer with her
bikinis ... or, strictly, with the delights that these revealed.
Her body had been sketched with a rosy pencil by someone
who had an idea of slenderness more plausible than anyone
else's. At the centre of the lawn, itself at the centre of some fine
busy Sunday, her navel was a tender smudge that made a blur
of the entire garden. Charles Hickman found it necessary to
repaint his windows, reconstructing the clever scaffolding that
enable him to do this in mid-air. He must have been one of the
loftiest of voyeurs, 1954.

More remarkable perhaps than Caroline's beauty was that
she gained and held the affection of most of the other women
on that summery scene. She was courteous and amusing and
considerate, and was liked almost as much as if she'd been
plain. The trouble was that she sharpened another difference
of style between us.

Simply, she made it possible for Ben and Marie to go out.
In brilliant displays of this freedom, they went to theatres,
cinemas, art galleries. They vanished for whole weekends.
And they talked about it all with enthusiasm: even saying that
we must see ... we shouldn't miss. ... Occasionally, coming
back from some grand event, they advised us on no account to
see ... to make no mistake about missing. ...

It was absurd. There was no reason in the world why they
shouldn't have an *au pair*, or use the freedom she provided,
shouldn't talk of plays, films, paintings. ... The problem was
that Kate and I were prisoners, and felt, wretchedly, that the
freedom of our friends was like another layer of walls round
our scrupulously painted domestic jail.

143

Whenever we did arrange to go out, having fixed that the Fletchers or the Hickmans would listen for us, ready to step in if Tom woke or Dan, we'd be presented with architectural problems by our particular flat, and by Dan especially with problems of escape.

Dan had been born with an inbuilt detector that told him when adults who should have been straining their nerves to care for him, were nursing the intention of nipping out to see Paul Scofield in something by Anouilh. It was pretty well as specific as that. The trouble would begin when the idea simply occurred to us, days before. He'd be sulky, madly suspicious, and disinclined to let Kate out of his sight. On the evening itself he'd detect that she was changing into unmotherly forms of dress before she'd even approached the wardrobe. And as to leave the flat by its front door it was necessary to pass the door of the children's bedroom—and as Dan turned out to have an unerring ear for the faintest squeak of an evening shoe—it was always necessary for us, if we'd got through earlier obstacles, to leave by the living-room window. This did not count as a suitable start to an evening out. No happy woman, Kate held, was ever required to set out for the theatre by way of a sash window. The window somehow cocked a snook at her evening dress. And there were terrible evenings when, incredulously prepared for music or drama, we'd get half out ... and from the other arm of the flat a fatal wailing would begin.

I'd think that marriage was quite simply a means by which I'd defrauded this passionate theatregoer and music-lover, this cursing livid lady, Kate, of her rights as a citizen. Certainly I'd embarked on a course that had converted the charming person of half a dozen years before, who'd barely been able to find words for the admiration I caused in her, into this flaming termagant who, one leg out of our living-room window, with Dan or Tom or both systematically howling in the background, was addressing me in terms falling far short not just of admiration but, I'd think for a desperate moment, of mere liking.

When we did get away, it was memorable. I recall an evening when we saw the Spanish dancer, Antonio, and his company of foot- and finger-clicking, marvellously howling, skirt-flicking, imperious women and short, plump men, and, absurdly inhabited by the spirit of flamenco, arrived at Kings Cross in its near-midnight sootiness, and danced and howled on the platform; and behaved, roughly between Finsbury Park and New Southgate, in a manner that might have led, on conviction, to our spending some time in a prison less well painted than the one we occupied at 1 East Drive. ...

But envy rather than arithmetic suggested that Ben and Marie had seen Antonio a dozen times. ...

How, Kate and I wondered, had we been converted into such moral mediocrities, jealous of our friends? Kate wept once with the thought of it—with enormous vigour, a cloudburst. It didn't seem possible that anyone could produce so much by way of tears in so short a time. Dan was in her arms at that moment, and regarded her with alarm; then decided to be amused, instead. Amusement reminded him that he was hungry. He passed from a tremendous enjoyment of things to absolute misery with no observable transition.

Oh, the lucky—or, of course, unlucky—dip of parenthood! And the time it took to pass beyond the point at which you were merely in possession of a mysterious parcel! It was months after Dan's birth before it dawned on us that we'd encumbered ourselves with a clown. Suddenly this was as clear as if at the end of his nose one morning there'd appeared a red knob.

Earlier he'd shown severe symptoms of hair fetishism: any accessible lock or tress making him tremble with lust until it was seized and he'd simultaneously and violently thrust a thumb into his mouth. His eyes crossed, his ears turned red: one felt one ought not to look. One must grant this mad little pump some dignity! Almost at once he seemed to become aware of the absurdity of being himself; any act whatever being followed up with vast, unfocused smiles, and noises in which there was an alarming link between chuckling and choking. He fetched up sighs from distances not to be accounted for by the very limited confines of his small body. He then discovered his utopia and inhabited it: it was wherever it was possible to make oneself free of fragments of biscuit and to mumble them to infinite pulp. There was no level of soppiness beyond which he could not reduce a biscuit.

This was the point where his clown's nature declared itself beyond doubt. Aware that he was being eyed, and coated with a general vague plaster of biscuit, he'd wink, crow, testify to his amusement with crazily rapid rotations of arms and legs, and set out to complete the compulsive process of which the desired end was his entire encasement in biscuit pulp. ...

Tom had seemed at first to regard tolerantly the appearance of this vile usurper disguised as that charming thing, a baby. He'd professed to being much struck by Dan's having arms, legs and private parts. A delicious little innovation: well done, the acquirers thereof! There was an almost instant reversal of policy: he became furious when Kate prepared to remove her dress in order to feed Dan. Nothing more disgraceful had ever been brought to his attention: 'Put it back! Put it back!' Dan became quickly used to the world, and was inclined to be extremely benign and happy ... and fierce. Tom's outlook moved in the other direction. Despite the care we took to modify the enthusiasm we felt in respect of Dan, Tom was perfectly aware of the process by which the attractive newcomer causes attractiveness not to leak but to flood away from the oldcomer. There was no way that Tom could persuade himself that he had the glamour of this grinning novelty ...!

It grew worse as Dan began to communicate, a matter of half a dozen onomatopoeic hisses, and Tom concluded that the labour he'd put into mastering the English language had been misspent. What was the point of making yourself at ease with the relative pronoun if adoration could be commanded with some unhygienic splutter?

Upstaged by Dan's tremendous act, Tom fought back with hurried turns of his own, all of a displeasing character. Dan, wonderful grinner by day, took to howling at night. The crying of a small baby, I thought, might destroy the nerve of a moral Samson. In my diary I found surprising phrases for our children: 'Debilitating exasperations', for example.

Suddenly we had two tormentors, which turned out to be much more than twice as bad as having one.

And it was, after all, I thought, simply a conflict of styles, again. Possessors of *au pairs* v. non-possessors of *au pairs*: children v. non-children. ...

146

3

I had become aware of different styles of marriage, too.

There was old Mr Ryall-Musk, across the road, who simply couldn't endure anything that was said by Mrs Ryall-Musk. I thought of her as a kind of very anxious fire-engine. That is to say, she clearly regarded any statement made by anyone as a spark dropped carelessly into the social brushwood. She'd hastily ride forward and damp it. 'Bad news from India,' someone might say, vaguely enough. It was probably a matter of a cricket match. 'But if there's bad news from one place, there's good news from another, I've always found,' Mrs Ryall-Musk would hasten to say. 'Children are at their best at a distance,' Ben said once at a local party. 'I'm thinking of a distance of about a hundred miles.' 'Nice to be free of them now and then, but all the nicer when they're back again, the little dears,' said Mrs Ryall-Musk, hosingly. Her husband was a man of the coarsest opinions, largely in the fields of Rugby football and politics: a committed social arsonist. He'd dropped into the nervous habit of attempting to jam Mrs Ryall-Musk. As she spoke, he'd hum, actually sing, loudly kick any furniture that was around, bang on a table with spoons, forks, knives.

I'd been astonished to discover that this display went generally unnoticed. Or it might be conceded that *she* was a warm little woman, and *he* a fidget of a rather jovial kind. I thought it obvious that in marrying each other they'd embarked upon a course of mutual destruction. She might have been happy with anyone but a man of aggressive opinions. Perhaps only a nervous temporiser like her could have made him maritally miserable. It didn't seem fair that no one at the very beginning had pointed out their glaring incompatibility.

'It's not as easy as that,' Ben said. 'The trouble is that we marry children, and marriage keeps them children. ...' I didn't see why it had to do that; but saw it could be a string that made sure you were never anything much but the parcel it bound. ...

Then there were the Quints. Mr Quint, from somewhere on the elbow of East Drive, was always warning us against plays currently running in London, to which Mrs Quint had dragged him. To each he had the same objection—which he was confident would be yours, too. 'It's all dialogue!' He seemed to regard drama as a form that was methodically abused by dramatists, imposing speech upon it. His ideal— and he knew it was yours—was a theatre in which verbal exchanges were cut to a minimum: as, it sadly appeared, they were in the Quint household. I find it difficult to believe that I ever heard the Quints addressing each other. The time came when Mrs Quint silently commanded him to accompany her to a performance by Marcel Marceau. It should have realised Mr Quint's ideal, but didn't. He seemed to have concluded that the great mime had absurdly insisted on appearing whilst suffering from some complaint affecting the voice box. Mr Quint felt for the man the whole evening, and hadn't gone there to do that. 'Got by with making faces,' was his verdict.

If he vastly preferred human action to human speech, he also had a distinctly limited view of the former. There were two main achievements open to man: he could secure a bargain, or he could waste money. To an amazing extent, Mr Quint's account of things divided them into one of those phenomena or the other. To the idea that money might have been wasted he brought qualities of indignation, compassion and anger that others might bring to, say, the idea of someone being struck down by grave illness. Mr Quint busily talking in the B----- W--- Stores, his face white and drawn, was as often as not a man telling a neighbour the story of another neighbour who had handed over more money than he might have done. And Mr Quint so happy that he'd dance a little on the spot as he spoke was a man with the tale of a penny saved.

About Mrs Quint it was impossible to discover much. I remember her simply as very tall, enormously silent, and

148

plainly unhappy.

And then, in this range of marital styles, there was what went on between my friend Philip, who'd come to live on the edge of Barley Wood, and his wife Ruth.

She was beautiful, and had been superbly courted, won with interesting difficulty, and tucked under Philip's bright wing. For many of his friends, she was the archetypal wife: a wild angel half-domesticated. They had for me, together, something of the witty beauty I found in Ben and Marie. It was somehow not likely, given their cleverness and attractiveness, that they should have offered their wrists to the marital handcuffs: and so they gave marriage an unorthodox cachet. As married persons, there was something about them of the recently erected Royal Festival Hall: they constituted a new view of an old idea.

I'd met Philip when he was teaching art, and I was teaching some kind of confusion, at a London prep school. He was a struggling painter—or, I think, looking back, a struggler who painted. His gift was for trying but not succeeding. He was marvellously interesting about the picture to come, the next he would paint, the breakthrough. Bound for failure, he gave off no air of it. He made—and for some time was to go on to make—achievement out of its absence. I look back at him and think of an under-described biological cruelty: the offer by nature of a half-gift, the boisterous shadow of a talent.

But that charming marriage, I discovered soon after he'd come to live five minutes from East Drive, was under immense strains. They seemed chiefly to spring from Philip himself. 'I'm coming to feel,' he'd murmur, 'that one needs a wife for every phase.' Or: 'One ought not to expect to take any mate the whole way.' He complained that Ruth had come to look at the world through his eyes, or had rested her chin, for life, on his shoulder. 'I wish she could be herself.' It seemed to me that Ruth, a great reader, an amused observer, was very much herself. Her worst characteristic was a certain occasional indifference to surrounding, an obsession with whatever was in her head. I used to think I'd be glad not to be with her if the world came suddenly to an end. She might well, following some line of talk, fail to notice that this was happening: which would mean that, doomed to politeness, I'd have to give her my attention when I'd desperately prefer to give it to the final cataclysm as it had its interesting way with Barley Wood. I thought her, all the same, no more dependent on her mate than you'd expect a married person to be. After all, marriage in its nature was the reverse of a bid for total independence. And *that*—relying for one's composure on no one else—I couldn't imagine. I wasn't convinced that Philip could imagine it, either. What he was really after was surely a constant renewal of sexual pursuit and conquest.

He had a salty longing to sleep with as many women as he could. Or—to have regard to an objection to that phrase expressed by Ben—to fail to sleep with them. A strange evasion of a plain fact, Ben said of the other usage. What the deceived husband should surely cry was, 'Dammit, sir, I hear you've been remaining awake with my wife!'

When Philip complained that Ruth was not completely herself, I was beginning to think, he was really complaining that she was his wife. He and I had always had an amused and lively relationship—it was the best thing of its kind in my life after my relationship with Ben: but a strange tartness and hostility were now entering it. And it was our different approaches to marriage that lay behind that. Somehow Philip was drawn to a notion of marital brokenness as I was drawn to a notion of marital wholeness.

What surprised me about this was that, as with other conflicts of style, the temptation was to treat such differences as having their roots in philosophy rather than in temperament. In the end it seemed to me that Philip argued against marriage, and I argued for it, not out of any kind of rational objection or acceptance, but because he needed to be largely free, and I needed to be largely bound. He was not a brutal man, but he found it easier to think of hurting Ruth than I of hurting Kate. There were hundreds of ways of phrasing the difference between us, but all led back, not to some thought-out position, but to chemical accidents of character.

Well, I'd think, being beaten over the head by Philip with some densely documented refutal of marriage, in the end it was perhaps a matter of my being Lizzie Pye's son.

4

'To be in love with someone new is to be a bit renewed oneself,' Philip said. And for a while he embraced a theory that behind every good painting by a wedded artist lay some dazzling adultery.

It was one of the few techniques I'd not got round to using in my attempt to write my novel. This experience of, in fact, *not* writing a novel reminded me of an occasion when Freddie Dew introduced Kate and me, in a field somewhere in the West country, to toxophily.

Freddie had been a colleague of mine when I first went to teach—or rather, to discover that I didn't know how to teach—at Stonehill Street School. He was one of only two men on the staff to whom it was possible to talk about classroom problems. Many of the rest, in a school where nothing was easy, pretended that difficulty didn't exist. 'Just let them see that you intend to be firm,' the deputy head would say: and might as well have said that you should just let them see that you intended to be incredibly beautiful. Well, he himself had once laid down a line of behaviour for the school at assembly: 'I insist,' he cried, 'that you lads be sincere!' What I found the lads were, most of the time, was damnable, though I confess there was some evident sincerity in that. As I limped into the staffroom, I leaned heavily on Freddie's understanding of my miseries. 'Some of the best teachers have the worst beginnings,' he would say. Or he'd tell one of his stories, all of which amounted to hints that, some time or other, laughter might become an ingredient of my life at Stonehill Street. Well, there was the one about the class with whom he'd made a great clay map of Islington. 'If anyone's got a board ... an old noticeboard, something like that, we could build it on. ...'

he'd said. And that afternoon one was splendidly in place in the room when he got there, the clay heaped on it ready for moulding. It was a year later that he reluctantly decided he needed the space: so demolished the map and turned the board over. It bore the name of one of the local hospitals, and had clearly stood, until he'd inadvertently brought about the change in its use, at the main gate. ...

Freddie had taken an external degree in psychology, and his use of its special language in discussing children made the staffroom frown. 'No substitute for ordinary common sense,' old Slough would growl: being himself a man who kept order in the classroom by the use of scorn. I found it a curious gloss on the toughness of the Stonehill Street boys: that they shrank from the desolate withering quality of Slough's tongue. He could take the shine out of the sun; and I'd shudder to think of the simple despondency he'd caused in forty years of teaching. 'I don't suppose you know what you mean yourself when you say the fellow's—what is it?—schizophrenic,' he said on one famous occasion when Freddie was discussing one of our unhappiest boys. 'The blunt truth is that the lad's barmy.'

Too soon Freddie left to be an educational psychologist somewhere else. ... And it was on one of our visits to his new home that we were taken into that field, with a target and bows and arrows, and Kate and I were discovered to qualify, as archers, for erasure from the roll of Englishmen. Kate's disgrace was slightly more remarkable than mine, her first effort being with the bow reversed. Had it been possible to fire from this position, Freddie, standing directly behind her, would have been split in two. ('Schizophrenic!' would certainly have been his dying mutter.) I knew the back of the bow from the front, but found it impossible to release the arrow. Freddie said I went through the motions splendidly: but the arrow stayed with me. It was an awful thought that had I been at Agincourt I might have been rewarded for my services ... by the French. ...

Trying to write my first book was very much like that. And now I *was* actually making the attempt.

A letter had come from another publisher. 'You might,' it said, 'like to make a book out of your experiences, either compiled from existing material or written afresh. ...'

It was another open goal, a new ball. I prepared once more to run foolishly about in the neighbourhood of the goal-mouth. But this time there was instant money—an advance of fifty pounds—and a meeting, at which I was asked under what heading in their catalogue my book would be best placed. Would it be Fiction, or Autobiography: or would it be more exactly described as, hmm, Education. How did I see it?

Not seeing it at all, and overwhelmed by the thought of being in a publisher's catalogue—I could bear to be known for the rest of my life for nothing more than having stood on that peak—I was grateful to the publisher's literary adviser: a man who made, alternately, good novels and good gardens. He was a vehement man, and I remember the brief, cheerfully bristling speech in which he invited the publishers to consider how they might act if bloody Homer came through that bloody door with the idea for writing the bloody *Odyssey*. Would they announce this work under Fiction, Poetry, Travel, or Bloody General Adventurousness, whatever we called that category in this firm. 'Announce it in a general way. Let the poor fellow find out, as he goes, what he's writing.' He pointed at us a sharp witty face, with its whitening expletive of a beard.

So I floated on air, and then fluttered and fell, and desperately contrived to float again, a tipsy Icarus. This time I was bound over in the sum of fifty pounds to do *something*. And the contract sharpened the definition of it: a work of 80,000 words. Ah! Well, a *Guardian* piece was nine hundred words. All I had to do was to compose about eighty-nine *Guardian* articles! Laying them, of course, side by side in some significant manner. I told my diary how it would be: 'A forward-moving mosaic of sketches. ...' The trouble was that the mosaic, as it developed—and like all known mosaics, had I thought about it—was indisposed to move in any direction at all. 'This dishevelled heap of bits and pieces ...' I wrote in my horrified diary. I began to think of myself as a literary bricklayer. Brick laid on brick laid on brick. ... But then I thought I should cast about for another image. The complete similarity of one brick to the next was not what I was after. In any case, if I *was* the bricklayer, I was also the man who carried the bricks up the ladder on a hod, and the man who received them off the lorry and stacked them ... and I was the man who dug the foundations and I would be the plasterer and the tiler. .... The enormous size of the enterprise made me think of myself (another image) as an Atlas, supporting the world I was creating. I wondered that there was no change in Kate's attitude to me. Did she not know what a hero she had on her everyday hands? I walked about looking like anyone else but was engaged, surely she understood, in unthinkable triumphs of construction. ...

Well, no: not really triumphs. The images for my despair changed from day to day. 'I seem to be writing on my rims.' 'For seven weeks now the book has been beached.' I entered a period in which various ploys, devices, changes of habit, random stimuli, seemed each at last (my diary cheered crazily) to have solved my problems. Writing with a pen in the first place instead of typing: a breakthrough that lasted a couple of days. There was the effect of other people's work: 'Having read a really very funny and eminently disrespectful new novel called *Lucky Jim*, I feel suddenly better, looser and freer about my own, and less inclined to crawl miserably along trying to link together my existent sketches.' Alas, after a few days of imitating Kingsley Amis's loping stride, I was to be found by the roadside, nursing a more awful cramp than before. I thought for a while that it was better to write at weekends than on weekdays: on Mondays, Wednesdays and Fridays rather than Tuesdays, Thursdays and Saturdays. I wrote a prologue, which was to make the purpose, movement and connectedness of my pieces blindingly apparent. Alas, when that light fused, it became *very* dark.

In the middle of it all, I had the oddest relief. I seemed on suddenly good terms with the boys who were largely my subjects. I had a series of greatly enjoyable lessons in which they contracted to write stories ... about three hundred words long. One boy actually said, at the end of a lesson: 'I enjoyed writing that, sir.' I thought wildly of putting them, as a consortium, to the job of writing my book. I did not tell Ben about this. I could imagine his response. 'Well, I think you couldn't do better. They've not been rotted through by literature, you know. They'd probably go straight to what, as someone who reads far too much, you're trying to reach by crooked means.' And so on. My dear—but in this case, very carefully not to be consulted—friend.

Kate and I had a stupendous quarrel—I left her for ever and was a couple of miles away before the discomfort of taking to the roads in my slippers began to register—and then made it up in a fashion disgracefully majestic ('like love between elephants,' says my gasping diary): and that seemed to make me light-heartedly able to write, full of what felt very much like new ideas. Yet another hint to struggling novelists: Row with your wife, and beautifully, pachydermatously, make it up.

Two days later I was groaning: 'Not a touch of energising fiction.' I was becoming aware of the current limits of my resources of language. Writing so much, I was gloomily sensitive to twists of sentence and phrase that repeated themselves—as I felt, again and again and again. ...

And I saw, fearfully late, that in writing a book that was transparently about the school in which I was teaching, I was doing something that might be described as travestying my own nest. Well, I'd have to leave Stonehill Street! perhaps London! perhaps teaching! I'd be ruined ... and massively sued!

Libel! My goodness, yes! Here I was, struggling to cope with thickets of repetitiveness, dangerous torrents of inconsecutiveness, landslides of sheer inadequacy of language, and I turned round, sweating and bleeding, and there, in front of me, or all round me perhaps, were the volcanoes of potential libel. ...

5

The garden was still to me the most astonishing thing I'd ever part-possessed. After summer rain, the damp leafy extravagance of it! I'd stand and be aware of the whole garden audibly shaking water off itself! There were the looseboxes we'd painted white and green—white doors, green hinges, green bolts. There was the greengage that had fruited once and would never fruit again, and had yielded small globes of a sweetness without rival. We knew not only what was to be seen, anarchies of orange-blossom, bright red puffs of japonica, strict cones of lilac, but also what was hidden, old nests, amazing fungus, plants existing in the folds of other plants.

Somewhere in a corner by the house a viburnum spread its big skirt, as if some vegetable dowager were bedding there, that green rump starred with creamy flowers that grew out of tiny pleated boxes, scarlet-washed. I'd observed over several summers how these flowers emerged, at first lime-green and shaped like the boxes they came from, and then turned into these spread stars, which in their turn grew whiskers, knobbed with purple seeds. In autumn the plant dropped a charming mess of scarlet and cream. And I'd think of all the years it had taken to grow to its present height, twelve feet and more: and how during that time there'd been so much aberrant human foliage, eccentric human flower, so disheveled and many-formed and strange, while the viburnum had grown, year after year, these repetitious leaves, these flowers of a single unvarying design, and had spread to fill the corner by the house. What I was struck by was the different ways that time could be spent, by different forms of life: how complex and confusing the human variety—well, all those Bens and Kates and Maries and Toms—while, in all that time, the viburnum had followed a single intention: expansive, but single. It had set out only to be a viburnum × burkwoodii: while we . . . what a wilderness of aims we had!

To Ben and me, that acre of garden was a kingdom. At fruit-picking time, we'd swarm into the trees and stay there long after the job was done. It was like, in our mid-thirties, having boyhood again, braced against branches in a rustling concealment, talking of poets.

Or discussing the attempts each made to wring prizes from the other in weekend competitions. We were now setting these, and were determined not to reward each other. It meant the submission of multiple entries typed on unfamiliar machines and sent from misleading addresses. On one occasion I kept Ben at bay only, as it turned out, by quoting three Bens as runners-up. In the end, it was my luck to break through his defences. He'd asked in the *Spectator* for some news item about Britain distributed by the Soviet agency Tass that only a Briton would realise was false. At the last moment, on a postcard, I'd submitted a piece of sports news: 'There was play today in the Test Match at Old Trafford'. Ben, to his subsequent chagrin, awarded me ten shillings. ...

His novel about life in Barley Wood had been set aside in favour of a book, urgently sought by a publisher whose importance made us laugh nervously among the leaves of the apple-trees, about ways in which raw human beings were converted into civil servants. This had followed from a prize essay Ben had written—two thousand words about the condition of being a bureaucrat that made me feel that my brain, the precise grey matter, was guffawing. Ben, I thought, could make the intellect itself bend double and slap its dignified knees. The sound of his typewriter, heard of an evening above our heads, had become relentlessly continuous. For my part, I'd been translated into a broadcaster. BBC Schools had written—it was a single producer, but I preferred to imagine an entire institution—to ask if I had ever thought of writing scripts suitable for broadcasting. It seemed, at this point in our progress, very much the sort of inquiry people wished to address to Ben and me. It was as if we'd had letters from famous beauties asking if we'd ever thought of making love to them. I replied that I'd not altogether avoided such thoughts, and the result was an audition at Broadcasting House. The producer invited me to read a piece I'd written for the *Manchester Guardian*: I did so, and he offered the opinion that I took to the microphone like a duck to water. Totally amazed, I wrote a twenty-minute script about books: and found myself recording it. Becoming a broadcaster was then a greater matter of astonishment than it is now. At a parent-teacher's meeting the headmaster was moved to refer to me as 'our Mr Blishen.' I had never expected to be laid claim to in this fashion. 'May I tell them?' he went on. 'He is *broadcasting* next week.' There was applause—or the cheerful ambiguous hooting that stood for it at Stonehill Street. At the hour of the actual broadcast, all normal school activity ceased. To my horror, a special timetable bunched the largely baffled boys round loud-speakers. Their ears had not been prepared for the sounds I made, in the company of actors who read extracts from the books I discussed. My friend Charles Radkin listened in the school hall with large parts of the third and fourth years, and reported that they'd not precisely been spellbound by it. 'All those careful refined voices, you see,' he said. 'I hope you won't mind if I say ... too polite for words.' The only real politeness I received uneasily in return was from a boy who asked how I'd managed to speak in so many different voices. There were for some days untraceable cries of 'Edward', and a moment of sternness on my part in a classroom was rebuked by the boy I was addressing: 'You mustn't think just because you've broadcast. ...'

On the whole, I felt this splendid recruitment had simply laid me open to charges of over-refinement and gentility extremely difficult to refute. ...

But on fine Sundays the garden could be a scene of anguish.

The ingredients of disaster, in themselves perfectly agreeable, were wives and husbands: children and the friends of children: *au pairs*: neighbours ... and a dog or two.

Seating was a problem. Our count of deckchairs was a fluctuating one. We had started out with secondhandness in a field where it is dangerous. Deckchairs bleached and dried by dozens of other people's summers would, without warning, collapse into rags and splinters. It might—too often it did—happen to Marie, who had a strong belief that the world was organised to her disadvantage. The puppetmaster who'd long been responsible for spoiling things for her would mutter: 'That's Marie feeling happy, and about to sit on that deckchair,' and the chair would snap into ruins. At once the sun would vanish. 'It just isn't fair!' Marie would cry. It would then occur to someone that someone else had fallen behind in the provision of replacements. Whose turn had it been to make up for the last disaster of this kind? A question to which there were many possible answers, all productive of misery and anger. It might be plainly known who should have bought a new deckchair: and for him the afternoon would

158

grow wintry with guilt. There might be a pointing of fingers at a culprit confident of his innocence, so that for him the afternoon was made hideous by his sensations of injustice. There might be no certainty whatever, and we would all be tormented by mixed suspicion and guilt.

And then our children, who would have been passing through a period of unusual primness, would degenerate together. Fighting furiously, making claims and counter-claims of unintelligible intricacy, full of ugly wishes, madly insolent, using vocal registers we'd never heard them use before, they'd come tumbling on to the lawn: and one's feeling that *their* children were behaving horribly was capped by the feeling that one's own children were behaving worse. One grew irritable with scorn for theirs, so uncontrolled, and contempt for one's own, so intent on giving a false impression of an absence of control. Sorting all this out whilst discussing acidly general issues of child-rearing, we would become aware that the lawn was now the setting for a conference of local *au pairs*. That's to say, these beautiful creatures were suddenly everywhere, their slendernesses insolent in bikinis, and their use of French, Italian, German and other languages a plain camouflage for satirical comment on the conduct of the inmates of 1 East Drive. The languor of *au pairs* would remind some of the hard labour to which they were condemned, and others of the languor of friends possessed of *au pairs*.

It was always the moment for the arrival of dogs, loosely attended by children of a half-familiar kind. The lawn would now be jammed from end to end, and the peace we'd all been seeking would be heavily overlaid with young screams, great barkings, the soft murmur of continental languages, the sound of slaps, amounting to a general thunder as of Utopia deferred. ...

6

There were many firsts: including Tom's first days at school. I remember the amazed anxiety with which we awaited his account of his very first day—well, of course, he was not the only schoolboy there had ever been, but Kate and I had never dressed our flesh and blood in a schoolcap before—and the meagre monosyllables with which he replied to our questions. If the day had been one long fascinating scandal he would still have given his entire evening attention to some urgent amalgamation of leisure activities, capped by train-spotting. It emerged in asides that he adored the school, the teachers, the routine, and could not express his delight in the ritual of putting your hand up when you wanted to leave the room. Who could have a harsh word to say about education, given this delightful business of raising the hand! Yes, his teacher, Miss Prowse, was plump. This again was to be taken as the highest possible kind of praise. An HMI could not have said more: 'Miss Prowse is plump.' On the second morning he wept bitterly on waking, after desperate attempts to present himself as one stricken with the incapacity to wake at all. On the second evening, after more intense play than on the evening before, he launched into an attack on the process of schooling that might have lacked philosophical fibre, but still left pedagogy with a case to answer. And within a week he'd become the most accustomed schoolboy in the world, though he bore no resemblance at all to the Tom we had known. It had been a mistake to allow him this glimpse of a larger world. He treated us like domestic pygmies. What virtue was there in creatures who knew nothing of life in the playground at Botany Bay?

One unlooked-for effect was that he was briefly bowled over

by ... one can hardly say religion ... the unfamiliar fervours of Religious Instruction. He became for a while hideously holy: speaking of Jesus as some new acquaintance who made family and friends seem very small fry. Kate reported that he'd suddenly, in the High Street, clapped hands together and prayed for us all. The prayer had apparently not been offered in any sanguine spirit. Tom's teacher, Miss Prowse, Tom himself and half a dozen classmates had a reasonable assurance of God's good opinion. For Kate and me there was minimal hope, but no hope at all for anyone else about in Barton High Street on the day in question. A little later we overheard Tom trying to catch Dan in his pious net. 'Nice Dot,' he was, after lights out, suggesting as a rubric for Dan to echo. 'Nice Minnie.' Two pleasant aunts cunningly named, he added; 'Nice God and nice Jesus.' Enthusiastically Dan echoed him, but threw away his chances of immortality. 'Nice God,' he chuckled, 'and nice Gee-gee!'

Ben's daughter Sally responded in her own way to the new stimulus. With a gesture embracing Barton High Street, clearly for our children a branch of the road to Damascus, she informed Ben: 'God made all this.' 'He must have been very busy,' said Ben. 'Oh no,' said Sally. 'It's easy. Abradacabra— Barton-on-the-Hill! Abradacabra—Barley Wood!' 'What about High Holborn?' muttered Ben from his position on the ropes: having his own obsession, at that moment, with the failure of a much worked-over parody in the *New Statesman*'s weekend competition.

Another effect of school was that we now had three writers in the house, and that Tom, the new recruit, reinforced literary postures with teacherly ones. Spotting his approach with a thick notebook, I'd look round for an escape route.

He was a pasticheur of promise, and his stories were made out of narrative clichés laid lovingly end to end. Given that I hadn't eluded him—and usually I hadn't—he'd say: 'I've written a story. It's called "The Adventure of the Boastful Hedgehog." Shall I read it?' There was no despicable pretence of waiting for an answer, as with adult writers in similar circumstances. He'd begin at once. It would be an enormously long amalgamation of themes and incidents from all the animal tales he'd ever read. Owing to one of his few inefficiencies of style, it was sometimes difficult to know who was speaking. '"It's a lovely day," he said,' Tom might read. '"Yes, it is," he said. "Are you coming out?" she asked. "Of course I am," he said.' Here Tom would pause and eye me severely. From school he'd already taken a strong sense of the need to couple literature with interrogation. No substantial amount of reading should ever occur without visits to the dungeons and an application of hot pincers. 'Why did he say that?' 'Why did who say what?' He'd look at me aghast. 'You're not following!' Displaying another side of his gift as a pasticheur, he'd take on the personality of a small round teacher, a kind of motherly wasp, who relieved Miss Prowse now and then, and whose name was either Miss Skipton or Miss Skippingrope: one of these was a nickname, and Tom used them both with such versatility of tone that I was at times genuinely uncertain which was which. 'You've not been listening,' he'd snap. 'Tell me what I've been reading to you.'

Kate said it served me right. I was always approaching *her* with some equivalent of a thick notebook, and confessing that I'd been ... writing, as if it had been some rather disgusting activity quite out of character. Might she at some time, but I really meant *now*, be in a position to ...? Here I'd be vague, as if my not absolutely defining my requirement would make it easier to accede to. In the nature of things, Kate was rarely in such a position. As often as not she'd make herself available with a mad-eyed resignation that was completely at odds with my dream of an eager, lovingly critical audience.

Settling wearily once to listen, her flour-covered hands an accusation, she asked: 'Do you want me to say what I think of it, or do you want me to say it's good?' A question to which the only answer was a ridiculous one. What I wanted, of course, was that she should praise my work to the skies in the context of the most rigorous and even pitiless criticism.

It was what childhood was: a traffic jam of first occasions, a nightmare of initiation. Well, money, for example.

Kate spent part of one day in 1954 running in and out and round and round the drive after a wailing Dan. Having acquired two halfpennies, a penny, two farthings and a sixpence, he'd decided to indulge himself massively in Miss Fluster's shop. He'd concluded after long thought that the coin he'd miss least was the farthing: so he'd armed himself with one of these and prepared to set out. Kate intervened and proposed he use the penny and the two halfpennies instead. Dan had an instant fit. He had resolved to splash out, all right, but he was not going beyond the surrender of a single 'little one.' Kate's attempts to explain that the currency was not based on charming notions of coins as 'little ones' and 'big ones' were unsuccessful. And so the chase began. 'I don't want to, I don't want to!' Dan screamed. It was open to any passer-by to infer that his allusion was to some threat to put him down. Kate had summoned up mammoth powers of diplomacy in persuading him at last (and to launch on the delicate process whilst on the run wasn't easy) to accept five big ones and two smaller ones for the despised (because very small) sixpence. Dan immediately brimmed over with pleasure: but returned the two halfpennies with grateful scorn. Such a glut of big ones made small ones more than usually despicable.

And there was Tom's first visit to the theatre. I'd always remembered my own—at perhaps the same age. About 1924: a pantomime. I see now a fishing rod in gleeful hands—I see the hook catch in a red wig—I see the wig (which I thought to be the man's true hair) rise and separate itself from his head. I hear my own appalled screams. I imagine the chagrin of my parents, who cannot have enjoyed finding money for that visit and then having to leave early with a child who'd encountered the stuff of lifelong nightmares. Even now I don't care for the detachability of wigs.

Tom's first experience was one that seemed safe enough: *Toad of Toad Hall*. However, given the difficulty the young have at the best of times in distinguishing between reality and make-believe, it was impossible to be sure. Tom was aware of the theatre as a mysterious promise which was also a frightful demand: you had to experience it—it must be endured. They were all awfully bright about it. But what was *it*? The very excitement with which playgoing was announced filled a newcomer with alarm, on the grounds that such fanfares had often before proved themselves preludes to horrors officially

163

endorsed.

The Silence Muselum, for example: as Tom ominously took it to be. I'd dreamed from soon after his birth of taking him there, to press knobs and set the Industrial Revolution dancing in miniature—tiny wheels revolving, minute pistons throbbing. And so we had set off from Barley Wood one morning, three or four years too soon. Before the train left the station, Tom had been sarcastic about the outrageous length of the journey. Between one stop and the next on this relatively short suburban trip there was a Gobi Desert, and between that and the next again a couple of Pacific Oceans. By the time we arrived in Kensington, Tom had aged beyond recognition. But he allowed himself to be led on ancient legs into the main hall of the Museum, the home of the best of those responsive models in their glass cases: and there he announced, with his usual damnable clarity: 'I think I feel sick!' There was about the announcement the finest possible shade of artful uncertainty, coupled with the subtlest insinuation that only a fairly bestial parent would have taken a very small child ten miles in order to nauseate him. ...

In the theatre Tom said, squarely: 'I wish the play would begin and we could get rid of it.'

Again I remembered *that* feeling. There'd been that respectable old man who'd waited for us after school, a retired official, blamelessly related to one of the town's best families—yet somehow blameful, old Trott, so kindly, so gentle, in his lodgings a cupboard full of boys' comics; and given to taking a little mob of us, a mob of angels (all blonde or blonde-ish), to the Palladium; cinemas otherwise outside our range; grand teashops; and first-class football and cricket matches. I was puzzledly aware of old Trott being probed by parents, investigative steps being taken; but he clearly passed all the tests (they didn't know about the Bombay duck he would sometimes eat in our presence, which vaguely I understood to be at the bottom of his mild uncertainty of reputation), and he did nothing harmful to any of us; unless you hold that he harmed me by taking me to great football matches. I could never reconcile myself to the strain of standing for hours in cold weather and trying to keep my mind on the game, which was like fixing my attention on the activities of twenty-two balls of mercury rolling about some surface, even given that the balls of mercury wore football shirts. How pleased I was to be there, and how I hated it, and longed for the final whistle so that I could ... get rid of it. Tom's phrase was well chosen.

And then ... the play dismissed all his fears; he was enraptured: and at the end he declared a surrender as excessive as his reluctance has been: '*I wish we could stay here for ever and never go home!*'

7

No doubt about it—it was a damnably difficult business, being a child! Well, there'd been that earlier first for Tom: a first visit to an art gallery.

We'd not meant to take him: but there were no baby-sitters ... or one with room only for Dan, an understandable limitation ... so there was nothing for it but to set out to the Tate in Tom's company. He was enchanted by the approach along the river: but his mood changed when we entered what must have seemed to him the mysterious prison of the gallery. He began at once to negotiate for a more sensible climax to the journey. We understood, did we not, that what he liked best at the moment was collecting train numbers. Indeed, this was a study to which he would fail to measure up if he did nothing ever but stand with his notebook at Barley Wood Station. So why didn't we go at once to where there were trains? We tried to make the difficult case for remaining in the gallery based on a preference for staring at pictures. He resorted to loud and, he must have known, embarrassing ironies. So he collapsed on a bench in the centre of one of the rooms, adopting his carefully studied pose of the Small Child Insensitively Treated by his Parents. (Dan was in due course to be even better at this, inventing at least one striking advance: the pose of the

165

Small Child whose Father has Just this Moment, and most Cruelly, Broken his Arm. ... Even on this he improved, adding gestures that amounted to saying '... a Brutality totally Unsurprising to the Small Child in Question, who has long since Deduced that the Police are in His Father's Pocket'). Tom then began to comment on the pictures: pointing to them one by one and crying: 'I *hate* that!' 'I hate *that*!' He gave his noisy approval only to a painting of a lionhunter by Monet (and that only for the dead lion's sake) and, without explanation, one of a tree by Chaim Soutine. His sense of satire sharpened, I guess, partly by the amusement of some of the gallery-goers around him, partly by the heady certainty that he had his parents against the ropes, he finally cried: '*I'm not old enough for this!*'

It was gallery-going under a handicap—perhaps a little like making love whilst beating off a charging rhinoceros. Except, of course, that our small rhinoceros was a droll and charming one, and that it would have been possible to be far less interestingly tormented.

When we went home by way of back streets, he took against the sudden looming appearance of Westminster Abbey. 'I don't like big churches,' was his comment on this great building. 'They make me look small.'

I often thought of that remark of Tom's. Of course, a child *so* small had not yet plumped for a clean separation between the inward and outward views of himself. It must be an odd and difficult feature of childhood—your consciousness so often slopping over, like a jug that was being asked to contain too much. Well, you had not yet made an efficient inward container of it. What should be inside was always making its appearance on the outside. So, where someone older might say that a large building, ecclesiastical or otherwise, made him *feel* small, Tom (spilling over) said it made him *look* small. He hung out his feelings on the outward walls.

But great amounts of outsideness would get inside, too. He had developed over the years a small litany to preserve himself against the tendency for external objects to climb into him and conduct campaigns of terror there. 'Don't hurt you, Father Christmas,' it began. That generous saint came down the chimney, and to Tom this unorthodox entrance, by what amounted to stealth, however benign, down those terrifying black narrows (a plump benefactor in serious danger of being trapped there and suffocated), was a torment. It might not have been so, perhaps, had we not, one summer, had a bird caught in a chimney. There were desperate flutterings one morning, a downward spiral of them as the bird, a thrush, fought its way to the hearth, where it appeared as a sooty panic of wings. ... The chimneys at 1 East Drive were astonishments to us all. More than anything else they seemed to speak of those domestic giants, the Edwardians, whom we'd so trivially replaced. My own attempts at making fires had often collapsed into beads of exhausted redness, and then into miserable feathery black ruin. We were, as far as chimneys were concerned, living far beyond our means.

'Don't hurt you, spiders,' Tom's litany went on: 'Don't hurt you, Barton Fair.' That famous annual event, in fields a quarter of a mile from where Kate's parents lived, making the valley at the foot of Barton Hill cheerfully hellish with light, flooding it with noise—a mixture of many contradictory kinds of music and the huge shuffling mutter that was the composite sound of the crowd ... from my own childhood I knew how stunning it could be: deeply exciting, deeply disturbing. The familiar world, tested for safety, suddenly went berserk.

'Train won't come in garden!' The final item in Tom's litany was, I suppose, aimed at keeping at bay any tendency for the railway to behave as Barton-on-the-Hill behaved during the week of the Fair. It was a prayer against untoward conduct, in a world spectacularly difficult to trust.

I crouched down one evening in noisy circumstances to hear what Tom was saying to me, and suddenly saw how far away from each other we ordinarily were. I'd taken it we had the normal propinquity as between two companions—but it wasn't so! We were as distant from one another as if we'd been standing on opposite banks of a river. Even his face looked different, down there!

I puffed nervously at my pipe. Tom sniffed nervously at any little ball of wool he could make by raiding a blanket, a garment. He held it in a particular way between his fingers, and his eyes, as he brought this odd narcotic to his nose, became very distant. Reasonably robust, both of us, but much in need of puffing, sniffing forms of support.

Though it had to be said that I'd been around for some time, and had worked out at least an elementary map of probabilities, likelihoods. I thought what a hero, or heroine, a small child was, exhibiting usually some degree of poise in a world that was so ferociously unfamiliar: that made great claims to reasonableness and put on great exhibitions of irrationality ... and that was on a scale so different from the child's that only Captain Gulliver in Brobdingnag had it worse.

8

Books were other refractory children being produced. Ben was having trouble with his. Largely it was a matter of the publishers wanting endless revisions, most tending to the removal of colour and story. Ben was suffering from a massacre of his anecdotes and images. Well, he'd written an account of training in the Civil Service which at all points was struggling to be a novel, of a comically serious kind. There were long arguments about a story he told of an old, archetypal clerical officer, alongside whom he'd worked as a new entrant. This man had been, in everything, ploddingly punctilious: greatly efficient, greatly lacking in imagination. He was admirable for his professional rigour and abominable for his professional conservatism. Ben remembered how this ageing man would fall asleep over his lunch-time sandwiches, and Ben and other youngsters would creep up and, very gently, apply the office date-stamp to every quarter of that nodding bald head. I thought this passage might have been written by Gogol. What a feeling for the tragi-comedies of official life the Russians had always had! The droll sorrows of the humdrum! Ben wrote here as if belonging to that tradition. The publishers were uneasy: could not the point about the old clerk as a symbol of fossilised officialdom who nevertheless represented important qualities of conscience and care, be made without ... oh, stories!

I remembered a boy who'd said he was grateful I asked so often for the writing of stories—'We always used to have to write about ideas, sir. Our opinions about this and that. Well, that's all right. But don't you think sometimes you only have ideas because you know about ... something that happened to somebody?'

Ben said: 'I feel as if the book had begun as a beard and I'd been obliged step by step to trim it down to a hairline moustache.'

The question of Ben's value, not simply as a writer, but as a person, had been raised in a doubtful manner by Miss Furlong when Kate and I went to lunch with her.

Ben had long since deserted her class for one in painting, where he caused extreme rage by producing cryptic spontaneities that owed nothing to the instruction he was receiving: or—the general impression seemed to be—to any instruction received by any artist at any time in the entire history of painting. My own stint under Miss Furlong's care had come to an end a year or so before: I missed the strange happiness of being required to read according to a scheme and to write about what I'd read. All my life I'd nervously shuffled and reshuffled the cards of literature, and in Miss Furlong's Thursday-evening company I'd had to play a literary game or two right through, methodically. Lately we'd been discussing, by post, a common interest in Aldous Huxley: who, during my adolescence, had been virtually a schoolfellow of mine: that is to say, I'd thought of him as as rebellious crony aged, more or less, eighteen.

'Bring,' said Miss Furlong when she issued her invitation, 'your wife.' Then, in the manner of someone who has just invented a totally imaginary creature, 'She *is* interested in Aldous Huxley, I imagine?' 'Well, indeed,' I fenced. Kate, in the context of the extravagances we exchanged during our wooing, had held that I closely resembled the novelist in appearance. Making this assertion had certainly been a point in her favour. 'She *must* be,' said Miss Furlong, unconvinced. Kate threatened to pretend that she thought we were discussing, not the novelist, but the zoologist. 'I go along with him when it comes to monkeys,' she'd say. I said this remark would do equally well for Aldous. Very well, said Kate: she'd fall back on asking: 'How can I stop my husband reading so much, Miss Furlong?'

It was a splendid lunch, as to food, on an immensely hot day at the top of a tall house, under a roof that had a special relationship with the sun, so that Kate and I rapidly became visiting beetroots. Time ceased, or went unkindly into recess, while Miss Furlong attacked us with the story of her life, laced with her opinions. Born out of her natural time, she had inevitably figured in many private tragedies, most of them occurring far from these banal shores. Well, in Italy, Greece, and what vaguely might have been India, but Miss Furlong didn't seem to be quite sure. The Far East, say. Very late in the afternoon, when we knew our babysitter would be in a state of rebellion—and still we had to get home—she butted at us with her whirling idealisms. Surely we agreed that there was no sense in the current attempts to educate the ineducable? And was it possible that I could deny a pervading consciousness in the universe? 'I don't know what you think, Mrs Blishen?' Kate half-framed a perspiring reply, but Miss Furlong had dashed on to a consideration of Ben's character. 'So truculent and, one suspects, a *bit* of a Philistine?' She did not wait for an observation on this judgement, and I gave my boiling attention to Miss Furlong's use of the word 'bit'. Well, dammit, Ben was either a Philistine or he was not. Could she see him being a *bit* of anything? 'Woefully lower-middle-class,' she seemed to be saying; but whether this was a reference to Ben, or to Kate and me, Miss Furlong's exhausted guests were not able to decide.

Set free, we walked towards the tube station. It was a Bank Holiday, and among the people sunnily sprawling on the grass in a public park we were passing through, a woman was breast-feeding her baby.

'While Demos behaves like that,' declared Miss Furlong stoutly, 'I can never be reconciled to it.' It had a quality of challenge; for a wild moment, one thought the rebuke might have its effect on the holidaymakers lying with such happy untidiness in the sun. There would be at least a widespread tucking in of breasts; and Miss Furlong might then have to reconsider her position. There might be some extraordinary tableau: Miss Furlong Reconciled to Demos!

She was murmuring something about the culpability of William Godwin. 'This has been extensively discussed with Mr Fletcher,' I said, meaning I was on Ben's side. 'Yes, and to no effect,' she exclaimed: meaning that she could imagine me being on no side but hers. 'Mr Fletcher seems the complete Philistine!' I was relieved that she was now granting him barbaric wholeness. 'An odd man. Is there some problem in the background?' I wondered what she had in mind. An unsatisfactory wife? Ben's judgements entirely the grotesque fruit of domestic unease? 'Distinct limitations of sensibility,' she cried, cheerfully. 'I suppose you are old friends.' Only enormous antiquity of friendship, I understood, could excuse the association. 'We limbered up together,' I said. 'Or, in fact, didn't, usually.' 'Astonishing,' said Miss Furlong, blankly. 'Well, it is useless attempting to discuss literature if one hasn't an ounce of poetry in one's make-up. Mr Fletcher is almost devoid of anima.' 'His psyche is hard to seek,' I volunteered wildly. To my surprise Miss Furlong agreed, with warmth. 'No better way of expressing it,' she said. 'Don't you think so, Mrs Blishen?' Kate, startled in the middle of thoughts of the children, uttered a shriek. 'We are all of one mind,' said Miss Furlong, happily.

9

I was in even worse trouble with my book than Ben with his. I had been shaken lately, aware of the shambles of it, to receive a letter from the publisher's sales manager: had I a title in mind—one to replace his own tentative suggestion: *Shining Morning Face*?

From the notion of drawing a title from *that* speech, I shrank. Indeed, from robbing Shakespeare at all: he had been so prodigiously ransacked. I'd always had in mind a phrase from Traherne, who the looters had on the whole left alone. Not taken from my favourite sentence of his, which I'd think of sometimes when I saw Tom and Dan and the other Barley Wood children offending the last representatives of the old dapper district by playing football or some unnameable game outside the station. 'Boys and girls tumbling in the street, and playing, were moving jewels.' Well, it was easy enough to see them as moving grubbinesses: little causes of annoyance, hooligans in the making ... or made. But look again and ... such brightness! such impatient, *tumbling* energy! We had these fresh stars streaking across a local sky that had seen a multitude of them flash and fade—among them the offended elders who threatened to ... oh, write to the Council! What in his vision of children was seen by the child for whom Traherne spoke was the state of Heaven in the state of Earth! And I'd seen it sometimes at Stonehill Street, when at assembly the head complained and his deputy lamented, and on the fidgeting uncouthness of our children fell the rays of the morning sun that the old building could never quite exclude. And there they were, momentary life, and I'd been struck by the marvel of it, this accident of being alive taking these forms: Bickers and Balding and Dilley and Moffat and snuffling sniffing Nye and mean-minded Wicks and, in our policemen's positions along the walls, my colleagues and me.

The phrase of Traherne's I had in mind was 'Roaring and swearing boys ...' Of course, it was the other side of his vision of 'young men' as 'glittering and sparkling angels.' I'd sometimes think that with that double view of reality Traherne must himself have taught at Stonehill Street. The only criticism I had of his phrase was that it might have been much extended. 'Roaring and swearing and groaning and shrieking and farting and screaming and tittering and tormenting boys ...' But *Roaring Boys* might be as much as they could find room for on the spine?

And, wrote the sales manager, perhaps I would provide a blurb for the next catalogue. By this request I was astonished. I had always imagined that blurbs were written by persons of extreme impartiality, trained over a large number of years in some very exacting religious institution. I was to write my own blurb? I set about it with passionate modesty, but then thought that work of one's own could perhaps be described attractively without hopeless untruth ... Anyway, *wrote* it.

I was now dashing off little pieces, sometimes basing them on an experience or feeling of that day, sometimes choosing them from a vague list I kept making and unmaking. In my diary I was furiously reviewing the book before it was finished. 'Horrifying in its shapelessness ...' 'Shockingly badly written ...' 'Something the appearance of which will fill me with abysmal shame. ...' 'Stretched-out tenuities.' 'Droning scraps.' 'Not a book at all, but a disaster ...' 'Not shaped, not made, not created ... And DULL!' With such a commentator so close at hand, who needed reviewers?

But a week later the same venomous critic was of another mind altogether. 'Excellent,' he found himself writing. 'Full of meat ... with a real, innate continuity.'

Why, I'd wonder, had we ever smiled at Freddie Dew's readiness to see so many human situations in terms of schizophrenia?

But I was oddly horrified to have a Christmas card from the publishers. My advice, if asked for, would have been for them to refrain from gestures even less friendly than this.

One of my problems lay in the spectacular sounds of typing that came from Ben's flat above. They were particularly clamorous on the evening of the day our court case came to a painful and thrilling end.

It had been a very long day and I had thought that perhaps the Day of Judgement would be like this, so economically being Hell at the same time: the interminably slow attempt to piece together some relatively simple series of events so as to adjudicate fairly upon it. But things grew brighter when the builder was taken by the electrician's counsel through a cunning sequence of questions that, as time went on, revealed themselves as falling into two parallel sets. These converged, an intellectually splendid pincer movement, towards a final question and answer, which left the builder with no alternative but to agree that, in the light of his own responses, an estimate which all had been happy to leave loose and elastic was precisely the same thing as a firm and final estimate. We seemed to be safe: but the judge had a game of his own to play. For three quarters of an hour he summed up most plausibly for the builder. He had to use half-bricks and splinters to do so, and the edifice was always, we realised afterwards, without foundations or damp course: but it seemed solid enough to the frightened listeners from 1 East Drive, and all three women found it necessary to retire, sick. The judge then summed up for another three quarters of an hour for the electrician and, incidentally, for us—unanswerably, we would have said, except that the word seemed to have applied equally well to the opposite case. In the end he let us off the hook with a single sentence: and we crept away to join our stricken women.

Ben recovered swiftly and celebrated by typing overhead with special fury. And it was the following morning that our ceilings began to fall. The first came down in our bedroom.

Dan being in the habit of waking early and putting on an instant hour of vaudeville, himself a whole cast of ventriloquists, bird and animal imitators, stand-up—and also lie-down—comics, with a striptease artist of formidable coarseness thrown in, we'd moved him into our room: there having been bitter complaints from his audience, Tom. Even Tom didn't want the day to start that early. Taking Dan into our bed at the first sound of tuning up from the orchestra pit had the unlikely effect of causing this versatile entertainer to doze again. I guess it was the warmth of Kate's body, which I too associated with a tremendously pleasurable kind of semi-consciousness.

The morning the ceiling fell we hadn't reached that point. The fall occurred precisely in the space between bed and cot. The ceilings were twelve feet high, the plaster two inches thick. Kate had a badly bruised thigh. If Dan had been struck he might not have survived.

Being attacked by ceilings was, for Kate, the last straw in a series of assaults by bills, shortage of sleep, my many inadequacies, her energetic children, and the constant proximity of dreadful accident; and the account of her given by Ben in the novel he was writing alongside his book on the Civil Service. It added to her feeling that, in having this flat, we'd been conned into inhabiting a monster of brick and plaster: it twitched clumsily all round us, every twitch a wall splitting, a door jamming—and now a ceiling down. She became shrill and desperate, and spoke of 'this bloody house.' To Ben it was as it might have been to Adam if Eve had talked of 'this bloody Paradise.' It seemed to him that the danger to Dan was probably exaggerated by us both—but certainly by Kate. Well, he had this view of her that he'd expressed, not particularly obliquely, in his novel. This was plainly based on life at 1 East Drive, and was intricately libellous in respect of all its residents—Ben included. Kate was represented as a woman always trailing children behind her. They included a small boy, clearly intended to be Tom, who spoke in 'sugary tones.'

The fact is that, to Ben, a woman who took children seriously, and almost any child, were natural objects of satire. Indeed, they satirised themselves. He merely came along and recorded the process.

In expressing despair at this moment, Kate seemed to Ben to be following the line of her character: profoundly domestic, her happiness ridiculously dependent on ceilings staying where they were and the lives of her children remaining unendangered. To her agitation he responded coolly; and that made matters worse.

Behind the growing disagreement between them lay, much of the time, a simple difference of opinion about children. In Ben they caused impatience, together with a horror that some day he might, if only for a moment, find himself speaking of them with the cloying indulgence and nauseous fondness of . . . well, the Pringles round the corner. *They* had a flow of rapturous anecdotes about their young, and often told them when the children were present. Grimly hostile to such squashiness, Ben opposed himself also to ordinary decent softness.

And Kate, alongside the practical tired fury children caused in her, had a deep sympathy for the condition of childhood.

175

She enjoyed the idea, and much of the reality, of children. These feelings made her positively in favour, for example, of Christmas: the year's supreme exhaustion, a general huge anxiety as to presents, decorations, meals ... but still a children's festival. She thought tenderly of Christmas Eve excitements, having the keenest recollection of the thrills she'd felt herself as a child. I was less convinced: worried about the over-excitements, greeds, ugly frustrations that emerged in Tom and Dan alongside the real and acceptable satisfactions of the season. At times it seemed that we provided children with a stimulus beyond all bearing, and then became angry when they ... couldn't bear it. And the stuffy sweetness of it made me feel I was buried up to the neck in Christmas pudding: I'd long for the sour, the dry and the sceptical. But much of the time, Kate's delight was my delight. She had an innocence that matched the innocent idea at the heart of Christmas. I'd wish it could really be the season she imagined. ...

Ben, in our kitchen in late December with one of the communal bills that helped to make the ideal Christmas difficult of attainment, lectured Kate on the season's horrors. Well, yes, he said, in the Middle Ages it had been a patch of brightness in a dull year; but now that the whole year had an abominable brilliance about it, Christmas ought to be the most sober and quietest of occasions. 'Without,' Ben added, knowing what he was adding, 'the children.'

Kate was furious. If there were to be no children, you might as well get rid of Christmas altogether!

'That's a very good idea of yours, Kate,' said Ben. 'I must dash up and tell Marie.'

And now there were all Ben's machines, his dryers, his wetters, waltzing around overhead, loosening still further our treacherous ceilings. Kate had barely time to put the accusation into words before there was another fall—in the kitchen: smashing down on the sink, which it tore from the wall. At that very moment, as it happened, Ben's typewriter could again be heard, being used by a man evidently in full literary flow. Too easily Kate imagined him adding a touch to his portrait of her as a total housewife. At the same time she attributed to that familiar creative clatter my own impotence

176

as a novelist.

Well, I had indeed at times been unnerved by that sound; since it seemed never in any ordinary fashion to be subject to interruption. The most confident writer in the world, you'd have thought, must pause from time to time, if only to rest his fingers. But Ben seemed to suffer from no intermission whatever of the literary flood. Once or twice I'd suspected it was some sort of machine he'd devised and set up in the room above, precisely in order to make me feel ineffectual. I'd imagine him groaningly composing by hand in an armchair, while on the table the typewriter chattered away under mechanical propulsion, producing nonsense. . . .

'This bloody bloody *bloody* house!' cried Kate. 'And that *bloody* Ben!' Our sons wept. The cat leapt through a window into the garden, not to be seen again for days. But in all the stunned confusion and uproar, a welcome note made itself heard.

Or rather, an unwelcome one made itself unheard. That bloody Ben had stopped typing.

IO

Looking back, I see there were other things, infinitely grimmer than Ben's harmless typing, that in those 1950s seemed immovable elements of life, but in the end were to stop.

In a school hall filling with fog, a boxing tournament. A boy whose glove revolved perilously round the tip of his own nose—the action of a fly with enormous feet. Though he seemed always about to fell himself, he boxed effectively, and the audience wept with admiration and amusement. I tried to imagine a world champion whose action was such that, as he stormed to his victories, great arenas rocked with laughter.

Another very little boy had legs that seemed to have been, in the woodworking sense, turned specifically for boxing purposes: with such legs, there was nothing for it but to be a boxer. He had steady, fierce boxer's eyes, and needed them in the yellowing hall, which in the end suggested such darkness outside that the afternoon was brought to a sudden close. We must all, said the Head, make our way home as quickly and carefully as we could. Parents were already at the school door: and we scurried out into what seemed very much like a huge unswept chimney. It eddied and swooped, a stinging grit, this fog that had a kind of solidity about it, as if it had only just turned into vapour from blocks of filth. Somewhere inside those grimy billows, traffic groaned: there were cries of dismay, alarm, warning. Under lamplight, the obscene stuff oozed at us. ...

And I remembered out of a lifetime of fogs one of the earliest I'd known. It was soon after we'd moved in 1926 from East Barton to Barton-on-the-Hill, and for the journey to school of a mile or more I was under the wing of a large girl, the daughter of a neighbour, whose attitude to me was not inhumane but not totally kind. Well, I guess she hated the job. I can still remember the puzzling sensation of surrendering myself those early mornings and afternoons to someone who seemed so motherly, and was not. Doris would seize my hand in hers and set off, not speaking, not pausing. I saw nothing like it until years later; and that was at the New Theatre, just after the war, when Ralph Richardson, as Falstaff, gave Laurence Olivier, as his old tittering friend Shallow, a final handshake that he instantly forgot he'd given: so that he left the stage with Shallow's hand still in his. And Olivier had somehow reduced his substance to that of a feather, and he floated out in the other's oblivious grip. ... Doris was much like that.

But I longed for her, I sobbed for her one home-going when there was fog and I altogether failed to find her: missed the girls' gate; missed the entire known world, as it seemed to me; and somehow, by desperate indirections, on a basis of landmarks half-recognised or wretchedly guessed at, scampering between grunting cars, confusing roads and pavements, made my way home. I have never in my life been so lost, and recall still a sense of disorientation so great that I would not have been surprised to discover I had come home upside down. ...

There were times in Barley Wood when our tall red house and wide green garden were wrapped in a sallow greasy muffler of fog so settled you thought it would never shift. ...

And another day when Georgie Ring arrived in the classroom with a red, swollen face. 'What on earth has happened?' I asked. In his nervously abrupt fashion this dull boy said: 'My father passed away yesterday, sir.' He went back to his desk, sniffing; and returned a moment later with another detail: 'He had an ulcer, sir.' Again he went away, and again came back: 'He bled to death, sir.' Later he visited my desk to tell me about his father's watch: it would now be his. 'It cost ten pounds, sir.'

In the afternoon he played football in the playground with his usual eagerness, the unforgettable horror half-forgotten. At some moments during the day you could see that his misery was balanced by a sense of strange importance. Having a father who died was an attribute that turned the rest of us into nobodies. But then much of the day he was simply a shocked boy with a red, twitching face, in whose eyes the tears came, flowed, and then went away, in just the rhythm of coming and going in which he'd told me the story of his father's death.

And that evening on the train to Barley Wood they were discussing the last-minute attempts to save the life of a dull boy who was to hang for the murder of a policeman—shot, not by him, but by his accomplice, who was slightly below, as the condemned boy was slightly above, the age at which one might be hanged.

My fellow-travellers, city clerks of one kind or another, had no doubt of the importance of this execution. Its not taking place would amount to an invitation to all such young ruffians to shoot any policeman they caught sight of. This would soon be followed by the irresistible shooting of city clerks, their wives and children.

'These do-gooders ...' said someone, referring to the attempts to secure a reprieve.

'Never hear of one of *them* being shot.'

'Worse luck!'

I remember how they talked with great confidence about the decline of religious instruction in the schools. Closely associated, as one would expect, with the decline of corporal punishment; which led, by a logical process only too familiar to comfortable people sitting in suburban railway carriages, to the necessity of capital punishment. They were quite clear that if you stepped up flogging you would have less hanging to do. A clear economy.

But after ten minutes or so someone reflected the general feeling that rather more than its due of discussion had been given to the question whether this boy should or should not be throttled at 9 o'clock the next morning. What would you do, he asked, about a sudden outbreak of mildew among your roses?

How odd! Fog, capital punishment—apparently fixed features of life! The murderous fog, the legal murder—as it seemed on those mornings when the bus entered the tangle of shabby roads around the school, and you knew at that moment someone was being killed in your name amid the sickest possible ceremony of death. Or anti-ceremony: all stripped down to grey suits, hoods, leather straps.

Even the worst of illegal murderers did not tell his victim he would die at 9 o'clock on a named morning so many weeks ahead; but that, of course, he would be thinking the matter over in the meantime: and might even at the last moment be moved to change his mind. ...

And clinging to those memories is another, of a day when one of my colleagues had confiscated a comic that was such a horror of ghouls and decaying corpses that, having made myself read it all through, I felt ill, as if the shriekingly decomposing skulls of the comic had taken possession of my own skull. Returning home in the train, I stared at a woman sitting opposite, and she seemed to be one of those horribly unreal women of the comic, bent on murder or risen from the dead—often both. My imagination was fouled by memory of the houses in which these creatures lived, or putrified ... and the omnipresent cemeteries out of wilful nightmare—on hilltops, under clouds and lightning. ...

But then into the carriage came five or six schoolgirls, creating a quite un-necrophilic atmosphere of chatter and eleven-year-old excitement. One of them babbled more than the others: and talked of a film, referring rapidly to stars whose names I didn't catch. 'Shan't see it—it's only Linda Darnell being chased by X ... and she meets Robert Mitchum ... and loves him ... and meets Y ... and he loves her! *No good!*' And when her friends left her at the next station she remained animated, humming softly to herself, as though she were a gathering of people in her own right. ...

II

Well, it struck me more and more that what human beings needed as much as anything was the capacity to switch from tragedy to comedy, and back again, without ever, in the process, quite breaking their necks—or their hearts.

'You've washed all the plates, you've done very well,' Kate would purr; whereupon Dan, indifferent to such encomiums, would elect to do something dramatically nasty, so that, with barely time for a breath, Kate would conclude: 'You absolutely beastly little boy!'

I did not understand, as life at 1 East Drive settled into its characteristic pattern, waves of marvellous happiness followed by waves of marvellous wretchedness, why we did not prepare ourselves for ordinary reality with courses in, say, Confusion Management, or Disaster Accustomedness. The first would be concerned with the smoothing out of marital and parental and inter-neighbourly disarray; the other with making oneself ready, as on the whole people amazingly did not, for the inevitable occurrence of the undesirable event at the inconvenient moment: indeed, for the withdrawal from circulation, for whole periods at a time, of the very idea of convenience.

Kate dropped a bowl of porridge, intended for Dan, and it spattered carpet and walls. She wept. I begged her not to be silly; not to cry about nothing: and whistled as I cleared up the mess. Kate told me not to be so damned cheerful. I instantly became cheerless, and a little wheel of dark thoughts began to revolve in my head: she was lacking in courage, I was an ass, I was more courageous than she was, I'd had a bad day too, cheerfulness was the only counter to such days, her bad day was much worse than my bad day, I must kiss her at once, this would be misinterpreted, we'd reached the point where kisses could be turned against the kisser, I would leave and find a room somewhere and write, I was the soloist in the Saint-Saëns organ concerto and with clever famous fingers was creating enormous sounds in an incredulous concert hall—the Albert Hall, doubled in size for the occasion, partly in order to dwarf Kate, sitting sobbing in one of the cheaper seats and full of useless regret. ...

In some sense it was always April with us, and there were times when we'd simply lost our capacity to tell good weather from bad. We'd go on being happy when we should have turned to being miserable, and vice versa.

Having quarrelled bitterly, Kate and I would make love in the Barley Wood moonlight, flooding through the blunted Gothic of our windows, and experience happiness so intense that it clearly wasn't meant for us—we'd intercepted some elation earmarked for our betters. There we'd lie, amid the tumbling shadows of leaves that made our bed seem out there rather than in here, and the latest appalling irritation, which had brought us sullen to the day's end, would seem itself to be the root of the enormous sensation of harmony that drove us to make love.

I was astonished constantly by it—the reparable nature of human relations. A dreadful feeling that one quarrel would destroy everything was what I'd grown up with. Yet experience showed over and over again that the end of things could be instantly followed by the superb recommencement of the same things exactly. I'd love Kate and hate Kate and love

Kate again, and you would not be able to put your finger on a single second of real inconsistency.

It was Kate who was slowly teaching me how to ride a quarrel. My inclination to leave by a window at the first cross word and become a pathetic refugee, or at best to retreat into a grim fortress of sullenness and sulks, was giving way to ... in essence, a growing mass of experience that proved such drama was not called for. Kate, I learned, could address me as if I were some worm compared with whom other worms were lords of creation, and this would not be at all incompatible with her thinking quite well of me.

In the middle of some typical confusion, largely a result of having to accommodate the wishes and needs of two small children alongside our own in an appallingly difficult flat at a moment in the history of domestic science poised between one form of technology and another fantastically different, we'd meet and glare at each other ... and it was like blundering into someone in the middle of the roar and smoke of a battlefield and realising—from some single bloodshot look you were given—that this was the person you loved and who loved you, and that this ghastly uproar was the precise consequence of your having these feelings for each other. Heaven knew how you'd read the destination board when the journey began, but this was not where you'd expected to end up.

But I found myself drawing on memories of being a young cyclist. I began to think of marriage as a sort of inner tube. The road of life, dammit, was macadamed with tintacks; but the human spirit, given half a chance, was an absolutely inexhaustible puncture outfit.

I wonder, with an awareness thirty years older, how Kate could have stayed: a domestic drudge, a maternal labourer, a prisoner in the Railway Hotel-that-never was! But then I remember those aspects of having children that I could never talk of to Ben because, having taken against cloying talk of children, he'd concluded it was not possible to talk of them uncloyingly.

A few months after having Dan—feeling like someone with a new lover. First, the stranger: then you exchanged smiles, and suddenly between you there was, all the time, a warmth of smiles. You had with you this sweet smiler. ...

Much later he presented himself with an urgent message. He'd come with it out of great distances of garden. 'I been talking to the bees. Come and see the bees.' 'What did they say, Dan?' He made the lowest possible sound. 'Like dat.' You went to see his bees, and they were wood lice.

You read Tom some of W. H. Hudson's tales of friendship among animals, very much Tom's territory, and he went off to retell one of them to Kate—the comrades being a swan and a trout and the end coming when the fish was hooked. Tom told the story with the smiling energy he brought to such a task: a tale was always a spendid thing and you were always lucky to have it to tell. He came to the end, paused brightly: and broke down. His tears were wild. The tale had turned terrible on his tongue! Kate said hastily: 'But I know he was sent to join some other swans, and then he was happy.' Tom's misery worsened. 'But *I*'m not,' he pointed out.

We saw a swan asleep on a pond on Barley Green and Tom said he was his own pillow.

The children leading their mad life among the budding trees. ...

Dan, full of idiot good-humour, marching about at the heels of Tom and Sally and others, shouting as they did: 'I'm a soldier! I'm a soldier!' And long after the others had oddly changed this to 'I'm a stamp collector!' and vanished, Dan stumping up and down alone, loyal to the original chant, his face ferociously set: a creature made crazily content by his new-found pleasure of endlessly repeated statement. ...

And Dan for a while being always on Kate's track; and his fury when I tried to keep him at my side, to prevent him from trailing after her. He'd discovered the power of a fiercely uttered 'No!': delivered like a warning shot fired across the bows of the entire world. Here was Kate telling him to stop swinging on her chair—'No!' he cried, and roared menacingly at her. She smacked his hand: he was more furious still; shouted a louder 'No!'; was smacked again: and acting on some red-hot blurred notion of what would be the most appalling action he could take, one that would bring the world to its knees, fumbled at a cupboard door in an ill-executed attempt to make a screen of it behind which he'd withdraw

184

from us and from the whole injustice of things. ... Those gestures that small children make and that fail because their ideas are huger than their capacity to convert them into acts!

One's simply being an adult must at times be maddening to a child!

Tom with a proposition for Dan: 'Let's have a rough-and-tumble!' His reminding himself instantly that the word 'rough' was one of which Kate, at the other end of the room, was a massive opponent. 'Except that it's not really rough, just a tumble.'

There was a view that children were fairly intolerable until they grew up: so full acceptance of them must be reserved until they were ... moustached, or whatever was the female equivalent. (I myself had dreams of Tom and Dan passing me silently in corridors, eyes lowered. I simply imagined them fairly speechless and unwilling to put to me any question whatever.) But the problem was that growing up is not like that. At no point can it be announced: This child has now grown up! Instead there is a continuous process from the beginning, and there ought probably to be a steady acceptance of a child, from birth onwards, as a complete human being. Well, how much unhappiness in grown-ups, and capacity to cause unhappiness in others, rested on their having been subject to ungenerous, unaccepting judgement in childhood?

Of course, some form of special sympathy might be in order, seeing children were undergoing an astonishing crash course in giving up the right to screech and scream and clamour and fume and wallow in jealousy and hate and smash things up and bite and kick. ...

Dan, under Tom's now professorial influence, issued an invitation. 'Come and see my Nature!' On a bedside table, three dilapidated leaves, a sordid pebble, an unhappy worm.

However badly things went, however dingily imprisoned she felt, Kate wasn't going to give up her share of our muddled governorship of these exhausting inventions of ours!

12

'Well, yes,' wrote that boundlessly helpful man, the literary adviser to my publishers, 'it's all right: all you've missed, and all you need now, is the very simplest element: a feeling of movement. This need not be at all complicated, and might amount to no more than this: that in the first chapter you have the leaves on the trees, and in the second chapter you have the leaves falling off the trees.'

There were no trees in Islington, so I could not adopt this hint in any literal fashion. But I understood, suddenly, that it was indeed a matter of movement, of a change being brought about: I saw as if there'd been thunderclaps and lightning flashes (to this day I'm not certain there weren't) that my book might be the story of movement on the part of the teacher at the centre of it—how, from being hopeless, he became, alarming step by alarming step, hopeful. It was the dawn of a view of the writing of books as a process by which a beginning might be converted into an end. Having written the first sentence, your sole business was to make your way by some kind of intent navigation to the last; the author to be plainly discerned by even the most churlish reader as someone who was running purposefully from A, on the left, to Z, on the right. Z should be implicit in every revolution of his shapely legs. There should be a general whisper—which now and then might become a rather loud general shout—of: 'There's someone who knows where he's going!'

A suddenly happy man delivered the manuscript, and a man suddenly in despair waited for the proofs. Well, I thought, fancy becoming widely known as the author of a ludicrously bad book! If no glory had attached to me until now, there'd been no serious blots, either. Perhaps gratuitous-

186

ly I had converted myself into a blot.

Had I spent those anxious months in the construction of my own stocks, my own pillory? Might I simply have laboured over a device for making myself, in a twinkling, *passé*?

I received with awe the first copy of the book. Here was another startling question: Could mere print and binding give authority to what had hitherto lacked it? I felt as if my book had been promoted beyond the sphere occupied by its author. I had written a book that, by the fact of being printed and bound, was in a league its creator could not aspire to. I'd been cut dead by my own product.

And then I had my first experience of being reviewed. This is much like being pointed at in the street, and made me aware that I had no natural enjoyment of being even the periphery of attention. Perhaps it was related to those days, long gone, when I'd tried to get home from Barley Road School without being shouted at by Brian Green and his friends. The disunity between Brian and me sprang from the unity of our feelings about Jean Rawlins, the belle of the class. Given the cultural atmosphere of the back streets of Barton-on-the-Hill, Brian was in a strong position when, standing with his mob on one pavement, he was able to accuse me, scurrying past on the pavement opposite, of gaining full marks for my compositions. 'Excellent!' 'Very good work!' he shouted, as if these were scurrilities—as indeed they were.

I cowered, now, as Brian Green of the *Observer*, on the heels of Brian Green of the *Manchester Guardian*, prepared to reinforce (in shouts across the literary street) the blistering verdict of Brian Green of the *New Statesman*, who would be totally in accord with Brian Green of the *Times Literary Supplement*.

But it turned out that Brian was otherwise engaged, and they'd asked for reviews from ... well, it seemed in nearly every case to be Jean Rawlins, in one of those moods when, in answer to the question 'Do you love me?' scrawled on a dangerous piece of paper (the property of the Hertfordshire County Council), she'd write: 'Yes.'

There was a general air that was not one of disapprobation, and, for all the precautions I took against conceit, I found myself carefully pleased. My mother would have liked me to be more brash. 'When I talk about the book,' she said, 'he looks so embarrassed.' She had set herself up at once in what for the rest of her life was to be one of her roles: as an extremely eccentric barker outside my shy tent. She clearly lost me more readers than she gained, being inclined to urge the virtues of my books, of whose titles she made dreadful jumbles, on anyone she caught reading. The drift of what she said to each of these indignant persons was that he should at once shut the wretched book in his hands and look for. . . . The titles she invented at this juncture were beyond belief.

Questions of libel seemed to vanish, not as a result of any conclusion that they did not exist, but because those libelled had their own unexpected approach to the matter. Since it was not one of the common hazards of being a teacher, the offence lacked definition; and the notion of some legal issue being involved occurred to no one. A colleague I had identifiably caricatured asked me to sign his copy affirming that he was the original of the grotesque concerned. Astonishingly, I did so. By the headmaster a whole range of attitudes was adopted. They included delight at the idea of *attention being drawn*—he had a simple belief that no school could fail to profit from publicity: horror when he discovered that this attention was not everywhere thought to be favourable ('a social sore'), though his horror remained curiously poised at the same level as his delight: and the view that the scene was transparently recognisable in every particular, combined with the opinion that the headmaster in the book was a plain invention, quite ridiculous—thought not wholly unlike certain ridiculous headmasters he had himself encountered in his time.

Some of my colleagues hinted at an obscure anger which I at last traced to its source: they belonged to that large part of the human race that would rather be libelled than left out.

None of this terribly troubled me, since I knew that not one of them had been really hurt, and that some had taken obvious pleasure from the affair. But I was distressed by the reaction of one of my closest friends, Mark Hawkins: not the least of whose qualities was that he was the only Old Etonian on the Stonehill Street staff.

Mark and I had taught together before, at a prep school not far away in geographical space; in social space, very distant.

Being egalitarian in politics, and having a family to provide for, Mark had moved to Stonehill Street the year before I arrived there. In its account of his departure in the school magazine, The Vale could not bring itself to spell out this shocking Odyssey. From Eton to The Vale to Stonehill Street was not an acknowledgeable journey. 'Mr Hawkins,' it said, 'has joined the Education Department of the London County Council.' He might ... one wasn't being explicit ... have become the Chief Education Officer. 'His beautiful smile will be missed.'

That was the worst of The Vale and the best of The Vale side by side. It was socially prudish, but given to candour in pointing to such things as Mark's smile. That *was*, simply, beautiful. He had a yellow mask of a face, usually set with pain or a habit of endurance. He had hurt himself irreparably, years before, playing Rugger: a ruined spine had become the home of all manner of weaknesses. He was bent, he shuffled. But he had a strongly gentle face: every feature definite, a nose that had no doubt about being a nose, a fine mouth; and it was partly because such a striking face expressed so well his long sorrow and disappointment that, when he smiled, people found themselves deeply moved. Years of bad weather, simple hideous bad luck, stood aside and you saw, shining, the lost Mark Hawkins.

His father had been a teacher at Eton, it was a teaching family: and Mark was a *dreadful* teacher. He'd done well by a handful of boys at The Vale, clever, odd boys with a passion for words, who did not depend for learning on orderly classrooms. Mark was incapable of keeping order. An effect of his long story of illness was that he yearned simply for peace. 'I'd like to sit for ever,' he once told me, 'in a deckchair in the sun, reading a novel.' He read nothing but novels, saying it was an odd effect of having been to Eton, which regarded English literature as a baleful modernism, that he came to fiction late, and was hooked, as he calculated, for ever. 'Or for as much time as I've got left.' Going day after day into classrooms was never anything better than an interruption. It was so at The Vale; it was more awfully so at Stonehill Street.

Mark told himself that he'd moved to Stonehill Street because he wanted to be among the bottom and not the top people. He wanted (he never spelled it out, but that was it) to bring fiction to the masses. But I think he moved really for the raw reason that, with three children, he needed more money.

At The Vale he'd been tormented, but within a pattern he understood. His ineptitude was inside the tradition. In Stonehill Street, he was lost. His very voice was a disaster. It was strong, pleasant—and sounded amazingly unsuitable in that battered North London world. It asked to be satirised—and it was. For some reason Stonehill Street thought that 'Monty' was a fit nickname for this alien who'd drifted into their midst. Being able to imitate Monty's voice was a fairly basic way of establishing your right to be a boy at Stonehill Street. When Mark appeared, the voice would break out everywhere, sometimes a hideous choral effect, Eton mercilessly captured and magnified.

So Mark, who'd come in order to break down social barriers, found himself crucified on those very barriers. To have Monty taking your next lesson was an intoxicant. And when he went into a classroom, and the class rose to the irresistible bait that he was, he responded in a manner that made his plight, already miserable, far worse. He stormed at them like some comic peppery colonel whose lawn has been invaded by ruffians. The upper-class voice became a travesty of itself. Vowels were dispensed with in exactly the fashion I'd grown used to among intemperate colleagues at The Vale. 'Y' j'll' w'll g't b'ck t' y'r d'sks!' It was a long rap of authoritative consonants: but alas for Mark, such vocal habits had no effect in Stonehill Street. Or rather, they had much the effect that would have followed if Mark had been made up like one of the pseudo-black comics of the day. The false coon language of *that* comedy was exactly of the order of Mark's disdainful, vowel-repressing angers. His tormentors, who were themselves vulnerable to satire on the strength of their remarkable diphthongs, destroyed Mark day after day for his submerged vowels.

When I began at Stonehill Street, I became Mark's ally as another man deeply in trouble. My own difficulties made me at times question my right to be Tom's father. How could someone coming from humiliations at the hands of so many boys in Islington pretend to have power over a single boy in

Barley Wood? Putting our despairs together, Mark and I cultivated a kind of snobbery of failure. To be an effective teacher you had to be a boring human being. Well, there was the headmaster we worked under in those early days. He'd come to this untidy, shabby, round-shouldered school and made it clear at once that he wanted to make his own impression on it. He was going to punch it into shape in such a way that the bruises were identifiably his. Mark and I found it easy to sneer at his ambitious briskness. I remember a morning in early spring, when the journey from home to school had been less painful than usual because the sun was common to both places, and in Stonehill Street made brickwork bloom and dismayed gardens perk up with the first dandelions. Birds were chirpy and bees buzzy: exactly the defects—chirpiness, buzziness—that the headmaster identified and named in the boys at assembly. They stirred with spring, and he hated it. 'I came here to enjoy my service to God,' he cried. 'Oh, that I could trust and believe that you did the same!'

It was precisely, Mark and I thought, what they'd been doing. But a chirpy, buzzy God—and probably round-shouldered, too.

As time went on, we remained close, finding comfort in each other's ironies; but I began to see that he was truly defeated, and that I'd only taken temporary refuge in the language of defeat. Oh, I still wasn't the headmaster's man. It was true that the school needed greater alertness. The round shoulders had become a slump and a slouch. But to demand shoulders squared was not the answer. In a more bracing informality lay some hope. In military crispness—none. I'd begun to feel I might engage in the business of bracing, myself.

Mark and I had both adopted the Hamlet view of things, that's what it amounted to: but I'd received an unexpected injection of Fortinbras.

'I was pathetic,' said Mark one day when he'd had to be rescued by the deputy head from a rioting classroom. 'I was awful. I knew Harris would come. All I could do was wait for him to hear what was going on and *ridiculously* pretend to write names on a piece of paper.' It was total surrender: and none of us knew how to make him take up the struggle again.

But when I wrote my book I drew a portrait of the valiant Mark, the ironist—so often quizzical about his own disasters. It was the Mark who, a few minutes after abominable experiences with old Slough's inflamed class, would be talking shrewdly about some new novel. I wrote of him as a martyr—but a martyr amused by the very arrows they shot into him.

And I found that I'd mistaken his feelings. I'd thought he would enjoy my portrait: but, misreading the comedy, missing the note of affection, he saw it as ridicule. He never put this into words—saying not much more than that he thought I'd portrayed the boys 'too rosily.' There, alas, lay Mark's problem: he was unable to think of them as anything but ogres, though to break your way through this view of them was an essential step in reducing their ogrishness. But the fact that he made no comment beyond this one amounted to a very dark comment indeed. I had hurt him; and nothing that happened between us thereafter—and within five years he was to meet his death in an accident as bitterly absurd as any of the accidents that composed his unlucky life—ever softened the outlines of that fact.

I seemed also to have hurt the London County Council, but this was less troubling. They were not opposed to having their schools written about: but wanted the results to glow, to have the polish of a prospectus. Difficulties might be hinted at, but only as reasons for recording the fact that they were being steadily overcome by armies of teachers with shining eyes, backed by administrators whose idealism was held in check only by their remarkable feeling for what was practical. I had said that the social plight of many of my boys was grim and that their educational experience was, to put it gently, mediocre. It seemed to me that improvement might come from a frank description of things-as-they-were. The LCC of the day held, or affected to hold, that an account of educational reality as it was in the Stonehill Streets of the capital could only create general discouragement. Teachers, deprived of their figleaves, would give up all attempt at decency.

What they really meant, I thought, was that any statement of awkward truths might lead to votes lost. Since the party in power was the one I was given to supporting, I felt particularly dismayed by such political cowardice.

Technically, I was in trouble. No teacher employed by the LCC was allowed to write about his teaching experience without obtaining permission and submitting the manuscript for approval. I had known from the beginning that I could not do this. My accounts of the Georgie Rings and Mark Hawkinses, battered boys and tormented teachers, would never be found acceptable by those who thought of attempts to tell the truth in terms of disloyalty. I'd be invited to County Hall and reminded that I was only a tyro in the teaching service, and that the truth was always terribly complex. It would be hinted that I was simply a pedlar of anecdotes. ... I didn't feel that the LCC had purchased my experience and my view of it along with my services as a teacher.

Ben, who was required to submit the manuscript of his own book to the scrutiny of his seniors in the Civil Service, said I had not given my attention to other aspects of the LCC's position. There were things to be said for their attitude. I knew this to be so. But I was moved by my own experience of that conspiracy of smooth silence as to difficulties that was so harmful to the young teacher. Things were not worsened, they were made better, by the teacher being prepared. If there were nasty aspects of the scene round the corner it actually helped if someone told you there were nasty aspects of the scene round the corner. It might help even more if someone said the nasty aspects had ... nice aspects. But to be left to discover the truth for yourself, in raging classrooms ... that was how teaching careers became rooted in shock and dismay and cynicism. There was such a gulf between the abstractions and idealisations of training and the blunt realities of life in the schools! The gulf was so wide, the crash-landing on the other side so shattering! Not that—in those bashfully exhilarating days during which the LCC decided that to take action would be worse than not to take action—I thought of the book in such crusading terms. What I largely felt was astonishment at having written a book at all.

13

And there was the party to think about that we had held in the
garden, and another sort of gulf opening up: between Philip
and me.

He and Ruth had come angrily to the party. Ben had
decided it should be fancy dress, and they came, they said, as
gangster and moll. It seemed to me that they came as Philip
and Ruth, inflamed: and their raw displeasure with each other
gave Philip a criminal air, and Ruth a bright flushed quality
that suggested the stereotype of a criminal's girl. Philip, I
guess, thought up these identities for them as they made their
warring arrival on the doorstep.

Not that we used the doorstep. People came straight down
through the garden to the basement, and were at once aware
of Tom and Dan, playing an uncontrollable part in the affair
from their bedroom window above. They lowered impudent
baskets, to be filled with offerings of olives, anchovies, cheese
dip. Light flooded out into the orchard, closely followed by
music, and soon by those billows of talk that make a party
sound like a sea unhinged. Ben's most carefully witty colleague arrived as a fancy waistcoat. The most beautiful girl in the
neighbourhood came as the most beautiful girl in the neighbourhood, and spent much of the early part of the evening
allowing her eye to run admiringly down the splendid slope of
her body. I was young in parties, still, and found the mere
filling of the scene almost intolerably exciting. It wasn't
always the obvious thrilling elements that contributed to this:
I was stirred to think of Mark Hawkins, in plain dress,
watching it all from a position he'd taken up in the courtyard.
'Don't often get out,' Mark had said on arrival. 'Just put me
somewhere in a corner and keep my glass filled.'

Ben and I had written, and we'd rehearsed, a short play, a midsummer satire, in the manner (in rapid succession) of Shakespeare, Chekhov, T. S. Eliot and Christopher Fry. It had been voted tremendously funny, and to this day I am unable to bring myself to think of it. Having insured against shyness by drinking before the party began, I found I had drunk the lines clean out of my head. The very idea of there being precise lines, to be remembered and reproduced, had become unlikely. I gaped dizzily on the stage of the lawn. ...

A plainly dressed figure said it hadn't moved from the courtyard, but had heard that I'd done rather badly in some other corner of the scene. I ran into Ben, who spoke soothingly in a manner that suggested to me that he was the worse for drink. I came within a foot, or it might have been a mile, of the most beautiful girl in the neighbourhood, and was minded to inform her of my opinion that she was ... odalisque-like. It was the exact term, and I intended, whatever the difficulties—and they seemed to be great—to use no other. I swam for a few moments through the deep sea of the orchard, and two small cheery fishes, having the faces of my sons, peered down at me from close to the surface. Kate, inexplicably dressed as a schoolgirl, rushed up in a manner suggesting clockwork, hurled hurried abuse, and rushed away again in the same manner. I found myself studying closely a man who was clearly trying his laugh out and didn't think much of it, and then, as a result of some catapulting action, was in the basement, intent on a girl whose skin was so tight that I knew her kneecap would at any moment come flying across the room.

And then I was in the company of Ruth.

She was bitterly wounded; and at once I became sober. She said Philip had vanished, and I recalled—less like someone drawing upon memory than someone magically summoning scenes from the past—that he and the most beautiful girl in the neighbourhood had made off in the direction of. ... They'd gone towards the bottom of the garden. I knew at once that the bushes down there were brimming with them. I was also terribly aware of Ruth's hurt.

We were joined by the husband of the most beautiful girl in the neighbourhood, who asked if we knew where his wife was. I proposed idiotically that she might have fallen asleep in some dusky corner. I then swam back into the orchard and found Philip. He was alone, and had about him an air of melancholy excitement. I begged him to go and reassure Ruth: 'You don't always,' I seemed to be declaring, 'have someone who will love you for years and years.' Philip muttered: 'I can't help it. ...'

The evening ended with a small storm: sudden dark blue rustle and hiss of wind, and then rain tin-tacking down in the orchard: and blanched faces among the bones of the party.

And Ruth crying: 'The heart is only a pump!': and Philip muttering, 'You're growing up, Ruth!': and a doleful voice, which seemed to be my own, singing: 'You are my pump's delight.'

And when we next met, Philip said: 'Your position as an advocate of marriage is philosophically indefensible, you know. You have no one to defend it. Bertrand Russell wouldn't. No one. Only Christ! And he didn't try it. ...

And I didn't know how to say that I wasn't in it for the virtue, or as someone with a general case to make out for marriage. I didn't even want Philip to be anything but his natural exasperating self.

What distressed me was the ease with which we all hurt each other. And I was struck by a feature of so many of the bitter quarrels that arose out of our being who we were: that they were cases of imperfect creatures accusing other creatures of being imperfect. ...

Philip hit upon a terrible term for me: The Diplomat. Well, it was partly a reference to an epigram I'd written for a *New Statesman* competition:

> Diplomacy's a means by which
> The nations (that, in brutal fact,
> Abhor each other) clothe with tact
> A tap upon a neighbour's snitch:
>
> It makes sedate
> The universal Billingsgate.

'Keep out of the fishmarket,' Philip said, 'if you don't like the language.' And we both laughed ruefully, because it really didn't wash, to accuse me of having a prudish ear. All that was happening, I thought, was that my love for Philip, added to my love for Ruth, together with a concealed inclination on their part to cast me in the role of umpire, meant that Philip was able to pose as a champion of emotional liberty, by defining me as one eager for emotional chains.

I was amazed, from time to time, by the sheer intricacy of the false positions into which, often in some muddle of helpless friendship, human beings were able to jostle each other. ...

14

It was Christmas—the bells of Barley Church had been clanging much of the morning like a collection of crazy tin plates. An infamous interruption, said Ben, who'd received the proofs of his book and wanted only to spend the holiday breaking his heart over them. He was distressed by the length of his sentences: without his noticing it, these had begun, as if animated by some actual immoral intention, to extend themselves—even to coil round on themselves in some sleek fashion he was inclined to despise. To me, they seemed as admirable as his sentences always were: spikily supple. I knew the splendid taps from which he drew his notion of the sentence: Bacon, Swift, Defoe. Ben had always read sparingly of the best, and hadn't my comprehensive stomach. He affected at times to think that I was ruined by indiscriminate reading. Anyway, Interruption Eve, we thought: Interruption Day. *That* was a day of strange beauty—early, a body of mist in which the branches of trees were black veins; and later, a sky daubed with red gold, among long scarves of cloud of the subtlest colours, especially mixes of grey and green.

After the usual ordeal by gluttony, I wandered into the garden, first into the orchard full of the ghosts of apples—it had been a great picking, that year—and on to the lawn; noticing how a few last roses, crumples of washed-out flesh held on to the briars by some glue of decay, were lit by the low sun. I thought of the seasons that lay waiting for us within the wintry covers of this garden, as in the pages of some pop-up book: springs to come, with their making of leaves and invention of flowers; and great moments of summer, the sun as bold as burning brass, the hot sighs of air. I paused at the closed umbrella of the weeping pear, and remembered how its slender silver-green leaves, falling sallow, turned as they lay there to a puddle of lead.

And I remembered, as the word 'sallow' occurred to me, my mother's recent statement about the pale face of a neighbour: 'A *salad* complexion!'

And a flood in the summer that had claimed as its most distinguished victim Charles Hickman's compost heap, which was a Rolls-Royce of treasured decomposition, a rich biscuit prepared over several seasons. There had been reports of it floating in a helplessly aristocratic way, and under a sky looking like a bowl of forgotten washing-up water, down the railway line towards New Barton. ...

Indoors, Tom and Dan had been made less than perfectly tractable by the arrival of this amazing day, the most longed-for day of the year: when possessed, as sad as it was splendid. Got, it was gone. Feeling it slipping through their fingers, they became, among other things, desperately boastful. I'd not made specific war on this defect since once upbraiding Tom for it. 'That's boasting! You mustn't boast!' Tom asked for a definition, and I offered it together with various narrative illustrations, designed to cause disgust. But Tom glowed. 'I *like* boasting,' he said.

Following the publication of the book—and though that in fact threatened, through some fiscal subtlety I had no hope of understanding, to make us even poorer than before—I'd bought our first stereophonic gramophone. Dan stood trembling beside me whenever I put a record on. He had the big hands of Kate's father, Jim, a mechanic by instinct, who'd been able to handle with equal delicacy the hugest nut and bolt and the tiniest; and promised altogether to be Jim reborn. Now Dan's hands twitched, in sympathy with the motor being switched on, the arm rising, the disc revolving. He *was* the gramophone. We listened to a recorded story, and came to a blameless moment in which the sale of a cow was discussed. Dan's eyes grew instantly damp, his mouth square. 'Why did they sell the cow?' he trembled. Brought up to think of tragedy in terms of the last act of *Hamlet*, I had not been ready to find it in this account of a simple agricultural transaction. Dan climbed on to my knee and wept a quiet half pint. But within minutes he was making untenable claims for the superiority of one of his Christmas presents over all other such objects: it was a fishing net, which for a very long time he was to refuse to submit to the degradation of use.

I had every reason to expect that my own best Christmas present was to come. The seasonal exhaustions had put it under threat, but there was a brightness in Kate, the promise of something that would see Fatigue off the premises. Well, I'd been inclined lately to give it the capital letter of personification, because of the nightly comedies of disappointment it led to. I'd come to think in terms of a long series of championship fights between Lust, in the corner nearest the window, and Fatigue, in the corner nearest the door to the children's room. Lust, a not unpromising contestant, well set up, surprised his backers again and again by succumbing, after a dreary round or two, to his pasty opponent. ...

It was another way in which the publication of the book had left us slightly worse off. Not that Kate's attitude to it was marked by anything but generous delight. All the same—and, I guessed, without her beginning to be aware of it—there was further underlining of the fact that I was free to create outside the family, and she wasn't. I felt that when I came home from a day in Islington. For me, there was the simple pleasure of doing so, added to that of the change of setting; but for her, there was no such renewal of scene. And to fatigue this must have added ... Fatigue. ...

The evening was spent with Ben and Marie. Ben said the stereo, heard for the first time, made him cross-eared. We told each other simple stories, the better for being familiar. Of Ben, for example, seen stealing in the embarrassed early morning down to his marrow bed, intent on fertilising a female flower with pollen taken from a male: a sort of vegetable pimp. Of the pea seeds I'd buried so deep that they'd not been likely to come up anywhere in the northern hemisphere. Of an occasional lapse in Marie's otherwise beautifully exact English; as when, moved by a notion of the spiral nature of larksong, heard high above Barley Wood, she'd spoken of the bird 'screwing away up there.' Of Kate's triumphs in the B-----W--- Stores, entirely due to her chance ability to make accurate totals of columns of figures upside down. There'd be Mr Robbins, doing his slapdash arithmetic on a piece of wrapping paper, and getting it airily wrong, always in his own favour: and Kate providing her cool correction. ...

And I thought of the war of styles that was emerging among us, and how we were slowly becoming accustomed to the fact that we were acutely diverse people, and how very astonishing such a fact could seem. Well, for so long I'd believed, for example, that if Ben held one opinion and I another, the probability was that I was wrong. I'd proved myself simply an inefficient version of Ben. How shocking, at first, to learn that you could have different views, and, in some essential fashion, both be right: and that between any two people, amity was not necessarily a matter of their being in agreement on important issues. ...

In our twenties—and even though half that decade had been held in the vice of war—we'd believed in miraculous escapes from erroneous situations. But marriage, the birth of children, the adoption of mortgages—and the constant payment of cheques for £8.13s.6d.—had made it clear that, from now on, if a situation was erroneous it might well not allow the most humdrum and laborious escape, let alone a miraculous one. It might be necessary to seek pleasure in closed options and in making a narrowed life grow broad from within.

How hateful the notion that the mundane was without glory, and that to work within chosen relationships was to be made incapable of marvels!

As Kate and I made our way to bed under the coin-spinning sounds of Ben and Marie doing the same above us, I remembered a moment that summer when, under the full stare of the sun, I'd been striding across fields from Barley Wood to Barton-on-the-Hill, feeling wonderfully aired and glowing, and had suddenly sensed that never again would I be quite so well as I was at that moment: so fit, so much at ease with my body or at home with the physical world.

Odd, and strangely satisfactory—to be quite certain that one had arrived at the hinge of life, on a particular summer afternoon in 1955; and to see the hinge glinting in the sun. ...

PART FIVE

I

Soda House, said my mother that first Christmas after she'd moved to the home, was (she lowered her voice) an institution. She had not expected to end up in such a place. We tried to persuade her that Cedar House, as it knew itself, might more attractively be called a place of convalescence and retirement for the elderly: as its prospectus held that it was. It was also far too expensive to be (we lowered our voices) an institution. My mother snorted, but admitted that it had its points. For example, the nurses and maids were united in their adoration of her, and the matron had once or twice found it difficult to contain her emotion, faced with such phenomena as Mother's spotless underwear. 'I find that a great *boom*.' Yes, it could be borne, Seidlitz House. If there was anything to mar it, it was the extraordinary number of old people who occupied the place. 'They're bonkers, most of them.'

Actually, as I'd noticed again fetching her for Christmas, it was a large sighing house, with an old person, usually helplessly silent, in each room. A paradoxical mixture: the mute and creeping, and the tirelessly bustling. Young girls in aprons, Mother's admirers, leapt up and down stairs, smiling. Old ladies crossed continents of corridors, deserts of landing, with each step slowly thought out, slowly achieved, and then slowly recovered from. They were all—the old ladies, and the few old men—distinctly middle-class. They were the ruins of people just like those who'd lived in the Avenues and Drives of Barton-on-the-Hill when my mother was younger and had lived herself at the bottom of a mere Road. Some, here as there, had double-barrelled names. Mother had once had such a certainty that living in an Avenue meant you had a double-barrelled name, that she'd try to create one where it

205

didn't exist—at times by simple echo. 'I passed that Mrs Jones-Jones. ...'

She sat blind among us at Christmas, smiling intensely, like some deeply affectionate spider, clutching at anyone who passed within range of her and drawing his face or hers down for a long kiss. Sally, our dog, old and bonkers too, stretched her terminal bones alongside my mother's—whose hand for much of the holiday fondled Sally's grateful ears. When she had to move, she did so in a slow, frightened shuffle, as if the whole world was a cliff-edge. At eighty-five she was ready to confess to intimations of old age. 'Shaky on my legs.' I carried her to bed, a giggling heap of bird's bones. 'You enjoyed that,' she said coquettishly. The coquette was wonderfully to the fore in her, during these last years. When I brought her tea up in the morning, she claimed that entering her bedroom made me shy. She then spelt out her gratitude for the pleasure that, in our vast magnanimity, we were providing. It was like nothing so much as having with us some eagerly grateful child.

Going back to Cider House was painful, but she smiled about that, too. She had no desire, she said, stroking my hand, to cause me worry.

Her world had dwindled to a little room in a strange house. It was a narrow room with cream walls; when she wasn't lying on her bed, she was sitting in an armchair with a table in front of her on which she kept her knitting. This had never been a passion of hers, but now she set about it with a furious intentness, making hundreds—in time, thousands—of tiny squares of all colours that she then stitched together into tea cosies, covers for hot water bottles, cot blankets: her industry becoming ours—that of finding recipients for this endless flow of largely unpractical objects. She conferred them on people, like honours—usually to their complete astonishment. They became marks of her love: as she'd smothered people with kisses, now she smothered them with tea cosies.

'I have to keep myself busy,' she said—defensively, as if I might think she ought to be idle. But I understood the panic in her: she was frightened of being melancholic, like her own mother, frozen for days on end into a staring sadness.

Terrible suspicions stirred in her. What had happened to the bungalow? to her money? She reminded me with some agitation that I was 'next of king.' I mustn't, out of preoccupation—'or because you're stupid about these things,' she said bluntly—allow unspecified elements to take her over. I realised that one of the ways in which she'd seen my father was as a bulwark between her and fearful shadinesses on the part of the State, or the local authority. Now, dammit, she was dependent on a son who she had reason to believe was abominably unworldly. ... At the same time, all this amused her. She'd lost her dignity, she said, and ended up in an institution; but it was all extremely droll, when you thought about it. 'Sometimes I think how cross *he'd* have been, and then I want to giggle.' She had dreams in which she wept for him, but others, I suspect (I remembered abrasive weekends from my childhood), in which his tragic wrath made her conceal her dream amusement behind a dream *Daily Express* held unnaturally close to her face.

Whatever happened, she dressed with her habitual neatness: being much attached, now, to that kilt she'd bought when on a tour of Scotland by coach with my father. This was secured by a vast safety pin, of whose glittering erotic potentiality I'd swear my mother was perfectly aware. I loved, in these last years, that defiant and faintly risqué dapperness in her. Her body was barely fleshed, her legs all but bone, but she retained, contradicting all that, a considerable self-regard. It wasn't anything as thin as vanity, thought that was part of it; it was, I guess, the operation of the life force itself. With her back against every kind of wall, and her dead heaped around her, my mother kept final ruin at bay with safety pins, well-chosen jumpers, her general militant neatness. Well, her own mother had done the same, eighty years earlier, with holy-stone and scrubbing brush; and nearly won through.

She longed to be with Betty or me—'Wouldn't it be nice if you had a shed in the garden and I could live in it?'—but understood, when understanding was possible in such a matter, that the cost would certainly be the destruction of our way of life, and almost certainly of the quality of our relationship with her. Well, my mother was the starer, and the tactless commentator. She couldn't live with us and not subject us to intolerable inspection. All her life she'd fixed her gaze on the people she was with, tirelessly attracted by their actions. At times it had angered good people as well as bad. I had been reminded of that cry of our childhood, addressed at anyone you thought had you excessively in his sights: 'Got your eyeful?' People had come close to that cry, feeling my mother's searchlight of an eye trained on them. Well, now, poor woman, she had no eye to train; but the doctor who attended her at the home had given her hope that she might see again. She'd said her only unhappiness was her lack of sight. 'Why not have the operation done then?' he asked. 'I screwed up my courage,' she told me, 'and said, "All right, I will."'

If she lived in a shed in the garden, we'd need a mother-sitter: and soon she'd be able to watch everything we did, and train on it her involuntary bluntness of comment.

At times, leaving Cedar House after a visit, I'd be heartsick at the thought of her loneliness, her valiant and puzzled occupation of that narrow room. But I knew that any other solution would have led to worse results.

Most of the time, I think, she *didn't* understand. She obeyed what must have seemed our inscrutable whim. And as it happened, compensations were slowly emerging for being at Cedar House. They took the form, not of the other inmates, but of the nurses and helpers.

Being a resident, at £70 a week to begin with, must have presented my mother with almost insuperable problems of social self-identification. She'd be strictly aware of her import-ance, as one of the pampered. No one, I suspect, made more determined use of the telephone beside the bed. If one was in touch with the kitchen, one was in touch with the kitchen, and it should be made unmistakably aware of one's demands in respect of midnight cups of tea and oddly-timed biscuits. I thought of my mother now and then as a sort of female Charlie Chaplin: come from much the same world, she'd make much the same response to finding herself suddenly sitting in Croesus's lap. Endless cups of tea, at the very least. I guess, cuckoo in the Cedar House nest, she kept that expensive institution on toes it had never suspected that it had. If she found herself among the snooty, she could be relied upon to be snootier than any of them.

At the same time, her deeper complicity was with anyone who waited on others. She'd done that all her life: as various kinds of housemaid, and then as my father's wife—and, for a long time, as my mother. I looked back with astonishment at those years during which I'd been able to be a reader barely stirring from his armchair because she'd been willing to be a slave barely stirring from her sink and gas-stove or from her shopper's trudge of the High Street in Barton-on-the-Hill.

Cedar House, like any such place, had a procession of ... ancillary staff was the term. My mother inspected them with an expert's eye. She knew the woman who gave more than she was asked for as distinct from the woman who gave less. It was a matter, again, of kisses given and kisses withheld. If you believed my mother, there were girls around the place whose delight in her kept them alive. More important functionaries found it easy to earn her scorn—'I think she's bonkers'—but women who appeared in the middle of the night, when it seemed that they took my mother in their arms in scenes of the most touching sultriness, had from her the loyalty of someone who was merely disguising herself as a paying resident. There was something about someone coming up from the kitchen, or being required to make a bed, that moved my mother deeply. Well, they were herself: occupying the position of mistress, she was wholly on the side of the maid; and she could deal with the complication only by hugging innumerable Annies and Betties and Maggies to the point of suffocation.

2

Tom came down from Salford and went with Kate and me to see a play of Harold Pinter's. It seemed a long way from *Toad of Toad Hall*—and obviously was. We enjoyed it greatly, but

Tom said he had not been able to suppress a longing for someone to dash onstage and cry: '*Sire, the French have landed!*'

We went to see my mother and she told Tom about her first visit to the seaside when she was nineteen. She remembered giving the sea her careful inspection, for it was what she'd come for: and her comment: 'I must say it seems to me it's only water.' It made us wonder what she'd have made of the Pinter, given that it had ever come under her blunt eye.

She told us, wryly, that they'd put her in mackintosh knickers. She'd conceived a horror of the niche in which her armchair stood, and now spent all her time stretched out on her bed. I saw that her unhappiness really rested on the failure of her sight, now almost complete. It was this that made her take against the niche, which she couldn't see— seen, it would have been harmless—but could only feel, as the very idea of an intolerable narrowness. It was a beautiful morning, as Kate and Tom and I sat with her, and the sun was a thousand points of light among the leaves in the expensive Cedar House garden; and I realised, on the eve of her operation for cataract, how like a broken puppet she was: unable any longer to support herself on her feet, deeply deaf, and in her blindness given to staring in front of her, never looking to one side or the other, her face lacking every scrap of that animation that arises from response to the incessant variety of vision. . . .

Hope for what the operation might do was high in her. 'I'll tell you all about it and then you can write a book,' she said. For a long time her puzzled view of me as a writer has been that she had some duty to provide me with material. . . .

The nurse said well, they didn't know. The problem was that there was so little iron in her blood that they dared not give her a general anaesthetic. It would have to be a local one; and it would depend on the surgeon whether he thought he could complete the operation on that basis. Meanwhile, would I sign the form consenting to the operation?

It was horrible, knowing this possibility that there would be no operation at all when she was so full of delight and interest and hope. She took enormous pleasure from the plastic bracelet round her wrist, with her name on it. You'd have thought that in getting her name right the hospital had paid her some deathless tribute. 'I'll be thinking of you all day tomorrow,' she said, in a characteristic reversal of the obvious: well, it would have been more natural for us to be thinking of her. My sister said she'd suddenly realised that she couldn't remember her as she'd been when our father was alive. It was as if the eponymous hero of a play had been removed from the scene and you realised that he'd been of vastly inferior interest to some apparently secondary character. And I thought how odd it had been, indeed: the sudden bringing of this valiant creature into focus.

And the operation was successful. She'd kept calm, she told us, and was only a little bothered by the sensation of clipping and snipping that was going on round her eye. In the end, one eye only had been operated on; the other had been declared dead, and she spoke of it for the rest of her life with a mixture of irritation and pity. She'd prepared a joke for us: that she looked, didn't she, like Nelson. She was anxious that we shouldn't have forgotten who Nelson was. She was profoundly happy, she said, about the hospital. She loved the food, adored the nurses. 'They adore me.'

And then the bandages were removed; and it was a new woman. Years had dropped away. She wore dark glasses, clipped over her own, but her face had totally changed—was relaxed and outward-looking. I realised how it had taken on the lines of the extreme tension of blindness. It was like ... oh, a girl's hair going up! As we spoke, she looked from one to the other; and we saw that she'd not done this for a long time. She had amazing triumphs to recount, in terms of her correct naming of the colours of nurses' dresses, a wall, the sky seen through a window. And suddenly I saw that the prison door her face had become had been flung open. ...

There followed minor operations: to repair broken stitches, to tidy the site. She rode every pain and setback on a wave of delight in her limited but definite return of vision. And when she returned to Cedar House, it became evident that the days in hospital had served another excellent purpose: now, Cedar House was home.

And slowly, as she waited for the arrival of her special

glasses, this Indian summer in her grew brighter and warmer. She walked differently; the old frightened shuffle had not been due to loss of the power of movement, but to blind fear. She was now immensely excited—bobbed up and down, clapped her hands, giggled. Again, I thought I saw what might have caught at my father's dark heart, seventy years before.

She went back to the hospital to have her sight tested. 'I'm not too good at reading,' she told the doctor. And to me she said: 'I was determined to get it right.' 'What sort of words did you have to read?' 'Oh ... "desire" ... "quality" ... I thought they might have read your books, and I didn't want them to think your mother couldn't read.'

Told that her glasses were ready, and would arrive in a day or two, she knitted two small flags, red, white and blue, and fixed safety pins to them so they could be waved. And so again to the hospital, and the vital glasses assumed. It was a moment made for her tactless candour. Kate and Betty had prepared themselves for that, but had not been ready for the remark she made to the doctor: 'You aren't as young and well-to-do as I thought from your voice.' 'You'd better take them off again, then,' he managed to say. Her companions were relieved that she waited till she was outside before saying: 'He had a *coarse* face!'

When we visited her next day, she was trembling with happiness. Her breakfast had arrived and she'd told herself she must not cry!—she'd been very lucky!—she mustn't spoil it with tears! ... but the plate had been so *white*, and for the first time she'd seen her name and room number printed on the edge of the tray! And there'd been the grain of the wood of the tray itself! And Kate—well, she looked handsomer than my mother had expected. Handsomer than me! Well, I was greying—and one eyebrow was growing higher than the other. 'Don't cut it!' With immense scorn for her former self, she was taking obtrusive threads of cotton out of needlework done unsighted, and tut-tutting merrily over irregularities in her knitting. She was also reading all the letters she could lay hands on, and gasping over innumerable newspapers.

The very young quality that emerged in her when she was happy made it seem that the world, marvellously repaired, had been returned to her like some lost toy.

3

Somewhere about this point I went off to Australia, and came back to find her sitting in our garden.

It was a fragment of what had been the garden of 1 East Drive: because the day had come when we'd sold that, and half the site, and they'd pulled the house down and built shops in its place, and we'd moved to new houses built in the tail of the old garden. Now we turned our faces to the fields, and sycamores saved from the old back boundary stood on our front lawns: in autumn, when the leaves had turned, making a thick honey of light in the front rooms.

It had been odd, moving such a little way, and then having a ringside seat when they destroyed the old house. There'd been a house-cooling, first, and we'd invited our guests to write or draw on the walls—it was all going, let them be as amusingly vandalistic as they wished. We'd forgotten that the moment would come when the house would be torn apart and our scribbles exposed. Old Mr Ryall-Musk's worst suspicions about our way of life would have been confirmed. But he was dead, and Mrs Ryall-Musk had vanished, and the Quints were dead, and so was Mr Robbins of the B----- W--- Stores, and Miss Fluster had retired. There were very few left to feel scorn for us in the old way. Barley Wood had passed out of the grip of the late Victorians and Edwardians and into that of the neo-Elizabethans: whose way of life would have caused that famous old evangelist—who'd forbidden 1 East Drive to be a hotel—to dissolve into ultimate thunder. Well, the district had grown by way of superior estates that, as the years passed, found it more and more difficult to accommodate their freight of cars. Garages sometimes dwarfed the houses themselves, and desperate amounts of expensive machinery occupied front gardens increasingly paved. There was never a bowler hat to be seen on the morning platforms, but many junior executives, schoolboys with moustaches. We were electric, and the old hoarse chatter and snort of trains had become silky sounds slicing through the suburb. ..

There had come a morning when the demolishers moved in and began the destruction of the old house with a surprising ceremony, dashing and impertinent. They'd all gone into the loft, and at a signal each of them had punched a hole somewhere along the ample slopes of the roof. From that point onwards you could say only that they pummelled the place to pieces, amid roars of laughter. There was a moment when they were all standing on torn towers of brickwork and suddenly the entire back wall fell, and dust rose, in a red storm; and when it cleared they could be seen conducting a perhaps very slightly chastened rollcall: but they were still laughing. And for some days our old life settled everywhere on our new, in the form of brick dust.

And now, more than ten years later, my mother sat on our lawn, once Charles Hickman's vegetable plot (his rhubarb had continued for several years to thrust itself through our startled grass), and I talked to her about Australia, while she murmured in a manner that suggested at once her desire to humour me and her sensible refusal to believe in Australia's existence. Much of what I did, I knew, put a severe strain on her credulity. What sort of life was it that required one to make ridiculous journeys to destinations that should stay where they belonged, in the atlas? I told her of my arrival above Sydney, in the early morning, when the lowest possible cloud was stretched over the city, a fine lace of it, and was pierced by tall trees, whose shadows lay on the cloud itself: so that it seemed to be pinned there with many black pins. I talked of the odd feeling I'd often had about flying: that it was to do something ridiculous and sometimes melodramatic as if it was commonplace. I'd never get over the way we'd made ourselves comfortable in those racing snails high above the highest cloud! My mother nodded and murmured and, I noticed, held her handbag particularly tight. I said: 'Would you be afraid to travel by air, dear?' She said, after a moment: 'I don't think I should allow myself to be afraid of anything.'

214

Her habit of staring at people was now fully restored. She raked you fore and aft, and was pitiless in respect of detail. She was impressed by Kate's teeth—'So white!'—but disenchanted by my shaving—'You never did bother enough ... Now, Daddy with his cut-thrusts. ...' I think it was pure tenderness that made her unable to say 'cutthroats'. I was suddenly a little boy when she spoke of those razors of his ... watching while the steel turned and briskly turned in the passage under his chin, and the hairs crackled as they were cut. ... His being immortal was promised by that deftness and those snapping hairs, the whole spring and skill of it, and here we were among the consequences of his mortality!

One of her brand-new energies, arising from that successful operation, was a brand-new energy of pure vanity. Looking through photos taken during her blindness, she'd come across one of me, or one of Kate, and busily sum up: 'Shocking! Oh, I say, how dreadful!' Then she'd come to one I'd taken of her, while my father was still alive, and she'd cry: 'That's nice! Oh, that's very nice! Not a wrinkle! It's a very nice dress ... Oh, I must say—that's a very nice photo! Isn't it?' 'Would you like to have it?' I'd say: but she'd be too busy stuffing it into her handbag to answer.

4

When she moved now, it was with astonishing turns of tottering speed. It was as if, going from A to B, she was really aimed at some mysterious letter halfway between. It ended in tears, as my father would certainly have foretold. One day she left her room bound for the lavatory opposite, and failed to notice that a vacuum cleaner had been left between the two. It was my sister's regular afternoon for visiting, and she arrived in time to board the ambulance. There, my mother expressed her regret for the incident. She'd spoilt Betty's afternoon! But she had to confess she was looking forward to the change of scenery.

A hip was broken. It must be set, they said, and that would take three weeks in hospital. Problems with anaesthetics? About that they could say nothing until they'd studied her medical record: but the alternative was six months in bed, which of course simply wasn't on.

I expected to find her gloomy and desperate. But she was merely grateful for this unexpected snatch of drama. There'd been no disposition on the part of nurses and doctors to differ from the usual opinion that she was a dear little woman. The discomfort of having to believe that she was nearing ninety was balanced by the admiration with which they contemplated her courage. For once she seemed not to be exaggerating. A young doctor told me she was in good shape, and there was no obvious reason why a general anaesthetic shouldn't be used. Her cheerfulness and pluck were remarkable, he said.

After the operation she put herself, as it were, on exhibition. 'Roll up,' she might have well cried, 'and see my bandaged hip!' It was frankly on show to the curious. There was much pain ... she made comic agonised faces. 'But they are so kind here! They're the essence of kindness!'

Back in what she was now inclined to call Sidney House, she was struck by the gymnastic possibilities offered by the zimmer they'd given her, that aluminium aid to walking. Pressing down on it, she could lift her feet from the ground and swing them from side to side. Drawing on a memory of athletes on television using parallel bars, she expressed chagrin because she couldn't hold her legs straight out in front of her. For a moment she was actually downcast: having this aid to gymnastics, she badly wanted to put on a show of amazing gyrations. You could see that in theory she was whirling round like some giddy ancient prayerwheel.

With new eyes and a renewed leg, she had several months of almost reckless vigour. Knitting furiously, she spared time for an old activity that had been dropped during her blindness. As long as I could remember, she'd cut news stories, articles, photographs, advertisements out of newspapers and magazines, each with an ideal recipient in mind. I'd always qualified for anything to do with books, education, music: but that was only the core of it. Let slip a reference to the most casual interest and you were a candidate for cuttings that might be thrust into your hand years after you'd forgotten how it all began. After every visit I left Cedar House weighed down with newsprint and tea cosies.

Remembering my bedroom forty years earlier, with its frieze of filmstars, she presented me with a portrait, snipped out of a woman's magazine, of an old sweetheart of mine, who'd never known of my love: Laura la Plante. 'Oh, she could have done anything she liked with me when I was ... nine, I suppose,' I cried in my astonishment. 'Big deal!' murmured Kate.

Many of the nurses and maids at Cedar House were coloured. Though she never stated her view—it was a matter of hints—my mother had always found it odd that there should be this variety of human pigment. *Why* wasn't there uniformity of hue, considering that those responsible could not have lacked the power to impose it? This doubt of hers caused her shame which grew greatly when I became involved, through the BBC's Overseas Service, with Africans and their writing. You might say that whenever the question of colour arose, she started guiltily: somehow, in her uncertainty, she was letting me down, she feared. It would be known all over Africa that my mother found blackness puzzling, and I'd be ruined. A remedy was to make it very clear indeed that she was untouched by prejudice. Her niceness to a nurse from Pakistan or Jamaica was spectacular, and must have caused amazement and a little discomfort to a number of innocent girls: since nothing but the most elaborate embraces would carry the meaning my mother intended to convey.

Betty was present once when a new nurse made her appearance: West Indian, sparkling, eager, and instantly subject to one of my mother's most brilliant displays of racial evenhandedness. 'Where do you come from, my love?' she asked.

'Ah ... *originally*—' the girl began. But got no further; for my mother gave one of her little handclaps and laughed in a manner designed to suggest a quite major order of satisfaction.

'A *very* nice place!' she cried. 'And *very* warm!'

She was so bright and alert that when a new arrival showed signs of being seriously disturbed by the strangeness of things, the matron asked my mother to pay her a visit of reassurance. And so, free now of her zimmer, Mother flew along corridors (her accident had not cured her of her scuttling ways) and found herself in the middle of a nightmare.

No one was to know—I think in advance she'd not have guessed herself—that this might happen. The fact is that the new arrival had been driven briefly out of her wits by the move to Cedar House. She believed there were hostile persons outside the door, and others attempting to break their way in through the window. She cowered in a corner, and was unable to recognise my mother's overwhelming harmlessness.

I imagine Lizzie Pye awfully worried for her, speaking at first in tones and terms of sensible pity and affection; and then, as the other woman's terror grew, being overcome by terror of her own. For what she saw now in the poor groaning creature was any inmate of the mental hospital where her own mother had spent the last quarter of a century of her life. Now both women were cowering and cringing. 'I couldn't bear it. I thought of dear Jessie,' Lizzie Pye told me. She now often spoke of her mother by her fond name, as if they'd become sisters—as I guess they had. 'I didn't know what to say. I felt such a coward. But I was so frightened and I had to get away.' She scuttled back to her room, in tears; to be found there, and comforted, by her favourite maid.

It was, I saw, what lay behind her talk of Cedar House as an institution. Any such place might always throw off the mask and reveal itself as a mental hospital. It was why she kept herself to herself, and held the other residents at a distance with her talk of their being 'bonkers.' It was necessary to make for herself a small secure cell of sanity in the middle of it all, and for this purpose her room was best.

She sat there day after day; and following the fright she'd had, her output of woollen products doubled.

Every tea cosy successfully completed was an assertion and assurance of sanity.

5

There was another reason why she rarely left her room. It was social. She was desperately afraid that the other residents with their posh voices would look down upon her; or rather, that she simply would not understand what they were saying. They had complex ways of framing any statement they wished to make. Confronted with such a person, my mother tended to put on a posh voice herself, astonishingly nasal, and to grope for unfamiliar words (which *she* never had difficulty in finding) and improbable ways of stringing them together. ...

At last the matron, afraid that she might go downhill fast if she remained a solitary, made deliberate occasions for Mother to go down to the lounge—in good weather, the garden. And suddenly, but briefly, she became an infatuated mixer. She took to it passionately. And that led to difficulties, arising out of her need to display—indeed, to *feel*—affection, and her lifelong uncertainty about names and identities.

She'd always gone through the High Street in Barton-on-the-Hill distributing kisses, embraces, and fervent greetings; often enough on some basis of simple wild error, so that there would be misnamings and astonishing confusions as to who anyone was: Mrs Samuels re-invented as Mrs Sandwich, Mrs Oliver as Mrs Livery—while she'd snatch at the name of a Mrs Margaretson with a general effect of calling her Mrs Maggots. Outside a core of close acquaintances, any woman might be converted into quite another woman: Mrs Smith became Mrs Robinson and would be the target of inquiries relating to the sad situation of Mrs Brown. It was, most of it, enormous affection; she was moved by a grand desire to love everyone and to demonstrate this plainly with jubilant pronouncement of names (so often wrong) and elaborate ceremonies of greeting, which could involve her in taking into her arms astonished women who, when it came to the practical question of the capacity of one person to embrace another, were outside her scale. Looking back on my days of shopping at her heels, I remember a small woman so often rapturously failing to encircle women much larger.

And now at Cedar House, where she really knew no one, and where most residents had insurmountable names, my mother added to that general lovingness that had always been her motive, a need to propitiate strangers she thought of as haughty. Her embraces now had some element of the intention of smothering criticism. 'Hello, my sweetheart!' she'd say to some little dowager priding herself on being able to walk as well as ever: 'And how are your poor legs?' Two of her gifts, that of confusing one person with another and that of inventing situations on the slenderest of evidence, would come together with a third—the use of tactless terms. 'And how is your boy friend?' she'd ask Mrs da Silva, thinking she was Mrs Bellamy, who was given to exchanging polite conversation with Mr Likeman, and nothing more.

For a while she spoke in a grand way of the impatience with which her appearance in the lounge was awaited. She was reported to be haphazardly kissing old ladies on a huge scale. Now she had a new cast of admirers. Her deafness had not prevented her from overhearing murmurs of 'Such a sweet little creature!' 'So clean!' 'What a very charming dress!' 'A splendid kilt! And amazing safety pin!' No one seemed to be put off by the activity of her hearing-aid; which she'd never managed to master, so that much of the time her ears emitted a high-pitched whistle. 'Such a very unusual little hearing aid! Expensive, I believe!'

But this new life ended as abruptly as it had begun. Impossible to be sure why. She had a story to tell of some tyrant of the lounge who'd accused her of coming from Barton-on-the-Hill; had insinuated that her family must always, and all of them, have suffered from ear trouble; had laughed coarsely when informed that my mother's son was a writer; and had forbidden her to sit in a certain chair. 'Go and sit over there!' 'She thinks she's the cock's whiskers!' said my mother.

And so she returned to her room: from which tea cosies began again to flood. ...

6

I think she was telling the truth when she said she wouldn't allow herself to be afraid of flying; but she was always terrified when she knew we were in the air.

I came back from a long aerial roundaboutness once, full of an exhilaration partly derived from seeing the world of humans from above as a world of fleas. I was an aero-addict: loved seeing the ocean as blue glass, scratched, mountains as brown scabs or puckered raw metal; the intricate stains and creases of the old carpet of Earth; hills lashed down by the pale rope of roads. But I was also wearied by that dribble of music in airports that never shapes itself into anything mildly noticeable ... the aching patience of these places. And a few minutes out of London the dapperness contrived for me by Kate became total crumplement. Everything I did led to a strain or a crease. ... My mother looked at me as she used to do when I returned from school, and said: 'I think you should stay at home.' She seemed on the point of offering me one of her laborious notes of excusal. She then asked for my forgiveness by way of a squeeze of the hand.

She didn't care for it when we went to that fiercely hot Asian island to visit Ben and Marie.

Ben, near the close of his official career, was looking after the British end of some great international project. His narrow clever face was now like some brown rock on which God knows what birds made their homes in the nests of white hair at his temples ... We'd go of an evening down to one of the seafront hotels—Ben and I, still incorrigibly literary, preferring the one they said Joseph Conrad used to hole up in, though no evidence was ever offered for this. And there, drinking just a little too much arrack under Kate's and Marie's indignantly indulgent eyes, we'd sometimes talk of Barley Wood. That was Act II sc. ii, and here we were at Act V sc. i.! And how very odd it all was! One hardly remembered from year to year what happened to oneself, let alone what had happened to one's friends! I'd sometimes thought I would make a time chart like those you see pinned up in primary classrooms; but instead of the History of Man, this would cover *our* history, Kate's and mine and Ben's and Marie's, indicating where we all were in particular years. Such a visual aid might help me to remember that 1960 was no longer (as for some reason I found it necessary to believe it was) yesterday.

Had there been any serious change in us? I doubted it. Ben said he could no longer bear tragedy: he would not go to see *Hamlet*, on the grounds that you needed youthful stamina to come out of the theatre whistling. They'd have to sweep him out of it, in small bleeding bits. But then under Ben's boldness, I'd always suspected, lay a great and touching fragility. Living at 1 East Drive I'd thought that if he came out of the house one day and found me lying in the drive, with a leg severed, he'd make a quick reference to the advantages of having only one leg, and then ... talk of other things.

Had we changed? There'd been that glimpse of a Buddhist festival that had led us to discuss an old theory of ours: that people caused things to happen around them that were in their own style. Did such gorgeous solemnities as this one usually include an elephant, in what was clearly a second-class caparison, suddenly driven wild by the need to piss? As he came round a great marble corner, followed by wonderfully fulminating drums and trumpets, he fidgeted and bucked and turned sideways on to the general flow of things, until they had to unhitch his huge faded cloth and leave him free to hose the ground in tremendous steaming relief. Ben and I thought it was the sort of incident our presence might well impose on a sacred event anywhere in the world.

And that time in a museum when we were followed

222

everywhere by an attendant who insisted ('Sir!') on informing us about each exhibit in exactly the words of the printed account attached to it. Ben glared at him: I smiled, pointed to the print, shrugged my shoulders—with what must have been the general aim, when I thought of it, of persuading him, at this late hour, that his attendance on museum-goers was unnecessary. Follow up my line of propitiatory protest, and it made sense only if it concluded with the man giving a smile of his own, one of delayed understanding, followed by some Asian equivalent of 'Oh, what an ass I've been!'

Ben's glare: my helpless smile. Had we changed?

Somewhere in the middle of the island, we encountered a young Englishman who was clambering all over it, testing himself against mountains, totally defeating swift-flowing rivers, causing the wildest breakers on the loneliest beaches to cry out for mercy. He was, I thought, the perfect Outward Bounder: and suddenly saw that Ben and I had always, from the sixth form onwards, been Inward Bounders.

We stayed at the Seagull Surf Hotel; which ought to have been called the Crow Surf Hotel, there being a total absence of seagulls and a total presence of crows. We lay on a burning whiteness of beach, and remembered old weekend competitions. The twelfth-century literary conference, for example, under the title Is the Ballad Doomed? Speakers: Anon, Anon and Anon.

Ben asked me if I'd ever been back to Stonehill Street, and I told him how, a few years before, I'd almost been unable, physically, to find it. Enormously augmented—it had built upwards, it had lost playgrounds—it occupied still the space it always had: but the simple approach through simple streets had been, in a nightmarish fashion, quite cancelled. Planning had settled on the scene like some leisurely spirit of confusion and alienation, and had replaced the rows of little houses with vast bewilderments of tall blocks of flats; half-completed centres of, and for, this and that; a drawing-board barrenness that had no relation that I could make out to the blunt people who'd lived there and presumably still survived somewhere in this oddly silent scene of, as it were, permanent impermanence. I longed for a sight of a single little garden of the kind I'd once deplored, half a dozen hasty asters and a dandelion or two set in a fond little patch of paving not so much crazy as mildly daft. ...

After a day among paddy fields, silver lip after lip locked together, we sat under immense moonlight and talked of marriage. The moon had first been seen lying fat and very golden on a bed of black trees, and then began climbing ... much too fast, Kate thought: it would never last the night out. ... All those old anguishings over marriage! It *was* a matter of temperament, of course. Ben considered himself held to Marie by bonds at once taut and slack. He was still opposed in theory to the nuclear marriage (which sounded much like the kind of marriage some of our friends had had, explosive). Well, perhaps tastes and needs were too various for general schemes and universal arrangements. I found myself thinking, as so often, that human beings are biologically absurd. Their wants are so contradictory that only saints or simpletons have half a hope of holding themselves and their little worlds together.

What had happened, Ben asked, to Philip and Ruth? It had fallen apart, *that* marriage? Well, oddly they had been looking for each other over each other's shoulders: the trick of living for both of them had been to turn what was within reach into the hopelessly unattainable.

It was temperament and style. Marriage had a disastrous record among the people we'd known: but then so had unmarriage.

As for me, I thought, I had this taste for continuity. I'd enjoyed being continuous for thirty years with Kate Brown. Anyway, she'd been a dozen different Kates during that time. Where now was the Kate of the kitchen at 1 East Drive?

But did we change? Still from time to time Kate and I had that experience when you walk about building up an immense case against the other, spectacularly unanswerable; and then the court is convened, the judge takes his place, the corridors are crammed with witnesses ...And as you rise to deliver the prosecutor's opening speech, a denunciation exhaustively rehearsed ... to everybody's amazement, but your own especially, you cross to the dock and take the prisoner in your arms. ...

I wondered how much my own desire to keep things

continuous rested on resolutions reached years before when I sat at the top of the stairs at Manor Road and listened to the sounds of quarrelling below. When I was grown-up, I vowed then, I'd revenge myself on compulsory schoolcaps by never again wearing headgear of any kind; I'd buy myself unlimited quantities of chocolate; and I'd *never* shout at my wife! I'd *never* turn any wife of mine into desperate weeping Lizzie Pye!

'He thought we were both fools,' my mother had suddenly said recently. 'And I was good only to have his babies.' Well, fifty years on *she* was still polishing the speech for the prosecution: and no one had ever clung more loyally to the prisoner in the dock.

All these bonds between people that changed without altering! Between Ben and me, for example. That for me had shifted from a young ground of absolute admiration to this present ground, a state of affection that could barely recall where it came from. From deep clashes of personal style, the bond had slackened again and again. But how tough human relationships could be! So that they could break and be trampled on and come to the grimmest of halts, and then out of some deep energy in themselves, and out of the respect survivors have for one another, and out of sheer forgetfulness (so much of the memory being a carpet for things to be swept under), all is alive again—white-haired, more watchful than thirty years before, inwardly ironic, but perfectly alive, and warm. ...

Something, thank God, tough and leathery about human beings!

7

As the fees at Cedar House climbed, so my mother's money ran out. She found this difficult to believe. The bungalow had been sold for £16,000. Having spent her active life knowing exactly the difference between 11¾d and one shilling, she took it for granted that you could make yourself at ease in any number of Cedar Houses for centuries on money like that.

But the possibility had to be faced that she might live to be a hundred. This she had the declared intention of doing; and hinted that it was only a beginning. She hadn't my father's consuming terror of death—but it was an event she'd be perfectly happy to dispense with. You could give her terminal congestion of the lungs, snap her hips, reduce the beat of her heart to a wayward flutter, afflict her with diverticulitis and drain the iron from her blood, and she would simply look the other way. No one was going to get her to accept an invitation to vanish. Another resident of Cedar House told her she longed to die. My mother said she'd cheerfully put up for ever with the pain she was in at that moment, hideous quarrellings in her tattered innards, rather than be dead. She snorted, as though presented with a particularly silly suggestion.

We discovered to our astonishment that down the road there was another old people's home, and this one had all sorts of subsidies, public and private, and cost a quarter of the cost of Cedar House. It had an instant air of cheerfulness and kindness; would accept my mother at once, given her age; and offered the final attraction that it would look after her to the end. Those who were dying were not sent away to hospitals. They were cared for among those they'd come to know. It was what my mother would have called the greatest possible *boom*.

That left us with the painful task of explaining to little, rooted Lizzie Pye, queen of her narrow room at Cedar House, that she must be uprooted. We all shrank from this duty but Kate: who since that long nursing five years before had become an object of my mother's passionate gratitude—touched always with amazement, since when my father was alive she'd 'not been allowed to know' Kate. Gratitude came easily to her, and again and again she'd make a sudden small solemn ceremony of it: once announcing that, for her, the term 'daughter-in-law' no longer existed: 'You are my daughter! I have *two* daughters!' Kate volunteered now to break the news on the occasion of one of my mother's visits. Then Betty and her husband would arrive, to reinforce our comfortable

226

account of the new home, and we would ask my mother to sign an application form.

It went well. She listened with interest to Kate, assented to all the propositions that led to the idea that this was a necessary and tolerable move, ate a cheerful supper; and then, when Betty arrived and produced the form, fell apart. Panic swept through her. She had become used to the nurses who bathed her, the girls who came up with her midnight tea! I explained again: a move was made necessary by the melting away of her money. 'Oh no!' she cried. And her voice, suddenly, was my father's. Inside her he was speaking of familial skulduggery. It was, I guess, the nightmare in the midst of which they had been brought up: the constant dread that some member of the family would cheat you of such wretched assets as you had. And the signing of forms had so often been at the centre of such villainies! She wept; grew faint; from pale, turned feverish. I said she must stay the night; she could not return to Cedar House in such a state of despair. 'Why,' she cried expiringly, 'can't I go back?' Everything that happened was an aspect of conspiracy. And then, on the immediate tail of such despairs, she took a hand of each of us in turn, and kissed it. She was sorry, she said, to have worried us with her behaviour!

The next day Kate drove her through the grounds of the new home: 'Elegant!' said my mother. Returning to Cedar House, she began at once to turn the disaster to dramatic advantage. If she had to go, there should be no indication that her departure was involuntary. Grandly she had decided on a move. Never were farewells more stately—or more often duplicated. She bowed out over what must, for the other residents of Cedar House, have been several exhausting days.

But she wept into the bosom of her favourite Indian attendant; and confessed that if she could allow her heart to be broken, it would be broken.

8

Life at Deansville was quite different. There was no hiding away in one's room, which was shared with another. Instead, we found her in a lounge, among other snoring or staring old ladies: her own mouth agape. She was not unhappy, she said. But it was clearly a move from a hermit's cell to the middle of some crowded beach. 'It's not as luxurious as. ...' she declared, hideously loud. 'But if you've got no alternative. ...' An old lady wearing a fat strawberry of a hat made her way slowly to a chair. 'She's been walking in the garden,' said my mother, as if she were admitting us to some sordid secret. 'She's walked too far!' And as the other lowered herself into her chair: 'That's right, my dear! Sit down! You'll be all right in a minute!' She was full of random ironies. In the direction of another old lady, owner of a canary in a cage: 'You talk to the dickybird, don't you, dear! That's right! You *talk* to the dickybird!' And so on.

The excitement of the move had brought out something in her that I thought must provide a backward glimpse of the Cockney child she'd been, holding her own among the satirical cries of street and school. The main technique, and it remained invariable during the year or so she had left to live, was to call out a description of whatever it was a person was doing in such a fashion that it could be taken as smart raillery. 'Reading a book then, my dear!' To me: 'She's always reading!' The old lady in question always *was* reading, and presented my mother with the problem of convincing her that it was silly to read any old book when you might be reading a book by her, my mother's, son. 'This is Edward!' she'd cry across the room on any of our visits, as if this clinched the argument. 'You're too shy!' she scolded me; obviously I should have rushed across and added my arguments to my mother's. Then she'd kiss me with a lover's intensity, and hold tight to my hand. 'I cling to you, you cling to me,' she said. Under what was happening on the surface, all those ironies, the little half-mad cries and the puzzlements that arose from her becoming deafer and deafer, there was shrewd, interested Lizzie Pye, I knew, and her kisses and the fierceness of her grip were messages from that increasingly sad prisoner.

For now she began to fade. To the decay of her hearing was added the final decay of her sight. I felt her vanishing, week by week. And at times, oxygen in sufficient quantities would fail to reach her brain, and she'd stop in the middle of what she was saying, baffled, like one who'd had something snatched from her open hand ...

But her relation with her room-mate, Mrs Lucas, was animating, much of the time.

On the very first evening Mrs Lucas had affirmed her astonished admiration of my mother's cleanliness, but had chosen what might have been taken as a satirical expression of it: 'Don't forget to wash your bottom,' she said. The two old ladies, both immensely deaf, obliged to share a room and expected to adopt a mature approach to the arrangement, resorted in their bewilderment to the wilder immaturities of a quarrelsome nursery. Each showered ironic comment on what she understood the other to say: which was never what was actually said. My mother's conviction that she was the lonely representative of a more gracious world, marooned among old ladies of uncertain sanity, gathered force. She spoke of Mrs Lucas's astounded pleasure when offered sherry. It was clear to her that her room-mate (whose side of the room was cluttered with pictures of her husband and herself, public persons, at dinners and receptions) had never before had the experience of drinking from a sherry glass. 'You loved it, didn't you, dear!' Mrs Lucas snorted. It was a small step for my mother to suggest that never before had Mrs Lucas even drunk sherry. 'It's nice, isn't it, dear! But you mustn't have too much!' In response to this remark, too, inaudible to her like the other, Mrs Lucas snorted. 'You must take her out one day,' she said. 'She'd like that.' It became a major item in Mrs

Lucas's strategy, to foster this view of my mother as someone who rarely, if ever, knew the bliss of being given a day away from the home. We'd bring her back to it after such a day, and Mrs Lucas would say: 'You must really take her out some time. She'd like that!' 'Old fool!' my mother would say, not having heard a word of it, and taking a fierce grip of her tormentor's hand. They held each other's hands constantly during their most withering exchanges: even punctuated them with kisses. It was not long before they were bound tightly together in a tangle of evident irritation but barely less evident love.

Another demonstration of the fact that if you said 'love', meaning some single thing, you had said nothing.

She couldn't easily remember recent events: she and Mrs Lucas becoming famous for their insistence, ten minutes after a meal, that they had not eaten for days. She came to us for her last Christmas; and found herself with a bodyguard, if a fickle one—Dan's son Tim, aged three, who was interested in the notion of a little creeping person who might be watched over, with the aid of some theoretical gun, as she made her way from living room to lavatory and back. He was not the most reliable escort, at times being unable to resist the temptation to pill her. This is what he thought you did when you levelled a pair of fingers and cried 'Pill pill pill!'

I had avoided being merely his grandfather by being his Bumper. He pilled me frequently, rushing away when I fell to announce the good news: 'Bumper's dead!'; and then returning to lie alongside me on the floor in the affectionate comfort of extinction.

Signallings across the years! Like his father, he'd discovered the enormous power of saying 'No!' 'You say "No" to everything everyone says,' I observed. 'No, I don't,' said Tim. On Christmas morning I found him in the larder, puzzled by the sudden multiplicity of biscuit tins. 'Mmm mmm mmm,' he said, as if being unintelligible would establish his innocence. I imagined such specific pieces of behaviour could hardly be inherited: but that *was* Dan, all over. ...

And other echoes! Like Ben, years before, I had the proofs of a book to attend to; and not being able to give time to it was like having a child in intensive care next door ... longing to be able to dash in and conduct blood-counts and carry out small desperate operations. ...

I'd become aware, as I knew more and more about myself as a writer, worrying over pages in pencil and then typescript and then in proof, of the oddest irony in that long history of dissatisfactions between my father and myself. He, always dapper, had particularly raged against what he held to be my lack of interest in any kind of neatness; yet I'd realised that, when it came to words, I was as concerned with the exact and the trim as he was. I was astonishingly in his line, unmistakably his son: and he'd not recognised it because for him there was no connection between spruceness in dress or the layout of a garden, and verbal spruceness. ...

Thinking it would be kinder to my mother's stomach, Kate presented her with a mild trifle in place of Christmas pudding; which was received with a whimper of distress, a tiny helpless childishness. Her eyes filled with tears, which were not those of greed—weren't really childish at all, I thought. Shut away from the world by so much, she wanted no extra separations from it. To eat Christmas pudding with the rest of us, whatever her guts made of it, was to be a little more than a ghost.

9

I was talking in a school in Pimlico, and on the way home called in at a local pub. It was full of warm, battered, ugly people—and of a rich stale smell. It was the smell I recognised first—that of all the little flats we'd visited when I was a child, my mother's aunts and uncles and cousins: a thick smell of old cooking and damp. Ugly in itself—but it had been a deeply interesting ugliness! And the men and women in the pub, making their wonderful heavy jokes, were my mother's relations: composing that world out of which she had come and which I'd visited as a school-capped outsider. God, how hoity-toity I must at times have seemed to those unpretentious people! As a boy I'd had a strong puzzled feeling about that improbable existence of my mother's, before she married and I was born, of which those fusty flats, those jocular, gently rough people, were a proof. And in that pub I thought how strange it was that I had this present sense of great closeness to Lizzie Pye, and yet knew so little of her—could not *really* begin to imagine her as she'd been any time between her birth in 1890 and my own in 1920. We were historically remote from each other, and education had added further distances. Much that she'd said in these last years had been a kind of semaphoring, I guessed, from that old existence, which to her must be still so fiercely real, to this one, the strangest of sequels. . . . Well, nowadays she remembered some moment in 1900 far more easily than what happened this morning in 1980.

It was months before she stopped introducing me to Mrs Lucas, but the monotony was eased by the variety of names she offered for her room-mate. Mrs Luton: Mrs Lupin: Mrs Lurid: even Mrs Lulu. One day she surpassed herself; choosing a moment when they'd given a display of the wildest mutual incomprehension to make her known to me all over again. 'This is Mrs Lucid . . .! she cried.

She had gained an admirer: the most gentle, courtly man, whose Christian name was of a loftiness that persuaded my mother to change it to Charlie. She teased him about his turn, not of speed, but of extreme slowness: he'd been reduced to inching his way along, and did so with great cheerfulness. 'I can manage the first hundred yards, but it's when it goes into a second day. . . .' he told me. He laughed and bowed a great deal, and blew kisses at my mother from great distances, as a warning that at any hour now he'd be alongside. It brought out all of her affectionate haughtiness. Her return kisses, thought they were never withheld, had nothing easily given about them. He called her Blossom. 'You've been seeing my Blossom,' he'd exclaim, meeting Kate and me somewhere along an agonisingly slow corridor.

Oh, that inching along corridors! There was a moment that printed itself on my memory when two old men were approaching each other from different ends of one, while another emerged from a second running into it. Both the first old men were like broken spiders or craneflies, insects with limbs that had been smashed and then allowed to grow crooked, so that they were obliged to move with total deliberation: in each case the legs, so elaborately distorted, moved if anything behind the torso, so seeming to be dragged after it rather than being the cause of its movement. It was like the converging of hideously broken insects. And then the third old man came between them; and he was slower and more shattered still. . . .

One of the more alert residents, Mrs Foster, who was our chief source of information as to what actually happened in Deansville—to rely for this on my mother was to be offered what sounded like the plot of a Marx Brothers film—said to me once, intensely: 'I wish people could see us as we were, in our prime!' And I thought suddenly of all these people trapped by the vile hoax of old age, made odd, hairy, bony, bloated, emaciated; and being with unbearable wistfulness aware of their brisk firm former selves, lost for ever.

After all, only the very old had become much accustomed to being old!

Mrs Foster told us that my mother was given to shouting in the early morning. She lay there, shouting unintelligibly. It seemed to me this must be the voice of all the angers and dissatisfactions of a lifetime—a furious attack on everything that had stood between her and being, and doing, what she might have wanted to be and do; though she'd probably never had any precise idea of what these were. The lack of any precision might be why she was shouting. Her life, when you thought of it, had been remarkable short of ordinary, let alone extraordinary, satisfactions. Given her qualities, it wouldn't be too much to say that she'd been monstrously cheated.

Small obsessive vanities possessed her now. She'd noticed a ring on a granddaughter's finger that reminded her of a ring much admired on Kate's, being blue; and the idea that she'd never had a ring with a blue stone, and that life without such a ring was nothing, grew upon her. At last one was bought for her. For months afterwards she'd be found staring reflectively at it, raising a crooked finger closer to her eye, dreaming that she had a ring with a blue stone and then amazing herself with the reality of it. She dispensed with the question, 'Have you seen my ring?' and simply held it up to be admired.

Her deafness made it increasingly difficult to talk to her. At best it barely amounted to communication. Kate would sit close and tell her some anecdote, some simple story about Tim, perhaps, and Mother would stare at her, mouth open, and make at last some response, usually a cry of astonishment: intended to cover any uncertainty of hearing. But there were long periods when, exhausted, one could only sit and smile; or be in the same room; and she sat, behind the blindness of her glasses, perhaps pleating her skirt with little lost pinching movements of her fingers.

Tom had a gift for making himself heard; but then they'd always had a specially happy relationship, from the very earliest days teasing and being teased. Her ear seemed to open a little further when he spoke. She had a joke about his being a barbarian from the north, and pretended to see sufficient evidence of that in his cheerful beard. Her admiration leaked out, all the same: 'You've a very good mind, Tom!' 'I got that from my grandmother,' said Tom. She was truly puzzled. 'I'm afraid I can't for the moment think who that is.' Then, as she was reminded, an endearment from Tom's childhood: 'You little worm!'

She passed on to him, but he didn't think he could use, a piece of advice she'd had herself from one of the nurses. Referring to my mother's dehydrating habit of letting her mouth hang open, the girl said: 'Keep your mouth shut and you'll never have a sore throat!' For some reason this struck my mother as a marvellous piece of wisdom; she passed it on to everyone she met, twice to most, but continued to allow her mouth to gape. It expressed, that hanging mouth, her being now a long way behind every piece of news, every event. We'd come into the lounge on a visit and there she'd be, a tiny spruceness in her invariable chair, often asleep. If she were awake, it took some time for her to believe it was us. She'd stare, mouth open, across the room, until the knowledge of

234

what she was seeing made everything inside her leap. Then she wanted to rouse the whole room, all those silent fading women.

She no longer read or knitted. She was said to have gone to bed with her shoes on. More and more often there was the attempt to say something, and the helpless, staring halt. She came to the same chair, day after day: a wisp, increasingly lost in sleep.

She began to get out of bed in the night and aimlessly to wander. They put her in the sick bay for a while, in a high-sided invalid cot. She told me of this with all her old energy of indignation. 'It's like being in a mousetrap!' I smiled at the image. 'You see the funny side,' she said. 'I don't.'

10

It was a Sunday morning: she was not in her usual place. On top of a heavy cold, they said, she'd had one of her turns: when her heart lost all notion of rhythm. When she appeared, she was steering herself with a zimmer. Her usually neat hair was wild. 'Look!' she croaked, as if the zimmer had been the most amazing acquisition. It was what she'd always wanted, she said, and she'd been jealous of others who had one.

She was clearly very ill and very frightened. 'I'm a coward,' she said to me in a terse aside. Another resident, a soft, gentle, grinning, small woman who had nothing at all to say any more, made her way to my mother's side. 'She clings to me,' said my mother, with a kind of demented protectiveness. She flapped her hands as if it would help the other's progress. 'Come on, my dear! I'll look after you!' Her cough shook her. She was not with us: her attention was fixed on desperations within. Oddly, I was reminded of the last hours of her old friend, our dog Sally: who knew there was something awfully

235

wrong—it turned out to be a growth in her stomach—and ran in and out of the house in search of normality and ordinariness ... shivering, her eyes wretchedly intense, fixed on the puzzle of things being horribly amiss. ...

The next evening we were called to the home: she was desperately ill. She lay in bed, without glasses, without teeth. She stared, her throat rattled. Her eyes were grey and remote. From time to time she struggled up from her pillow: '*I'm all right!*' she croaked. I was glad she couldn't see my tears. And in the other half of the room, behind a curtain, Mrs Lucas moved about heavily, sighing and sobbing. She confused my mother with one of her daughters; and Mrs Foster had told us that my mother showed signs of confusing Mrs Lucas with my sister. There was this heavy, desperate woman, moving about blindly, shocked by what was happening to this room-mate and sparring partner who was also somehow her daughter. Kate went behind the curtain to comfort her and help her to bed: where she lay, sobbing more quietly but desolately, as we sat and watched my mother's hands composing and re-composing themselves. In these last few days of her life I was to notice as never before how conscious she was of her hands. How well, how long, I'd known them, with their sensible small nails, the brassiness of the rings she'd always worn ... that were somehow at the centre of my childhood: engagement ring, wedding ring.

Now, as we made to go, she suddenly stretched out a hand and caught one of mine, bringing it to her lips. 'My dear boy.' It was the last thing she ever said to me. ...

Leaving the two women was oddly like leaving some scene of nursery despair where all consolations had failed. ...

An astonished matron rang the next day to say she seemed on her way to recovery. She was sitting up, had resumed teeth and glasses; and when my sister called in to see her, was full of plans for the bold use of her zimmer. She intended to put all other zimmer-users to shame. No one till now had seen what the zimmer could do! Betty and her husband had come up hurriedly from the country; and Mother counselled them not to stay with her long. She might be the host for a lingering germ or two: and they should go and rest after their kind but unnecessary dash. . . .

It was going to be like that other old famous illness of hers, we thought. Once more Death was going to be seen off the premises. . . .

But it was her last triumph. At once desperate illness took hold again; when next we saw her, she was as she had been, only her eyes were more cruelly bruised, and her expression was now wholly one of puzzlement and despair.

She was moved to the sick bay, into the high-sided cot. We were called urgently; her pulse had vanished twice, there could not be more than an hour to go. She did not recognise us: was all weariness and discomfort, and the effort to make herself easy; the aching bones turned themselves this way and that. From time to time came wailing cries. I hadn't guessed how painful it would be not to be known. She was fearfully frightened, I was sure; and to be so remote from her nightmare that you weren't heard or seen—I hadn't bargained for that! And she wasn't going to die quickly, for all the vanishing pulse.

We had the curious experience, over the days that followed, of being with her, but absolutely *not* with her: Kate and Betty and her husband and I, often in the weariness of our vigil talking of general affairs, laughing, exchanging follies; while she lay a few inches away, her eyes open but blind, looking deeply hurt as if some unpardonable trick had been played on her. She ought to have gone by now, but her lifelong habit of struggle was working overtime. I was certain that the essence of Lizzie Pye was clenched up inside those dying bones, intent as it always had been on not allowing itself to be dislodged.

She had two moments of revival. Once when Betty was there alone; my sister had bent over her and she suddenly stretched up her hands and caught Betty's face and smiled, said my sister, enormously. And a nurse said she'd smiled at her once, quite broadly and easily, and said: 'I love you.'

A parson visiting the home came in to see her and after he raised a hand in blessing my mother raised both hers: it would have been, I thought when told of it, a gasping effort to outbless him. She'd always, out of some mixture of courtesy and emulation, tried to outbid those who were the instruments of any ritual: would always, so to speak, have made a Dame of

237

the Queen before the Queen had a chance to make a Dame of her. And there'd been a conspicuous touch of the President of the British Medical Association in her attitude to Dr Mackenzie.

On the last day I felt her terrible awareness had begun to relent: she lay gasping, the movements of her hands very weak. Her huge eyes did no more than stare: there was a sweet bad smell.

And the next morning the phone rang early: she had died at dawn.

I wanted to look devouringly, as if at a work of art, as it seemed to me she had become: and was afraid I might ever forget what I was seeing. I went back again and again to that solid yellow stone into which her face had turned, with her eyelids so fiercely closed over her eyes, as implacably as if the face had indeed been stone and there were no real lids, only the artistic illusion of lids. Then I thought it wasn't so much stone as ivory. ... As I'd drawn the sheet away from her face the soft prettiness of her hair had stirred, and it was astonishing to observe this almost playful movement of fine hair as a feature of what otherwise had become totally solid. Her face wore the sternness of her death. The mouth was sewn shut—that is, fine lines radiated from it, as if they were stitches: and they were drawn fiercely tight. There was altogether a great fierceness about her. She'd become a little ivory warrior. It was what death said about her, summing her up: that she was a warrior. There lay, her chin a rampart, Lizzie Pye who at thirteen had left home in search of a better life; and at twenty-nine had entered into her marriage with my father, against all sensible and kindly advice. There she was, abandoned under a sheet. It was astonishing to find her under a sheet—as if she'd been drowned and I'd had to reach down for her into the sea. Even though I knew she was dead I'd felt a momentary anger as if from carelessness they'd left her to smother.

As I returned the sheet, drowning her again, I thought: How astonishing, that everlasting stillness! And then again: How amazingly odd to be in the world without her!

And I thought: Poor dear, she died in her mousetrap!

As we drove away a hand waved from a high window. It was old Christopher, whom she called Charlie: and who called her Blossom.

It can't have cost my mother more than a few pence to enter the world in 1890. But in 1981 it cost her £422 to leave it.

This did not include music; on which the crematorium may have depended to smother certain noises that arose after the coffin had passed through curtains and out of sight: small thuds, shufflings, flurries of raps and taps. Tom and I had the same thought. They were the sounds of a last scuffle with mortality—the only neighbour about whom my mother had felt as my father felt about all neighbours.

Lizzie Pye refusing to go meekly.